✝

POLITICS

AND

THE

CATHOLIC

CHURCH

IN

NICARAGUA

POLITICS

AND

THE

CATHOLIC

CHURCH

IN

NICARAGUA

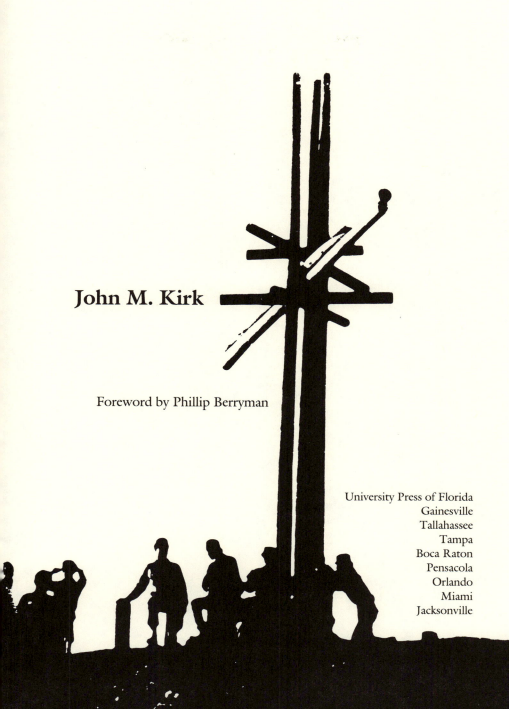

John M. Kirk

Foreword by Phillip Berryman

University Press of Florida
Gainesville
Tallahassee
Tampa
Boca Raton
Pensacola
Orlando
Miami
Jacksonville

Library of Congress Cataloging in
Publication Data are located on
the last printed page of the book.

Photographs by Deborah Barndt.

The University Press of Florida is
the scholarly publishing agency
for the State University System
of Florida, comprised of Florida
A & M University, Florida Atlantic
University, Florida International
University, Florida State University,
University of Central Florida,
University of Florida, University
of North Florida, University of
South Florida, and University of
West Florida.

University Press of Florida
15 Northwest 15th Street
Gainesville, FL 32611

CONTENTS

vii   Foreword by Phillip Berryman

xi   Preface

1   In Search of Stability: The Church in Nicaragua

7   1. In Search of an Identity: The Church in Nicaragua,
        1503–1936

33   2. The Institutional Church under Somoza:
        Accommodation and Complicity (1936–1969)

58   3. From Dictatorship to Revolution: The Church's
        Response (1970–1979)

100   4. From Jubilation to Despair (1979–1982)

141   5. Church-State Relations at Their Nadir (1983–1985)

176   6. In Search of Reconciliation? Church-State Relations,
        1985–1990

210   Prophetic Stance or Political Accommodation?

219   Notes

229   Selected Bibliography

243   Index

✝

FOREWORD

As we read John Kirk's book on the Catholic Church in revolutionary Nicaragua, many of us will find ourselves recalling events that we either observed personally or followed through extensive media coverage. What was this ten-year effort at revolution all about, and what was the significance of the highly conflictive public involvement of church people?

My own thoughts go back to a moment in early 1979 when the Somoza dictatorship was under attack but the outcome was by no means decided. While awaiting an interview with Carlos Tunnermann, then an exiled opposition leader, later to become minister of education and ambassador to Washington, I was thinking about what the Sandinistas were proposing: land reform, a literacy campaign, extension of health care, and so forth. Suddenly I was overwhelmed with the realization that these people really meant it—a government in a tiny Latin American country just might make changing the plight of the poor majority its top priority.

Over the years I had encountered a good deal of development rhetoric, and I was quite familiar with how it was contradicted by reality: the reality of governments run by pocket-stuffing politicians or the reality of the murderous military cliques then in power in most countries. I had seen Chile's experiment under Allende and had felt the crushing of the spirit under the Pinochet dictatorship. Throughout the 1970s military dictatorships had ruled most of the continent. Now in the small backwater countries of Central America, something different might be in gestation. A unique feature was the participation of some church people, both Catholics and Protestants, in this revolutionary endeavor. John Kirk traces here some of the outstanding examples of local-level contribution to the anti-Somoza movement, as well as the important role of Archbishop Obando.

It occurs to me that we can see the Nicaraguan revolution—overthrowing the dictatorship and attempting to develop a new economic and political model—as a wager. Many Nicaraguans, especially young people, were willing to risk their lives both in the struggle and in working either in the Sandinista government or alongside it, wagering that it was indeed possible to develop a qualitatively new kind of society. Although at times their rhetoric may have become somewhat utopian, they were striving to be realistic. They modestly hoped that the Nicaraguan economy could be reshaped to provide full employment and to satisfy the basic needs of the majority rather than enable small elites to live in luxury. Many church people believed that such a society would live with an austerity and equality closer to what Jesus preached and what the church is called to embody.

After an initial period of recovery from the anti-Somoza war, in which the people experienced improvement in their lives, the Sandinista government found itself devoting most of its resources to its own defense. Increasingly, their appeal was in the form of a promise: keep supporting us and when U.S.-supported aggression is defeated, we will all be able to return to the tasks of development. Those church people who had initially wagered now had to up the ante.

Has that wager been lost with the electoral defeat of the Sandinistas and the return to power of the old elites? As I write in early 1992, I note two signs in post-Sandinista Nicaragua. In one year the number of automobiles and trucks has risen from 111,000 to 175,000, and construction has begun on a new $3 million cathedral (80 percent of the cost to be raised by Tom Monaghan, the CEO of Domino's Pizza). Both attest to a kind of "development"—but not one likely to improve the lot of most Nicaraguans.

The basic commitment of those church people who "bet" on the revolution was not to a particular political program but to the people, and thus church workers continue to "accompany" the people they worked with during the decade of revolution. Will it turn out that the most enduring legacy of the revolutionary struggles in Central America will not be simply the memory of a leftist government in power but the steps of the poor toward shaping their own destiny?

In any case the future will continue to bring surprises. Certainly those who so triumphally subsumed the Nicaraguan election into a worldwide embrace of "democracy" and who assert that private-sector initiative will resolve the dilemmas of economic development will no doubt encounter many surprises.

John Kirk's book is the first scholarly study of the Church in Nicaragua covering the full decade of revolution. One of its merits is the attention devoted to the history of Church-government relations prior to 1970. Although the history related here is not likely to provide handy "lessons" for the future, since revolutions like those of Nicaragua do not seem to be on the horizon, the leitmotif of this book—that churches and politics are intertwined—remains valid.

Phillip Berryman

✝

PREFACE

THIS BOOK HAS NOT BEEN easy to write, having taken some ten years since the basic concept was first devised. I seek to cast some light on the political role of the Catholic Church in Nicaragua, a small and impoverished nation that had the temerity to undergo a social revolution after the overthrow of the Somocista dictatorship in 1979. It was a revolution like none that had gone before, and because it blended nationalism, Marxism, and Catholicism—a volatile combination in Latin America—it was destroyed. The revolutionaries had dared to be different, offering a dangerous example to other exploited nations of the Americas, and accordingly paid the price.

As the nation was torn apart by the so-called secret war stage-managed in Washington, the religious question grew rapidly in significance, and a tragic religious polarization—paralleling the deep political division—ensued. The role of the Catholic Church suddenly became "news" around the world, with extraordinary media attention being given to the struggle between the traditional, hierarchical Church centered on Archbishop—later Cardinal—Obando y Bravo and the grass-roots "People's Church," four of whose priests held key government portfolios. Yet a more dispassionate analysis of the role of the Catholic Church would reveal that this clear-cut politicization of religion was merely the last example of a centuries-old phenomenon. The Theology of Liberation did not, then, start with Gustavo Gutiérrez in the 1960s, while Oscar Romero had indeed many illustrious forebears who, over the centuries, paid with their lives for their own prophetic stances.

This book is the result of three long research trips to Nicaragua. It is intended to provide some basic understanding of the religious-political struggle that was the center of extensive debate throughout the 1980s, although it offers no definitive analysis proper of intra-Church dynamics: that is admirably undertaken elsewhere by Philip Williams and Manzar Foroohar. Its strength is that it seeks to situate the bitter ecclesial struggle against the backdrop of social polarization in Nicaragua and constant hostility from Washington.

The study of politics and religion is always a controversial matter, and this study will not be an exception. It is intended precisely to debunk the myth that religion is "apolitical," concerned with purely spiritual and pastoral values, and focuses on one case history—that of the Catholic Church in Nicaragua. I would venture that most—if not all—religions are also encumbered with sociopolitical concerns that go beyond the essentially "religious" and that the Nicaraguan case is not in fact that exceptional.

Many people have assisted in the production of this study and should be recognized for their support. Academic assistance and moral support were provided by others who have also studied this material, including Philip Williams, Manzar Foroohar, Ed Cleary, Michael Gismondi, Kirk Williams, George Gelber, Phillip Berryman, Max Azicri, Lou Pérez, and Peter McKenna. Material was generously provided by London's Catholic Institute for International Relations, by Philip Williams, Oscar González Gary, and Joan Campbell of Tools for Peace. The librarians at the Instituto Histórico Centroamericano at Managua's Universidad Centroamericana, and at both the Atlantic School of Theology and Dalhousie University, deserve recognition for their assistance in locating further information. Linda Cassels in particular was most helpful in tracking down material. Friends at the Jesuit Centre for Social Faith and Justice in Toronto have also been a great help: these include Michael Czerny (now teaching at the UCA in San Salvador), Tim Draimin, Joe Gunn, and Deborah Barndt.

In Nicaragua dozens of people assisted in a variety of ways. Friends such as Marc Allain, Susan Johnson, Geoff Clare, Betty Smith, Richard Donald, Mary Talbot, and Jennifer Watts provided transportation, accommodation, and general "infrastructure" during my three trips. Numerous Church representatives were extremely generous with their time and advice. It would be impossible to name them all, but special thanks are due to papal nuncio Paolo Giglio, Cardinal Obando y Bravo, archdiocese spokesman Bismarck Carballo, Ernesto Cardenal, Uriel Molina, Msgr. Arias Caldera, Alvaro Argüello, and Xabier Gorostiaga for taking time from their busy schedules.

Two further essentials required for any research project should also be recognized. Family support from my wife, Margo, and children—Lisa, Michael, and Emily—was extremely necessary, given the time spent away from them in Nicaragua. Funding for the project came from the Research Development Fund at Dalhousie University and from a generous research grant from the Social Sciences and Humanities Research Council of Canada.

Despite the support given by countless people (from a variety of backgrounds and perspectives), it is important to state that the opinions expressed in this book are entirely my own and that I am solely responsible for claims and interpretations found herein. To facilitate a broader understanding of the topic, all Spanish quotations have been translated into English, and, needless to say, I accept full responsibility for their accuracy. It is hoped that the study will add to the literature assessing the religious-political convergence, as Nicaragua struggles to achieve a modicum of the stable growth and tranquillity that it so desperately needs.

✝

IN SEARCH OF STABILITY

The Church in Nicaragua

In Nicaragua religious matters
are a concern for everybody.
To a certain extent in
Nicaragua today everything
has invaded religion, and
religion has invaded
everything.

César Jérez, *The Church and
the Nicaraguan Revolution*

DURING THE COURSE OF the last decade it became increasingly common to read about the polarization of Church-state relations in revolutionary Nicaragua and—as a consequence—divisions within the Church itself. Articles in the mainstream media highlighted the deeply rooted divisions in the Catholic Church, noted clerics from Nicaragua made countless visits around the globe lobbying for their own particular interpretation of the religious/political struggle, and President Ronald Reagan was not adverse to citing the (conservative) archbishop of Managua's words to support his arguments for contra aid. Among some of the more dramatic examples that may be remembered from this extensive media coverage were the Church's opposition to military service, the issue of several priests holding high-ranking government posts, the stormy visit of John Paul II in 1983, the refusal of Archbishop Obando y Bravo (whose very promotion to the rank of cardinal was seen by many as an overtly political move by the Vatican) to condemn the contras, the expulsion by the Sandinista government of several priests, the pressure by the archbishop's office on "progressive" priests and religious to leave their parishes and—in some cases—not to return to missionary work in Nicaragua, and the closing of Radio Católica by the government.

The list goes on and on, revealing just how deep the rift between the Church and the revolutionary government leaders had become and just how polarized the Catholic Church was—and is. (It is a phenomenon found in the Protestant Church too, particularly with the increasing influence of extremely conservative Pentecostal groups, but nowhere does it awaken the tension or the passion encountered in Catholic circles.) Yet in the wake of the Somocista rout of July 1979 this problem appeared to have disappeared: the Nicaraguan Bishops' Conference released (in November of that year) an extremely open and supportive pastoral letter encouraging the faithful not to be frightened of socialism, and the Sandinista government seemed intent on securing the Church's support (indeed key portfolios—including the Ministries of External Affairs, Education, and Culture—were awarded to priests, with dozens of other important consulting positions also being held by priests and religious). Within the Church itself, on the surface at least, there was also an apparent sense of unity, of common purpose, in the wake of more than forty years of the Somoza dictatorship.

Obvious questions need to be posed as a result of these clearly unusual circumstances: Just what did happen to change these circumstances so dramatically? How could Archbishop Obando y Bravo—so reviled in the Somocista media as a communist and a supporter of the Sandinista Front for National Liberation (FSLN) (he was often referred to as "Comandante Miguel")—suddenly turn on the Sandinistas and become their most outspoken critic? Similarly, how could the Sandinistas—who had personally invited the archbishop to mediate in several tense situations during the Somoza years—now decry him as an ally of the U.S.-supported counterrevolutionaries? When viewed with the value of hindsight and from a clearer geographical vantage point, it seems incredible that passions should have become so inflamed that Nicaraguans would have forgotten the pain inflicted on their nation for four decades by the dreaded Somoza dynasty and turn against each other so ferociously. After all, runs the argument, hadn't the entire population suffered at the hands of the dicatorship? Surely it was now a time of nation building, of seeking a wide-ranging national unity so that Nicaragua could rise from the ashes.

Putting this logic aside for a moment and examining the Nicaraguan scenario from a historical perspective instead, it is immediately clear that the ensuing bitterness and adversity that resulted within a year of the popular victory over Somoza was in many ways predictable. Indeed, if one looks at Nicaraguan history in the nineteenth century, or at least from the earliest days of the colonial period, it is striking to see how at key moments there existed fundamental division not only between Church and government leaders but also within the Church itself. Whether it be over the rights of the indigenous people, the struggle for independence from Spain, the invasion of Nicaragua by mercenary forces headed by William Walker in the mid-nineteenth century, or the nationalistic struggle in the 1930s of Augusto César Sandino to force out U.S. Marines, there has *always* been polarization of Church members (and serious difficulties between Church and political actors in these episodes) and a resulting period of bitter infighting among those involved. When seen in this light, the decade of hostility and religious polarization (mirroring precisely, of course, the political polarization found throughout the decade) is merely the last episode of a drama that has been unfolding for several centuries. "Plus ça change, plus c'est la même chose. . . ."

This study holds one basic thesis, around which the book's central argument is constructed: that the Church has always been a major political actor, something which is particularly clear in the Latin American scenario. Moreover, within the mainstream of this political activity, the hierarchical Church has traditionally fought to protect its niche in the bosom of the conservative sectors—a phenomenon sometimes referred to as the "comfortable pew." Of course, examples can be found to show that many priests and religious—and indeed some prelates—did manage to break with this ecclesio-political tradition, but they are a distinct minority. Instead, the dominant trend has been for the Church to defend a political stability that most clearly favored the middle classes at the social and economic expense of the popular sectors. This desire for accommodation with the status quo and for stability at all costs understandably led to ferocious debate within the Church as a whole, a process from which Nicaragua was not exempt. In sum, while providing all Nicaraguans with religious guidance, the Church has consistently been a major political actor, and in general it has sought to strengthen the status quo and thereby the middle class by urging the faithful not to follow "extremist" policies or tendencies—particularly when the hierarchy sees these as being in conflict with the Church's best interests. In doing so, however, it has also fomented division and polarization within its own ranks.

This desire for stability by Church leaders is only natural, of course, for like any corporate body they must defend their vested interests, particularly when they see apparently adverse political currents threatening the institution to which they have dedicated their lives. Yet such corporate conservatism is often vigorously denied by Church leaders, who consistently claim that they proffer merely "pastoral" advice and not political commentary—in other words, that they are "above politics." The line between the two is remarkably faint, however, and has been traversed consistently by Church leaders since the days of Jesus of Nazareth. The decade-long struggle within the Nicaraguan Church—portrayed in oversimplified form by the media as that between the "traditional" wing adhering to official teaching and the "People's Church" that seeks a parallel magisterium—is thus merely one last episode in an intense, centuries-old soul-searching within religious circles over the Church's mission in society.

The essential difference between the last decade and what has transpired in earlier times is that those clerics seeking a greater role for the Church in pursuing social justice now have support for their approach in Church magisterium—most noticeably in the string of progressive pastoral letters released by two remarkable pontiffs, John XXIII and Paul VI, in the 1960s. In the light of this radically new direction pursued by the Vatican throughout the 1970s, and following crucially important meetings of CELAM—the Latin American Bishops' Conference—in Medellín (1968) and Puebla (1979), the way ahead for a politically progressive and committed Church was clear. It is, of course, no accident that many of the main Church activists in Nicaragua were inspired in the 1960s by this liberating message of the need for a "preferential option for the poor" and the rediscovery of the radical (in the Latin sense of the term) message of Christianity.

The conservative upsurge within the Church, particularly noticeable since the arrival of John Paul II, has, on the other hand, strengthened the position of those who had looked askance at the liberating influence of Vatican II. The pontiff's considerable role on the international political stage, his appointment (particularly visible in Latin America) of extremely conservative prelates, and Vatican attempts to silence the leading exponents of Liberation Theology—all indicate an overtly *political* stance by John Paul II, despite protestations to the contrary. His emotional visit to Czechoslovakia in the spring of 1990 and his triumphant words on the necessary death of Marxism also reveal clearly the pope's political bent. In the case of Nicaragua the pope has done all in his power to delegitimize the "progressive" wing of the Church by demanding unwavering support for the Church's leader in the country, Cardinal Obando y Bravo.

Therein lies the dilemma for today's Church, for two very distinctive papal styles and messages have prepared the terrain for the current struggle. It is a contest that neither side will concede gracefully, since both have a decade of emotion and frustration wrapped up in the dynamic. Moreover, more than eighty thousand people lost their lives, first in the struggle against Somoza and then in the contra war, which devastated the country and polarized Nicaraguan families—and on which Church spokesmen from both camps clearly took sides, regardless of the rhetoric about being "neutral" and "apolitical." Understandably, it is a struggle that will leave political and personal scars for generations to come.

But as was mentioned at the outset, this dilemma is nothing new for the Church in Nicaragua—or indeed in Latin America as a whole. Since this situation is not novel, several key questions demand our attention: Precisely how did Church fortunes develop at those other times of inner, and national, crisis? What lessons can be learned from those traumatic chapters in the Church's history? In what ways is the most recent crisis—the focus of this study—different from earlier episodes? What can we learn from the polarized Church in Nicaragua? How have politico-religious matters developed over this past decade? What can we expect in the future? Clearly these issues need to be addressed if we are to understand the nature of this present crisis and the dynamics at play.

This study is divided into two sections. In the first I seek to present a historical overview of the Church's role at key moments in the national development of Nicaragua and, in particular, to analyze its political role(s). Its underlying motif is of a Church that—much like its counterpart throughout the 1980s—was divided at these important historical junctures over what political role to adopt consciously. Specific reference will be given to several Church activists who played a decidedly political role at key moments in national development. In the second section of the book, chapters 4 – 6, I examine in detail the nature of Church-state relations from the Sandinistas' arrival in power in July

1979 until their electoral defeat in February 1990, and in particular I assess the Church's role(s) in that turbulent decade. It is hoped that this detailed study, following the more general historical overview of the Church in Nicaragua, will make for a more balanced analysis of the Church's political role—a role in which all corporate bodies, whether of this world or the next and despite claims to the contrary, necessarily engage. . . .

✝

IN SEARCH OF AN IDENTITY

The Church in Nicaragua, 1503–1936

In Nicaragua, as in the rest
of Central America, a regime
of Christendom was
institutionalized [that]
legitimized the dominant
political power, be it colonial,
liberal or conservative. . . .
Taking full advantage from
the colonial domination, the
hierarchical Church preaches
an ideology that justifies the
oppression of Indians, creoles,
blacks, and mestizos, and
becomes an institution
that is both colonized and
a colonizing agent. It
participates in the prosperity
of the dominant classes,
covering up, blessing, and
legitimizing a shameless
exploitation of the native
peoples.

Oscar González Gary,
Iglesia Católica y revolución
en Nicaragua

Conquest and Colonialization

Comparatively little material on the role of the Church in Nicaragua exists from the first generation of conquest and discovery. In no small part this was due to the very dynamics of the rapid conquest of land (and riches), followed by a period of stabilization of political power through a process of colonization—a process in which the Church played a major role. Yet an understanding of the origins of Catholicism is truly essential if we are to appreciate the depth of religious roots in Nicaragua and the reasons why these developed so effectively throughout the colonial period.

Among the earliest references to the arrival of Catholicism in the region was the note that on his fourth—and final—journey Columbus visited what is now Nicaragua, bringing with him a Franciscan (Fray Alejandro). From the perspective of winning souls for Christ, early forays among the indigenous people were remarkably successful. Unlike Mexico, or indeed most other parts of the Spanish Empire, the evangelization of Nicaragua's native peoples went extremely smoothly and comparatively peacefully—"with little blood but lots of baptismal water," as it has been accurately described.[1] Massive baptisms were performed throughout the country,[2] and in one campaign reminiscent of the strategies of present-day televangelists, Fr. Francisco de Bobadilla allegedly converted 52,558 natives.[3] Not surprisingly, much of this evangelizing revolved around a superficial inculcation into the indigenous population of the most basic facets of Catholicism (a process in which priests often took advantage of native and Catholic customs to convince the conquered people of the inherent similarities of the religious philosophies). The imaginative and successful hybrid of festivities, beliefs, and ceremonies still survives in the deeply rooted popular religiosity encountered throughout Central America.

The first generation of religious life in what is now Nicaragua seems to have been extremely successful from the viewpoint of the Church—particularly if compared with other parts of the empire. By 1533, Governor Francisco de Castañeda had instructed some sixty-eight Spanish landholders to select the most promising Indian youth to be

educated in Hispanic customs and the Catholic faith at the San
Francisco de León convent. Four years later a royal decree was issued by
the Reyes Católicos requesting that a school be set up next to the
cathedral for the same purpose. These institutions would instruct the
children of the Indian leaders (*caciques*) in the ways of the conquistadores and ensure that the Church would be highly regarded by the
future native leaders. In this way the Church pursued a deliberate
program of co-opting the future indigenous leadership, a policy that
proved remarkably successful. The Mercedarians and Dominicans
quickly followed suit with the construction of their own convents. By
1550, the work of the Franciscans had thrived to the point that they had
already established a religious province (San Jorge); by 1586, they had
built twelve convents in Nicaragua, and some sixty-seven friars were
engaged in missionary work.[4] This was an exceptional situation (on a
per capita basis it represents perhaps a twentyfold increase in the
attention given to missionary programs) and helps to explain precisely
why the evangelistic campaigns were so successful in gaining converts to
Catholicism.

It is fascinating reading to peruse the variety of royal documents and
decrees that flowed from Spain to the colonies concerning the Church's
mission in the newfound lands. Common to all was a basic understanding that Catholicism had to be taught the "infidels" if they were to
emerge from their inherent ignorance. There was also an assumed and
underlying conviction that it was God's will for the new territories to be
converted to Christianity:

> It has now pleased Divine Providence that we should discover
> a large mass of land, beyond those islands and territories already
> found. This new land is inhabited by a great multitude who appear
> more reasonable and skilled, as well as better instructed in matters
> of Our Holy Faith than those we have encountered thus far. Since
> we desire to save such a multitude of souls . . . we have sent a large
> Armada so that, together with other soldiers already there, we will
> be able to subjugate those barbarous nations, and force them to
> obey Our Holy Mother the Church.[5]

Little attention was paid to the quality of instruction given the
indigenous population, and even less (despite the occasional concern
raised by well-meaning clergy) to what was, in effect, a legalized form of

slavery. Instead the Catholic king and queen, rejoicing that God had provided them with this virgin territory to Christianize (and exploit), forged ahead, encouraging a wave of enthusiastic evangelization. After all, they not only won souls for Christ but also won subjects for themselves, as well as land and riches never before imagined. All that was needed, then, was to subjugate the barbarian nations and "force them to obey Our Holy Mother the Church." While this was an effective and successful approach used throughout the empire, it was hardly the appropriate manner of developing a profound understanding of Catholic teaching.

But once the initial flurry of pastoral activity had died down, the Church found itself in a difficult situation. Its mission was to instruct the "newly discovered" population in the Catholic faith, yet it must have been immediately obvious that their evangelizing campaigns involving so many thousands of natives were remarkably superficial. (Writing in 1535, Fernández de Oviedo commented ironically on the mass baptisms that the clergy, caught up in a ritualistic frenzy of evangelizing, were performing: "It would be so much better for just one Indian to be properly instructed and a good Christian than a thousand of them baptized, since they do not know how to save their brethren or to live like a Christian.")[6] In an effort to win more souls, the Church emphasized similarities between indigenous beliefs and the Catholic faith, festivals accompanied by much pomp and ceremony were instituted, legends about miracles performed by priests blossomed, and a popular religiosity—a blend of Catholic and indigenous mysticism—flourished and indeed continues to flourish today. This popular religiosity might well have encouraged more natives to accept Catholicism, but it hardly constituted a solid base for orthodoxy—and much of it would have undoubtedly seemed heretical to European Church leaders. Nevertheless, Catholicism developed quickly and spread rapidly throughout present-day Central America, quickly cementing the political control exercised by the Spanish and in many ways legitimizing the cruel nature of the colonization process. From the point of view of establishing Spanish control (in both political and economic terms) over the area, Catholic evangelization was thus an exceptionally effective tool.

Yet despite this extremely astute harnessing of organized religion for clearly political ends, there was also present among many Church representatives a sincere, if occasionally naive, preoccupation about the rights of the native people, who were becoming increasingly frustrated at both the rapacious greed of the conquistadores and their own treatment at the hands of these "Christian" settlers. The inevitable question remained, however: precisely what was the role of the Church supposed to be in the colonies? It was fine for Charles V in 1527 to name Nicaragua's first bishop (Diego Alvarez Osorio) "Protector and Defender of the Indians," but what (earthly) power did he wield in the colonies, especially when the Spanish settlers were largely interested in getting rich quick, with little regard for the physical well-being of their Indian workers? It should be kept in mind that for the most part the colonizers were hardly the crème de la crème of Hispanic society: they had usually come to the colonies to escape a lack of opportunities for them in the motherland, and they were clearly unaffected by the appalling situation of the Indians—whom they exploited ruthlessly in order to increase their own profits. Given this situation, the bishop was in a most difficult predicament, particularly when many of his clerical colleagues were themselves not above exploiting the Indians.[7]

The issue facing the Church over what to do concerning the increasingly exploited native population was both an ecclesiastical and a political problem. Moreover, if all parties involved had been totally honest they would have agreed that it was one for which an amicable solution was simply impossible; their opposing positions allowed no middle ground. The dilemma was of an ecclesiastical nature in the sense that the Spanish monarchs (the Reyes Católicos) had specifically entrusted Alvarez Osorio with the spiritual and temporal well-being of the indigenous people.[8] It was also highly political in that—if effectively carried out—such a policy went directly against the vested interests of the vast majority of (Catholic) Spanish settlers in Nicaragua, who could hardly be expected to be loyal supporters of the very approach that threatened their livelihood. As a result of this inherent contradiction, there evolved a tradition of vicious infighting between, on the one hand, those clerics who took seriously their mandate concerning the Indians and, on the other, the Spanish settlers (often protected by the civilian authorities and supported by the complacency of other clerics, some of whom also had their own slaves). A double standard was established, one that continued unabated for several centuries. Lawsuits against clergy who did attempt to protect the indigenous people, lobbying campaigns back in Spain against their efforts, and direct force of arms were all tactics employed by the colonizers against this minority of clerics who dared to take their mandate seriously. Such was the case, for example, of perhaps the best-known advocate of native rights, the Dominican Bartolomé de las Casas, who was expelled from Nicaragua by the conquistador Rodrigo de Contreras.

Las Casas (who subsequently took up residency in present-day Chiapas, Mexico) and Nicaragua's third bishop, Antonio de Valdivieso, directed a petition to the Spanish administrative body, the Audiencia, in October 1545. In it they defined clearly their responsibilities vis-à-vis the native population ("since the Church has been charged with the protection and defense of these people, and through divine law is obliged both to shelter and defend them, as well as to investigate their complaints, and ensure that justice be done")[9] and appealed for support. Unfortunately, Bishop Valdivieso would live only four more years before being murdered by the Contreras family, who had become increasingly disturbed by his outspoken criticisms of their abuse of power.

Rodrigo Contreras was governor at the time, and his family held sway over the entire region, imposing his military might while owning approximately one-third of the country. Complaints against the manner in which they treated the Indians on their property were commonplace, and Valdivieso, armed with the 1542 New Laws that explained very clearly the obligations of landowners to their slaves, doggedly pursued Contreras. In the face of blatantly illegal actions by the governor, Valdivieso complained to the Audiencia, with the result that Contreras was replaced and his property expropriated. On February 26, 1550, some members of the Contreras family, convinced that they were a power unto themselves and supported by a gang of armed thugs, attacked the bishop and assassinated him.

The case of Antonio de Valdivieso is important in its own right, but it also sheds some light on the political role of the Church in subsequent centuries. First, it shows the example of a Church leader who believed in protecting weak members of his flock, in exercising the "preferential option for the poor" that was enshrined in the 1960s—in sum, in practicing what he preached. We also see the power—and the responsibility—of a prelate in a Catholic society that in many ways paid only lip service to Catholic values. In a letter to the king of Spain, for example, Valdivieso mentioned that many colonial authorities wanted bishops merely for decorative purposes and that, to their shame, many clerics played along with this game in order to protect their own vested interests. Valdivieso was fundamentally opposed to this superficial form of religion, commenting ironically: "The only reason they want a priest is to say mass for them and preach—but only then saying what they want to hear."[10] Moreover, several members of the clergy sided with the Contreras family (and their own interests), complaining about the bishop's meddling and political activities. While the Church was not yet deeply divided, it was clear that—just two decades after the Spanish arrived—there existed radically different views concerning the nature of Christian witness that the clergy were expected to bear.

After the murder of Valdivieso, colonial religious life in Nicaragua was in general characterized by a retreat away from protecting the indigenous population, a process that thereby protected the status quo and, as such, was indirectly a political action. The *encomienda* system (granting land tenure and the Indians to the conquistadores) continued, with minor amendments, for several centuries. How did the Church react to this system? The Mexican Church historian Oscar González Gary summarized this role succinctly, noting the "ideological manipulation of religion to cover up injustice. The Church thus became an essential partner within the colonial mercantilist structure."[11] Church leaders quickly realized that their own interests could best be served by collaborating with colonial authorities, and as a result the Indians' rights were quickly forgotten. After all, it was easier to preach resignation to the natives and engage in popular religious fiestas than to stand with them against the brutality (and the power) of the Spanish settlers.

This was a trend that, with a few important exceptions,[12] would remain throughout the colonial period. In essence the Church of the late sixteenth century was the same as that on the eve of the struggle for independence at the beginning of the nineteenth: despite the passing of three centuries, Church thinking remained mired in a semifeudal mind-set. Strengthened by the *Patronato Real,* according to which the Crown appointed Church leaders in the colonies (and paid for the upkeep of religious life, thereby directly co-opting Church personnel who were, in effect, their employees), an unspoken doctrine evolved whose basic tenet was that the Church's interests were best served by state support (and vice versa).

As Church and state leaders gradually forgot the aim and central thrust of the 1542 New Laws, a durable marriage of convenience was established that was mutually beneficial. On the one hand, the landlords were assured of a docile work force, reared on the platitudes of humility and resignation, while the Church was guaranteed a captive audience (almost literally). The ramifications of this mutually beneficial arrangement were witnessed on several occasions when the Church—acting in a clearly political fashion—sided with the status quo and sought to convince their Indian charges not to "get involved." When, for example, the struggle for independence erupted in Mexico in 1810 and then spread throughout the Spanish Empire, it was obvious to the Church authorities that they had to rally to the support of their allies, the colonial authorities. After all, the vested interests of both had thrived during the period of stability since the colonization, Church authority was at an all-time peak, and it would be a clear tactical folly for the Church to reject its ally of several centuries' standing. Accordingly, fearful of their own loss of standing and the dire consequences if the colonial authorities were forced to cede power to the rebels, Church leaders swung their power solidly behind the colonial authorities.[13] In their search for stability they mistakenly protected the status quo precisely at a time when it was abundantly clear that the ancien régime lacked any significant credibility (much less moral justification) and needed to be changed quite radically. Thus the Church hierarchy gambled, expecting the insurgents to be put down, and lost—badly. It was a process that would be repeated on several occasions in Nicaraguan history.

One important dynamic in these historical developments was the occasional division between the Church hierarchy and the lower clergy. Several variables came into play here, including national origin (i.e., Spanish-born versus Creole), wealth, dependence on the Reyes Católicos, the system of *patronato,* and the nature of the pastoral role. In general terms it was clear that, with some noteworthy exceptions, members of the Church hierarchy (most of whom were *peninsulares*) were unsympathetic to the claims of the indigenous population and chose to ignore questions of social justice. Conversely, while most of the lower clergy were apolitical, a significant minority (particularly native-born members) opposed the stance of their superiors and advocated a more progressive role for the Church. It is therefore significant, but hardly surprising, that the struggle for independence in Mexico should have started with priests like Hidalgo and Morelos, while the Church hierarchy was adamantly opposed to such an action. In Nicaragua the pattern was very similar.

The Struggle for Independence and the Church

By the time that the movement for independence reached Nicaragua in 1811, the Church had become one of the leading power brokers in colonial life and had extended its influence throughout all levels of Nicaraguan society. The bishop was an influential figure, present in all major social and political gatherings; Church schools catered to the families of the merchant class; and the Indian and mestizo natives also respected the Church's deeply rooted influence. Moreover, an entrenched popular religiosity had flourished during these nearly three centuries (which clearly remains to this day); the number of priests had grown significantly (by 1751 there were sixty diocesan clergy and sixty-four priests belonging to religious orders—for a population of approximately 150,000);[14] and the role of the Church (both at the level of the hierarchy and at the grass roots) was very highly regarded. It was obvious, though, that when the wars for independence broke out in Mexico—headed by a priest, Father Hidalgo, and subsequently led by a colleague, Father Morelos (both of whom were executed for their opposition to the Crown)—the Church in Central America would not be allowed to sit on the sidelines. When the demand for reform then spread to El Salvador, where once again priests were among the leading conspirators against Spanish domination, the Church in Nicaragua knew that it would have to take sides in the imminent war. Once again strictly political concerns would hold sway over religious matters, despite claims to the contrary.

In general there were two basic groupings within the Church as the winds of change blew through Nicaragua. On one side were the Church leaders, who in general were Spanish and strongly supported the monarchy's right to govern the colonies as Spain's rulers saw fit. Of a decidedly conservative background, they were in favor of the established order and feared for the Church (and their own interests) if the insurgency were to succeed. On the other side were many of the lower clergy, who not only supported the rebels but in some cases were also among the actual leaders of the struggle for independence. They viewed their role as catalysts for social justice and were determined to bear prophetic witness in this struggle. Included in their reform program were demands for an end to slavery, meaningful agrarian reform, and the substitution of Nicaraguan for Spanish rulers. This set of radical reforms contrasted strikingly with the mere tinkering that the Church leaders were willing to accept.

Among representatives of the hierarchy strongly opposed to the struggle for independence were Bishop García Jérez—the last prelate of the colonial period—and the vicar of Granada, José Antonio Chamorro. A study of their role in this decisive period is instructive, for it shows both how they went beyond the bounds of strictly spiritual concerns and how polarized the Church was on this political matter. In 1812 Chamorro roundly condemned the insurrection, stating that to rebel against the established order was "un-Christian" and encouraging all Catholics to lay down their arms: "The people have disobeyed the Spanish administrators—which means that therefore the people have disobeyed the king and queen of Spain. They have gone against their absolute rule. The people thus believe that they have more power than God, the Church, and the king. We can deduce from this that the insurgents have betrayed, and continue to do so, God, the king, and the fatherland."[15] Such a position was quite understandable for anyone steeped in traditional ecclesiastical thinking concerning the divine rights of power and authority. (A similar argument was pursued by Church leaders throughout Latin America in the 1810–21 struggle for independence, and even as late as 1895 when the insurrection broke out against the Spanish rule in Cuba.) It was, however, a strictly political stand, one that was deliberately issued to protect the status quo—and the Church's own vested interests.

At the other end of the ideological spectrum, many clergy played an extremely active role not only in the actual fighting against the Spanish authorities but also in the subsequent political reorganization after independence was declared. Among these can be cited Benito Miguelena, who stored arms in his convent in León and participated in the conspiracy along with clerics Tomás Ruiz and José Ramón Rojas; Benito Soto, who was one of the leaders of the uprising in Granada and who presented a successful motion to the reorganized junta to abolish slavery; and both Rafael de la Fuente in Rivas and Salvador Barrios in Masaya, who were elected as the towns' representatives in the wake of the uprising. There was thus a great degree of polarization among the clergy, ranging from an outright defense of the "God-given" colonial system to the active involvement of others among the insurgents.

A leading figure among the conservative wing was Bishop García Jérez, who was opposed to the insurgency but rapidly took on the role of mediator among the opposing forces. This initially occurred in December 1811, when the rebels surrounded the town hall in León, demanding the execution of the Spanish governor. The bishop intervened as mediator and played a major role in defusing a most volatile situation. Subsequently he counseled the election of political representatives to form a provisional junta—which he was asked to head—and later was named provisional governor. Bishop García Jérez was clearly opposed to the idea of political independence, yet he astutely managed to co-opt the rebels and to ensure that the radical restructuring being sought by them would not be realized: rather than a radical transformation, he preferred minor adjustments to the existing system. What he almost single-handedly managed to do, then, was to stall the demand for meaningful reform, emphasizing the need for reconciliation and social harmony and thereby derailing the insurgency. Given the official Church penchant for spiritual concerns, his was clearly a most political role.

Between 1811 and 1821 (when the Central American Provinces officially signed the Act of Independence from Spain), Nicaragua found itself torn apart in a series of plots and counterplots to overthrow Spanish control of the country. Mention was made earlier of the uprisings of 1811, and of the active involvement of clergy on both sides of the ideological divide—namely, of the active role of many priests in the actual insurgency and of Bishop García Jérez, who sought to defuse a potentially volatile situation by seeking certain minor local reforms.[16] Initially he succeeded, since the heady days in 1811 of massed insurgents on the streets quickly passed. Indeed, many priests were soon arrested: Tomás Ruiz, for example, who had taken part in the uprising in León, was arrested in Guatemala (only to take part in another attempt at overthrowing the Spanish) and finally was accused of being an insurgent by the archbishop of Guatemala—and was jailed until 1819.[17] Another key figure was Benito Miguelena, who was accused of disturbing public order, arrested, and sent to Guatemala. Later he, together with several other priests including Benito Soto, Victor Castrillo, and Tomás Ruiz, took part in the famous Belén conspiracy (named after the convent where the planning for the uprising took place). The actual goals of the conspiracy were radical indeed: to overthrow Spanish control of Nicaragua, distribute arms to the population, liberate political prisoners in Granada, link up with rebels throughout Central America, and proclaim political independence from Spain. However, as noted above, such plans for social transformation fell on deaf ears both among the Spanish colonial administration and within the Church itself.

When political independence from Spain was finally won (with the separation of the erstwhile captaincy-general into an appendage of the new Mexican Empire in 1821, followed two years later by the formation of the United Provinces of Central America) deep rifts clearly existed within the Catholic Church. On the one side were those religious who had stoutly defended the absolutist monarchy (such as Bishop García Jérez and the priests Rojas and Chamorro); on the other were clerics like Ruiz, Miguelena, and Monino who, echoing the call for revolution from other priests in Mexico and El Salvador, wanted radical social reforms and were prepared to fight in order to obtain them. Both groups were convinced that their political positions were based on their interpretation of the message of Catholic social magisterium and that their ecclesial opponents were opportunists lusting for power. Perhaps more ominously, there was clearly no middle ground in their political positions—as had been the case for Las Casas and Valdivieso and their detractors. The polarization between those two sectors was thus irreversible.

The Church in Postcolonial Nicaragua

Between 1823 and the Sandinista revolution of 1979, the political spectrum of Nicaragua was remarkably limited, in essence revolving around the Liberal and Conservative parties and their respective strongholds in León and Granada. The Liberals' central core of support came largely from those Creole producers and exporters who had been excluded from their fair share of commerce by Spanish controls, while their opponents had generally been better treated by that same Spanish commercial domination, particularly in the area of agricultural production. The Liberals "advocated reducing restrictions on trade and commerce, increasing basic infrastructure development (such as roads and ports), and ending exemption from taxes for the Church";[18] the Conservatives were in favor of altering the status quo as little as possible. The sectarianism that dominated Nicaraguan political life, compounded by the deeply rooted regional hostilities, further polarized the population (and the Church). The end result of this institutionalized tension was a series of bloody civil wars that continued virtually unabated from 1823 to 1857, wreaking havoc on the country at large.

The first round in this internecine struggle for power clearly went to the Liberals, who introduced a series of legislative changes that had a serious impact on the Church's status. In essence the Liberals wanted to destroy the old colonial order and replace it with a new (and more profitable) independent territory. Therefore, all that had cemented the ancien régime together—including the Church—now found itself marginalized and increasingly painted both as an anachronism and as an obstacle to change. The 1824 Constitution of the United Provinces of Central America, for instance, had recognized Catholicism as the official religion—and banned the practice of other religions—but when Liberal president Francisco Morazán took over the United Provinces in 1830, the Church's privileges began to disappear. Several convents (belonging to the Recollection, Mercedarian, and Franciscan orders) were annexed by the state, the clergy were dispersed, and the bishopric was left unoccupied until 1849. The first constitution of Nicaragua (which separated from the confederation in 1838) continued this trend, permitting for the first time the public exercise of religions other than Catholicism. The subsequent return to power in the mid-1850s of the Conservatives (whom many Church authorities had openly supported—for obvious reasons—throughout this time) marked a return to the privileges of before, as religious freedom was abolished and Catholicism once again became the official state religion.

The chronic political instability of Nicaragua was made worse by the injection of a further element in the equation: U.S. interests in commercial expansion, focused on the possibility of a canal across the Central American isthmus. The Liberals, itching to return to power, thus made an agreement with Cornelius Garrison and William Walker to overthrow the Conservatives in return for extensive land grants. The latter invaded Nicaragua with some fifty-seven Americans in June 1855 and seized power. Joined by an army of ruthless mercenaries, supporting the concept of legalized slavery, and fully prepared to execute all who stood in his way, Walker had himself elected president of Nicaragua in 1856. Later he left the country after a series of military defeats; in 1860 he was subsequently captured in Honduras and executed.

William Walker was a fascinating and paradoxical character. Fully believing in Anglo-Saxon racial superiority and in the doctrine of Manifest Destiny, he perceived the lands of Latin America as virgin territory waiting to be "civilized" by rugged entrepreneurs like himself.

He viewed slavery as the essential means by which the ignorant Indian masses would be saved from their own debilitating poverty and forced to enter the beckoning (and profitable) new industrial age. (The racist element of his program should not be underestimated, for he clearly believed white supremacy to be an essential factor in the development of nations. Indeed, many of Latin America's woes were to be blamed on the spirit of fraternity and equality that resulted from the struggles for independence: "Instead of maintaining the purity of the races as did the English in their settlements, the Spaniards had cursed their continental possessions with a mixed race," he noted).[19] Freedom and progress would of necessity follow in the wake of the progressive economic management instituted by the influx of (white) North Americans who would revive the failing fortunes of Nicaragua and fully modernize the nation.

How did the Church respond to the invasion of Central America by Walker and his crew of filibusters? Once again the response was extremely divided, with some priests angered at his military incursion and others seeing it as the necessary solution to the previous decades of vicious infighting between Liberals and Conservatives. (At the time, the Church in Nicaragua was without a bishop—a factor that probably contributed to the lack of a clear official position on the Walker invasion.) One keen supporter, however, was José Hilario Herdocia, the vicar of the Granada bishopric (the highest-ranking Church official in the vicariate), who was delighted with Walker's approach and provided him with moral and financial backing. The American wrote to him on November 27, 1855, thanking him for his support: "I had the pleasure and honor of receiving your communiqué of 26 [of November]. It is satisfactory knowing that the Church authorities support the existing government. It is not possible to govern well without the help of the religious sentiments and religious guides. Because the fear of God is the basis of all social and political organizations."[20]

Support for Walker also came from a priest, Agustín Vijil, for whom the American filibuster was both a "Protective Angel" and the "Star of the North."[21] He personally organized a thanksgiving celebration, a Te Deum for Peace and National Reconciliation. Moreover, when Walker needed funding to continue his military campaign, Church support was not lacking: Father Vijil, for example, donated his parish funds as well as almost one thousand ounces of silver taken from a statue of the Virgin on the altar of a church in Granada. As a reward for his support, he was sent to Washington as Walker's personal ambassador in the United States; he returned to Granada as the Church's representative after Walker's "election" as president.

On the other hand, several priests were fundamentally opposed to Walker's white supremacist message, his determination to reintroduce slavery, his unshakable belief in Manifest Destiny, and his brutal tactics. These priests included Rafael Villavicencio in Granada, Santiago Delgado, and Father Tijerino in Ometepe, who participated actively in the struggle against Walker. Once again tremendous religious polarization resulted over a clearly political matter as Church members aligned themselves with radically different positions.

The half century between 1857 and 1909, despite its two clearly defined periods of control by the Conservatives and then the Liberals, was a time of economic growth (due primarily to a massive increase in coffee production) and relative political calm for Nicaragua. Both features contributed to the solidification of Church-state relations, particularly during the thirty-year period of Conservative rule beginning in 1857. Once again the Church secured for itself a safe niche in the bosom of society, from where it sought to strengthen its social position (largely through its highly regarded schools) and promote a message of peace and reconciliation.

This newfound stability was in many ways typified by the signing of a concordat between the Nicaraguan government and the Holy See in 1862, which codified and regulated the legal relationship between Church and state. Among the twenty-eight clauses of the agreement were some that were crucially important for the Church: the official state religion of Nicaragua was to be Catholicism; public school education had to follow Church doctrine; the bishops reserved the right to censor books and newspapers; the government was obliged to sustain the Church (including the actual buildings, official salaries, and the seminary) economically; parish priests were to be named by the president of the republic; and the government exercised the right to present candidates for bishoprics.

The signing of the concordat was a significant event, for the agreement laid out coldly and categorically the basis for an effective Church-state relationship that would last for several decades. The overall objective was to ensure the stability of both Church and state as their fates became inextricably intertwined. More cynical observers might well claim that under the guise of the concordat both institutions were co-opted by the promise of support from the other leading social actor. Indeed, state authorities were obliged to pay for the upkeep of the Church as an institution but, in return for that stiff cost, could ensure the Church's future political direction since the state now controlled the nomination process of bishops and priests. For its part, after the vicissitudes of many decades of political infighting and resultant insecurity, the Church now enjoyed an economic stability heretofore unknown. Moreover, through the official acceptance of such rights as that of censorship (not to mention the declaration of Catholicism as the official state religion and the domination of the school system), the Church had assured for itself a powerful social and political base.

In short, any doubt about the Church's influence—both in temporal and spiritual planes—disappeared in one fell swoop. Admittedly Church influence was firmly subordinated to state benevolence, yet by the same token it had carved out for itself a niche of social respectability that had long been missing. Church leaders thus became powerful and influential figures, but they had learned that in order to survive they had to rise above the ebb and flow of secular politics. For leaders of both Church and state the amicable arrangement seemed to make sound economic and political sense. (In 1881 the strength of this union would be put to the test when an Indian uprising in Matagalpa was supported by the Jesuits. The government expelled them from Nicaragua, without more than superficial rumblings of discontent from Bishop Ulloa y Larios, who clearly understood that the Jesuits' actions threatened to derail the recently established working relationship with government officials.) At this point in its development, the Church as an institution had recovered practically all the influence and authority—as well as its monopoly on ideology—that it had enjoyed in colonial times.

The arrival in power of Liberal president José Santos Zelaya in 1893, however, signaled the end of this era of Church privilege and national stability. The basic tenets of Zelaya's reform program revolved around modernizing the coffee industry (by now the central pillar of the Nicaraguan economy), and to this end he set about dismantling the country's archaic sociopolitical and economic structures. In many ways it was a repetition of the 1820 Liberal domination, marked by the steady destruction of all that was perceived as having retarded economic growth. For the Church—long identified with the Conservatives—the subsequent reforms were quite shocking: the 1862 concordat was swiftly annulled, effectively wiping out the advantages the Church had so carefully cultivated for decades; the official separation between Church and state was instituted; civil matrimony and divorce became legal; cemeteries—traditionally run by the Church—became public property controlled by civilian authorities; the entry of foreign religious was forbidden; the Church's lucrative *cofradías* (wealthy holdings administered by lay Catholics) were annulled; Church-owned land was expropriated; several priests—including the bishop—were declared persona non grata and forced to leave Nicaragua (indeed, Bishop Simeón Pereira y Castellón was forced out of Nicaragua on two occasions); the Sacred Heart school in Granada was closed after it was discovered that the nuns who taught there had participated in antigovernment activities; the secular nature of education was established; and outdoor religious processions and services were prohibited, as was the wearing of religious vestments outside churches. (In León a priest named Ramón de Jesús Castro was beaten for wearing his habit, to which Bishop Pereira y Castellón responded by excommunicating President Zelaya.) Adding insult to injury, the president also encouraged and protected the entry into Nicaragua of foreign pastors, whom he apparently considered to be a more appropriate spiritual influence for his Liberal and allegedly progressive reforms.

The Church struggled to retain its former privileges,[22] but in many ways it was a losing battle, especially while the Liberals remained in power. Once again the Church, which in its cordial relationship with the ruling Conservatives had furthered its own ends—and acted in a consistently political fashion—saw its status rapidly erode. The explanation proffered by the Liberals for their steady dismantling of Church influence was not that they were antireligious; rather, they claimed that the Church's temporal, political influence had become too powerful and had retarded national growth.

Throughout the nineteenth century, Church fortunes waned and thrived, depending basically on whether their allies were in power. During this time the Church was actively involved in political activities that largely revolved around protecting its vested spiritual and tangible interests. It consistently sought to expand its influence, making pacts with political actors when it was in the Church's best interests to do so, and opposing those who sought to infringe on their rights and privileges. More importantly, the Church was itself an important political actor, often removed from the sacristy and actively involved in matters that frequently transcended its purely spiritual mission. As a political actor, the Church was often deeply divided—as we have seen, for instance, in the struggle for independence, the Walker intervention, and the ongoing struggle between Liberal and Conservative factions. This manifest polarization was due both to differing political positions and to varying interpretations of the role of mission—although the latter concern seems to have been a much more dominant factor, reflecting the inherent divisions among priests who sought to realize their vocation in widely divergent fashions. Indeed, just as there had been activist bishops like Valdivieso in the sixteenth century, there had been similar "liberation theologians" in every subsequent century; moreover, there had been conservatives throughout Nicaraguan history who sought to pursue a more traditional interpretation of the Church's mission. These two features—religious division/polarization and fundamental political activity—had been common denominators for almost four centuries; they would continue to be inherent characteristics of Church activity in this century as well.

The overthrow of the brutal caudillo Zelaya in the late nineteenth century was skillfully engineered by the United States, for whom Zelaya's plans to allow Japanese and German investors to build a canal through Nicaragua (thereby destroying the natural advantages of what would ultimately be the Panama Canal) were clearly unacceptable. A combination of U.S. and British interests supported an uprising staged by the Conservatives in the Atlantic port of Bluefields in 1909. The inevitable, time-honored scenario was then enacted: in response to a self-styled request for liberating forces, some four hundred U.S. Marines arrived—in theory to protect American lives and property, but in practice to warn Zelaya that his overthrow was guaranteed should he be foolish enough to remain in power. This was the logical twentieth-century version of Manifest Destiny as perceived in Washington: flushed with the success of its "liberating mission" in Cuba in the badly misnamed Spanish-American War, once again dollar diplomacy was rearing its ugly head.

The Church and U.S. Intervention in Nicaragua

The end result of the arrival of the marines was a quarter century of political chaos in Nicaragua. By 1910, for instance, the insurgents came to power—and the marines withdrew. The coalition government swiftly fell apart, however, and the new president, Adolfo Díaz, followed the only course open to puppet leaders in the Latin American mold: invite back the marines.[23] There followed a pattern of U.S. military occupation (the marines who landed in August 1912 remained until 1925, when they left for nine months—then returning to stay until 1933), shoring up unpopular and otherwise impotent political leaders, while the economy remained a disaster, leading to a growing dependence on external financial aid and investment.[24] The occupying U.S. forces imposed on the Nicaraguans their model for virtually everything from elections (which they supervised) to a national security force (which led to the formation of the National Guard, in theory a neutral paramilitary force distant from both the Liberals and the Conservatives).

Despite nominal Nicaraguan control, then, the real power behind the throne was now found in Washington. Given the fact that this U.S. military intervention was without doubt the major political development in Nicaragua for the first three decades of the twentieth century—one that permeated all facets of Nicaraguan life—it is interesting to ponder the Church's reaction to it. The official reaction speaks volumes about the way Church leaders perceived their responsibilities (be they spiritual or of this earth) and is a fascinating study of political accommodation couched in ecclesiastical terminology.

Despite the turmoil and political infighting, the landing of the marines, and the economic havoc as Nicaragua's future was mortgaged to North American and British banking houses, the Church's fortunes slowly improved during this period. This was largely due to the fact that there was little difference between the Church's interests and those of the Conservative oligarchy, which led the country for most of the subsequent quarter century. Indeed, by this time there was also little difference between the Liberals and the Conservatives in the manner in which they perceived the Church's influence. While the Liberals were, at least in theory, more anticlerical than their Conservative counterparts, in reality the parties' shared interest in a harmonious sociopolitical development—as they collectively defined it—superseded the traditional nineteenth-century distrust of the Church. In the final analysis, their shared class interests—as determined by their respective leaders—and desire for tranquillity constituted the dominant factor in their generally collegial relationship. In essence the nineteenth-century anticlerical Liberalism had been replaced by a more pragmatic twentieth-century version, and the differences between the Liberals and the Conservatives quickly dissipated.

In the wake of Zelaya's despotic administration, the chain of weak rulers who succeeded him generally proved beneficial to the Church's previously waning fortunes. Indeed, the Church now entered a period of unprecedented growth, quickly adopting a mantle of respectability it had not possessed since the mid-nineteenth-century Liberal reforms. In 1913, largely because of this growth, the diocese of Nicaragua was restructured with the establishment of three smaller dioceses (Managua, León, and Granada) and the vicariate of Bluefields; the archbishopric of Managua was also to have an auxiliary bishop based in Matagalpa. This was an important structural change, for prior to this time the diocese had been an appendage of the archdiocese of Guatemala. Relations with the Holy See—broken off by Zelaya—were reopened, and foreign religious (including the Jesuits, who exercised great moral authority in the country) were allowed to return as missionaries to Nicaragua. A variety of schools were opened by several religious orders, including the Instituto Pedagógico of the Christian Brothers (and a smaller school for poor children), the Colegio Centroamérica and the Escuela Loyola of the Jesuits, and several trade schools of the Salesians (as well as their San Juan Bosco secondary school). In addition, several Conservative governments, recognizing the important contribution of these schools to Nicaraguan society, made donations of land, buildings, and money to the Church. Furthermore, the development of Catholic Action programs—particularly during the period 1910–40—sought to extend the Church's influence among the working sectors. These programs were designed as a practical Church response in the modern era to deeply rooted socioeconomic problems and were clearly targeted at the working-class population. Moreover, Catholic media interests also began to grow, with the inauguration of the daily newspaper *El Católico* in Granada in 1920, followed by other Catholic publications such as *Acción Católica* (León) in the 1930s, *La Luz* (Managua) in 1940, and *El Sembrador* (Masaya) in 1942.[25]

Finally, while the second version of the 1911 constitution reaffirmed freedom of religious choice, nevertheless it formally stated the obvious: "The majority of the Nicaraguan population believes in Roman Apostolic Catholicism. The State guarantees the free exercise of this religion, and also of the other religions not opposing the Christian morality and public order. It is prohibited to favor or restrict any determined religion."[26] After the excesses of Zelaya, all these changes offered a welcome respite, and once again the Church sought to regain its authority and status. To a large extent it once again realized this renaissance by means of a political accommodation with the status quo and, especially at the level of the hierarchy, by deliberately abstaining from anything that could be perceived as criticism of the political masters of the day.

Significantly, this growth in Church activity and the development of its fortunes took place against a background of U.S. intervention. National sovereignty was clearly ignored as U.S. commercial and political interests took precedence in all major governmental decisions. Yet, with very few exceptions, the Church made virtually no official commentary on the U.S. intervention in Nicaraguan affairs. This silence can be explained by the fact that the various Conservative governments provided extensive material benefits for Catholic activities; the Church, grateful for this financial support, clearly preferred not to risk disturbing this alliance. The Conservative rule, it must be remembered, was kept artificially alive by its own political backers, the occupying U.S. military; it thus behooved Church leaders to refrain from criticizing their allies' patrons, even when this inevitably led to incursions by foreign Protestant missionaries. Such was the price paid by Church leaders in order to retain the support of the Conservative governments. And in the wake of Zelaya's attacks against the Church, the newfound social authority and privileges were delightful indeed to Church leaders, who were understandably fearful of losing their influence and respectability. Once again, then, an implicit political arrangement was reached, with the influential Church hierarchy largely supporting the foreign military presence in order to protect its own vested interests as a pillar of the community. It was an alliance that would reappear in the 1980s as the interests of Nicaraguan Church leaders and U.S. politicians again converged in an attempt to replace the Sandinista government with a more conservative alternative that was far more preferable to the leadership of the Nicaraguan Church and the U.S. government.

One notable exception to the Church's support of U.S. military intervention earlier this century was Bishop Pereira y Castellón of León, who, in a remarkable letter to Cardinal James Gibbons of Philadelphia dated October 9, 1912, explained in detail his own frustrations at the U.S. presence in Nicaragua. In part Pereira y Castellón's reaction reflects the Catholic phobia—common at the time—of Protestantism: "There are other, more important interests than these fleeting mundane concerns: in the wake of this material conquest will come the spiritual conquest . . . the wave of Protestantism is seeking to advance by first sending the dollar ahead to our fields and towns—and thus opening a breach in our defenses."[27] There was also a fiercely anti-imperialist component to the bishop's long letter, however, as he sought to explain to his North American colleague the seemingly irreparable damage being done to Nicaragua: "And so, my dear brother, your nation has imposed upon our small country the weight of its immense wealth and military power. And your powerful country has dominated our weak country with its warships and powerful cannons. And the vaults of the bankers in the North are swollen as a result of the daily and destructive squeezing by them of our hard-pressed resources—the result of burdensome loans, unjust treaties, and unfair contracts" (p. 80). Given the strong anti-imperialist tenor of this letter, it is understandable why President Daniel Ortega should have publicly read it in welcoming Pope John Paul II to Nicaragua during his stormy visit of March 1983.

In his extremely informative study of the Church in Nicaragua, Philip Williams notes how the official silence of the Church in the face of U.S. intervention became an act of straightforward complicity after the National Guard and U.S. Marines decided to pursue the rebel leader Augusto César Sandino. Sandino was a Liberal general who fought against the Conservatives in 1925–26. When the marines returned to shore up yet another corrupt administration, a deal was worked out according to which the Liberal general Moncada would become president, providing that all hostilities ceased. Opposed to the pact and to the U.S. military presence, Sandino continued his guerrilla struggle in the northern Segovia mountains until 1933. A clear threat to the status quo, he gained the disfavor of virtually all the powerful sectors of Nicaraguan society, including the leadership of the Liberal and Conservative parties, the occupying forces, the National Guard, and the Church.

The Church hierarchy was totally opposed to the Sandino-led revolution and did everything in its power to see him arrested. In 1928, the bishop of Granada, Canuto Reyes y Valladares, actually blessed the arms of U.S. Marines marching to do battle with the insurgents. Elías Beadle, director of the National Guard, also met with Bishop José Antonio Lezcano y Ortega in order to enlist the collective support of priests throughout the country—and was warmly received by the prelate. Subsequently Msgr. Lezcano sent a form letter to all priests requesting their support for the Guard. Beadle had referred to the influence exercised by the clergy, and Lezcano was apparently prepared to see this influence co-opted: "Sr. Beadle himself is requesting this influence in order to use it in organizing the National Guard of Nicaragua. . . . It is eminently desirable that the National Guard should take advantage of this favorable attitude of the Catholic Church. Officials of the National Guard will visit priests at their official residences, and they should establish cordial and reciprocal relations."[28] In addition, in May 1931 the clergy in León initiated a political campaign to discredit the rebels, provoking an angry retort from Sandino: "At this time the clergy are allies of the Yankee bankers and . . . that's why so many Church officials and other miserable types have come to the Segovias, preaching meekness to the humble residents there—so that they'll accept humiliation at the hands of the Yankee bankers."[29]

On October 26, 1930, in a purely political ploy, the Catholic hierarchy once again took sides in the dispute by issuing a collective pastoral, calling for the necessary reconciliation and peace and inviting the rebels to lay down their weapons. Significantly, the Church hierarchy had never implored the invading U.S. forces to leave Nicaragua (even when they engaged in the world's first episode of aerial bombing) or censured the National Guard for clear abuses of human rights, much less criticized the various corrupt Liberal and Conservative administrations and their inherent lack of political legitimacy. Against Sandino and his band of followers, however, Church leaders made their opposition extremely clear. Their appeal to Sandino to lay down his arms was couched in terms of compassion: "The cries of suffering and of compassion from various locations have reached us, exhorting us to employ our authority as pastors in order to issue a paternal appeal to our sons who still remain in the dense mountains of the north, a rifle over their shoulder. They are prolonging a desperate struggle which, when viewed in an impartial manner, can only bring misfortune in its wake—both for them and for the Nicaraguan people."[30] The political intent, however, was quite clear. For the Church leaders, then, despite their claims to the contrary, the struggle was not seen "impartially," and the hierarchy once again swung its collective support behind the occupying military forces and the government. In doing so they were clearly pursuing a political path—one that they correctly viewed as most likely to further their own stability and authority, not only in spiritual but also in earthly matters.

The Church on the Verge of Somocismo

As Anastasio Somoza García stood poised to take over the reins of power in Nicaragua in the mid-1930s, the Church had finally regained its position as one of the major political actors on the national stage. As has been detailed here, however, a price had been paid for this renaissance—for, particularly since the early nineteenth century, the Church had seen its fortunes swing violently between Conservative and Liberal administrations. Racked by divisions over matters of a political nature, the Church had been both the victim of ferocious Liberal purges and the recipient of extensive Conservative largess. Throughout this process a difficult lesson had been learned by the hierarchy: in order to survive as an institution, the Church simply had to make an accommodation with its political masters. (In many ways this was merely a latter-day version of what Church authorities had done for the preceding three centuries of colonial rule, which was to acquiesce to the domination of centralized power in return for government favors.) At the same time, however, there had consistently been a minority Church interest that had opposed this logic and had fought tenaciously to implement social justice concerns. This religious polarization (which had often pitted religious and clerics against each other over political matters) would continue throughout the twentieth century.

But by the time of Sandino's appearance in the late 1920s, the rules of the political game had changed dramatically. The Liberal and Conservative parties now pursued similar goals for the future direction of the country, and the survival of either group depended on the support of Washington. Thus the lines between the two parties became quite blurred, and their respective relationships with Church authorities were remarkably similar. This was, of course, advantageous for the Church, which no longer had to fear for its institutional life with the rise to power of their erstwhile foes the Liberals. Symbolic of this new relationship were the events surrounding the Primer Congreso Eucarístico in 1930: Liberal president Moncada held a reception at the close of the conference that was attended by Nicaragua's four bishops—who in turn presented him with a commemorative medal.[31]

Indeed, for the Church leaders, unaware that four decades of Somocismo lay ahead of them, their main objectives and enemies were remarkably clear now that they no longer had to fear for the Church's institutional well-being. Instead, they now shared with the government a common foe: social unrest sparked by an "alien ideology." The potential political danger inherent in communism and anything that smacked of it thus united Church and government leaders, both because of its atheism and its unsettling social doctrine. The Cristero war in Mexico (1926–29), regardless of why it had actually been fought, was widely perceived as being a typical Bolshevik development, and, fearful of social unrest in Nicaragua, the bishops began their campaign against the evils of communism—a strategy that was successful (given the influence of the Church) and which was greatly appreciated by the nation's political leaders since it helped to defuse pressure on them. (In the Somoza years this would become an even more pressing concern.) The Church also became increasingly afraid of the dangers inherent in the spread of Protestantism, which had flourished during the U.S. military occupation. Echoing this frustration with the spreading of the Protestant faith, one commentator revealed the widespread phobia in 1924, in an article provocatively entitled "Why Aren't You a Protestant?":

Because, to be the founders of religions, God has always chosen saints—as is seen in both the Old and New Testaments. And in addition the founders of Protestantism were depraved, perverse men. History does not lie. . . . [Martin Luther was] dishonest, and lived with a former nun whom he took away from a convent. He sated himself with food, drank excessively, used foul language— swearing like a trooper. Violent, haughty, intolerant and cruel with people. . . .

And if the founders were perverse individuals, the means used to spread their faith were even more perverse. They forced their religion upon people with violence, killing, persecution, robbery, vileness, internal wars, treason, blasphemy. The entire history of Protestantism is one of abominations and injustice.[32]

Within the realm of what could be called the social gospel, one searches in vain for prophetic commentaries by the hierarchy. It was something that clearly did not interest Church leaders, much to the relief of the *hacendados* and landed gentry. An example will perhaps suffice to show the general thrust of the hierarchy's concerns at this time. At the first episcopal conference, held in 1917, apparently the most important conclusion of the bishops' deliberations revolved around an exhortation to the faithful to respect Holy Days of Obligation, while in the second meeting (1923) it was concluded that "the sustenance of the Christian spirit within the family" was the fundamental ingredient of both public health and social well-being. Msgr. Reyes of Granada included among the social ills listed in one of his pastorals rebelliousness, children's insubordination, and even basketball, while in 1931 Bishop Lezcano commented that a recent earthquake was a form of divine punishment for "public sins or offenses against God."[33] This can hardly be termed illuminating theology; indeed, it reveals the conservative and stodgy mentality that pervaded official Church thinking in the pre-Somoza period. As Anastasio Somoza García prepared to take power, these trends would continue—as the Church sought to cling tenaciously to its status of social respectability. Its approach, in sum, was not remarkably different from that encountered since the earliest days of the conquest, and—consciously or not—the Church continued along a remarkably similar political path, despite the attempts of a vigorous minority to develop a more socially useful approach.

✝

2   THE INSTITUTIONAL CHURCH UNDER SOMOZA

Accommodation and Complicity (1936–1969)

The Liberal-Conservative
rivalry came to lose even
more significance under
the Somoza regime which
followed. In return for
continued religious
instruction in the schools
and the guarantee of other
privileges, the bishops
maintained almost total
complicity with the
government of Anastasio
Somoza García.

Philip Williams, *The Catholic
Church and Politics in
Nicaragua and Costa Rica*

The Early Years of Somocismo

When the occupying U.S. forces left Nicaragua in January 1933, Liberal president Juan Bautista Sacasa was left nominally in command of the nation's destiny. The real power behind the throne, however, was Anastasio Somoza García—better known as Tacho—who was married to Sacasa's niece and had parlayed this relationship, along with a good command of English, into being named director of the National Guard.[1] When he took charge of the nation as constitutional president in 1936, he was without doubt the most powerful man in Nicaragua and would remain so—through his control of the armed forces (who brutally repressed any opposition to the caudillo) and through a process of institutionalized graft (with which he skillfully co-opted any aspirants to his position). Until his execution in September 1956 at the hands of poet Rigoberto López Pérez, Somoza ruled Nicaragua in a brutal, uncompromising fashion while greedily helping himself to the national resources, thereby becoming one of the wealthiest Latin Americans in the world.

Three characteristics typified Anastasio Somoza García's tyranny: (1) his slavish admiration for the United States; (2) his inherently corrupt, self-promoting style of government; and (3) the level of repression he used to retain power. An uneducated, impoverished, and exploited populace was the victim of his reign of terror and corruption. Somoza's obsession with promoting U.S. cultural and political models has been well documented. Perhaps no more fitting epithet to his style could be cited than the well-known observation of Franklin Roosevelt: that he was "a son-of-a-bitch, but our son-of-a-bitch." With the onset of World War II, Nicaragua's declaration of war on the Axis powers was a natural step for Somoza (as was the opening of U.S. bases at Corinto, Managua, and Puerto Cabezas); it also gave him the opportunity to expropriate the property of wealthy Italian and German immigrants. (His younger son, Anastasio Somoza Debayle, was an even more flamboyant "gringophile" during his own brutal reign, speaking English better than Spanish, referring to himself as the "Latin from Manhattan," and even offering to send Nicaraguan troops to support U.S. policy in Vietnam.)

34

Somoza García's corrupt style of government was quite extraordinary. Through kickbacks from foreign and national businessmen, a series of taxes levied on state employees' salaries and a host of products, an institutionalized protection racket, and his all-encompassing control of the principal national industries, Somoza gradually carved out an impressive business empire.[2] He retained political power through a series of sham elections and political protégés (when constitutional niceties necessitated his temporary absence from the presidency). And on the few occasions when he was directly challenged by political foes, there was always the National Guard—an institution he took particular care to pamper—to call on in order to "shore up the democratic traditions" of the nation. For all who opposed the dictatorial style of Somoza there awaited inhuman prison conditions, torture, and execution. With the advent of the Cold War following the Allies' victory, fresh opportunities for repression—in the name of the "anticommunist struggle"—became apparent, and the level of terror (particularly under the brutal administration of his son Anastasio ("Tachito")) increased.

Given the rampant corruption of the Somoza clan, brutal repression by the National Guard, rigged elections, widespread poverty, and generally immoral leadership provided by the Somozas and their cronies, it is important to note the official Church stance in Nicaragua during the Somoza years. We have seen that the Church had in general fared badly at the hands of various Liberal governments (with the exception of the Moncada administration): Church properties were expropriated, priests and bishops were deported, and wide-ranging religious discrimination was institutionalized under Liberal rule. So just how did the Church fare during the longest period of Liberalism in the nation's history, namely, under the Somozas?

The question is somewhat rhetorical, since despite its political label the Somoza style of government was quite distant from the traditional Liberal model. Indeed, one can argue quite convincingly that *any* label or political identification was merely coincidental for the Somozas. Greed and corruption, supported by a policy of brutality and repression, were the order of the day, and old-style schemes of political differentiation exercised remarkably little influence on the Somozas' philosophy. As a result, there would have been essentially little difference in the treatment meted out to the Church had Anastasio Somoza García and his sons been Conservatives. What was important for them was to maintain a good working relationship between the government and all influential political actors—including the Church and in particular its leadership—in order to ensure the continuance of the status quo. This objective inevitably led to the co-opting of any potential opposition; if this tactic proved insufficient, there was always the National Guard to neutralize the political threat.

The Church Co-opted

When Somoza García finally took the reins of government in 1936, it was quite clear that Nicaragua's principal Church representative, Archbishop José Antonio Lezcano y Ortega of Managua, was himself more than prepared to provide the new president with the Church's moral support, thereby bestowing official ecclesial legitimization of the dictator. Both men were of a naturally conservative bent; in addition, both could see that a strong and harmonious interinstitutional relationship could be mutually beneficial. Moreover, in the wake of the Spanish civil war, the need for a strong response to the spread of international communism became particularly clear to the Church, many of whose priests were originally from Spain. In many ways, then, members of the Church hierarchy were psychologically prepared to accept Somoza as something of a "Nicaraguan Franco" and hence turn a blind eye to his excesses. Indeed, their pastoral letters of this period reveal that so great was their fear of communism they were basically prepared to accept anything about Somoza's style of government—provided that he was not a communist.

As a result, representatives of the Catholic hierarchy once again became conspicuous fixtures at presidential inaugurations, official ceremonies promoting important government works, and the like— thereby signaling to the overwhelming Catholic population their moral support of the dictatorship. In return for legitimizing Somocismo in this fashion, the Church soon accrued a variety of tangible benefits ranging from favorable treatment in constitutional amendments to gifts of money and land. Philip Williams, in a detailed analysis of this period, commented on the widespread nature of this support for the Church:

> Looking through various years of correspondence between the Somoza governments and clergy, one can find numerous instances of priests and bishops being granted personal "favours." These ranged from free airline passes for travel abroad, to gifts of

automobiles, to outright cash advancements. In May 1965, for example, the Archbishop Mons. González y Robleto was sent a "special contribution" of $1500.00 towards his expenses while he was in New York for a week to have an eye operation. Of course, his airfare had already been covered.[3]

In sum, the Church hierarchy during this first stage of the Somoza dynasty readily mortgaged its spiritual leadership for a fistful of temporal advantages, in much the same way as opposition political parties and the poorly organized labor movement also sold their influence. Although there were some important exceptions to this trend—such as the views of Msgr. Calderón y Padilla, who for more than thirty years showed his open scorn for Somocismo—the dominant position of the Church hierarchy was to seek accommodation with the Somozas.

This de facto political accommodation between the Church hierarchy and the Somozas was based on a remarkably simple premise: in return for legitimizing the dictatorship, various tangible benefits would be provided the Church. The end result was an intermeshing of influence and a process that could be described as mutual legitimization. Archbishop Lezcano y Ortega, for instance, sat on the National Lottery Board to emphasize its "honest" administration and was a member of the (essentially ineffectual) Chamber of Congress—whose inaugural sessions he blessed with much ecclesial pomp and ceremony. In return, the government received moral support for its blatantly corrupt administration and, in a throwback to the colonial style of the *Patronato*, even influenced Church policy and appointments. This influence can be seen from the transcript of U.S. embassy intercepts of a 1945 phone conversation (raising the question of why U.S. officials would be tapping phones) between acting foreign minister Barquero and the Nicaraguan diplomat based in Costa Rica, Pallais:

> Barquero said he wanted to pass on an order from the President [Somoza]; that Pallais should at once visit Monseñor Taffi [chargé d'affaires of the Holy See in Costa Rica] and tell him that the President wants Padre Octavio Calderón, nephew of General Padilla, named to León; that it should be handled very discreetly. Pallais said it was for the best, due to Liberal ties. Barquero also said that the President would also like Alfred Reyes moved to

Matagalpa, as Reyes was an enemy. . . . Barquero said . . . he was sending a recommendation along these lines from Señor Lezcano; that this also had the approval of the Archbishop.

That same afternoon a reply was forthcoming from Costa Rica: Pallais said that "he [Monseñor Taffi] would with pleasure communicate the nomination of the person Barquero mentioned this morning [Padre Octavio Calderón]."[4]

Shortly afterwards Calderón y Padilla was named Bishop of León but, in a quirk of history, was to prove one of the few prelates who refused to be co-opted by Somoza. In fact, he remained an outspoken foe of the dictator, even refusing to meet with his son Anastasio Somoza Debayle in 1967 because of the atrocious human rights situation in the country. The point to be made here, however, is that the government exercised an extraordinary influence over the Church hierarchy, which was more than prepared to accommodate Somoza's wishes.

The nature of this essentially subservient Church can be gleaned from a reading of pastoral letters and other official documents of the time, as well as by examining the popular media. Typical of the former is a collection of Archbishop Lezcano's sermons from the late 1930s. One searches in vain for anything that vaguely smacks of social commentary; no mention is ever made of social justice, nor is there any criticism of institutionalized brutality, problems facing the nation, or widespread poverty. The archbishop does mention poverty, however—not to condemn it, but rather to counsel the poor to be *proud* of their pathetic living conditions: "Let us rejoice in the happiness of those princes and gentlemen who became poor in order to imitate Christ; and the millions of Christians who, through religious beliefs, embrace the poverty of Jesus."[5] Significantly, he does not counsel Somoza and other "princes" to emulate Christ's example, preferring instead to encourage the poor to accept with resignation their lowly social status. For them, poverty in this life was something to rejoice about (and indeed to aspire to) because it would lead to greater rewards in the next.

A similar note is sounded often by the archbishop as he consistently preaches the related themes of resignation and humility, sacrifice and suffering. A true Christian, he notes, "has, necessarily, to suffer and weep for all his life" (p. 87) because this is God's will. In words that must have sounded magnificent to Somoza García (whose extensive business interests benefited directly from the Catholic population taking the bishop's advice to heart), the prelate continued:

> The true Christian weeps and suffers, and has to part with his material goods. He is ready to lose everything rather than offend God, whom he has to love above all else. He suffers and weeps upon entering the narrow gate and following the chosen path— which only a few follow, and which is the only one to reach eternal life. In order to reach those heavenly delights it is indispensable for us to suffer; and, the more we suffer, the more we will enjoy later. . . . Let not the true Christian be afraid or surprised by daily sufferings, which have been arranged and ordered by divine providence for our benefit. The disciple of Christ has to bear his cross every day. . . . Without suffering, we cannot enter the glory.[6]

Significantly, Lezcano concludes: "To think otherwise is a sign of foolishness and disobedience, and goes against what our faith teaches us" (p. 89). Here the archbishop is actively preaching resignation to the faithful, advising them that their duty is to accept adversity in this vale of tears because such is God's will. Moreover, if they protest against injustice, or if they choose not to suffer (by improving their living conditions, for example), their possibilities of gaining entry to heaven are immediately reduced. Indeed, should they be foolish enough to believe that poverty and repression do not fit within the divine plan, they are going directly and arrogantly against their Catholic faith—and God's will. In adopting such a stance, Lezcano is repeating the general tenor of the observations made by his predecessors at the time of the struggle for independence some 130 years earlier. Common to both is an exhortation to accept with stoicism the vicissitudes of life because they represent divine will. To seek justice, then, is to go directly against God's master plan for the universe.

When the faithful are faced with any social difficulties that may exist, the archbishop counsels the power of prayer ("fully proven in the Holy Gospel" [p. 95]). If, however, prayers remain unanswered, Christians should not despair "since God, putting to rights the true object of our petition, denies us what is not appropriate for us to have and, by contrast, provides us with what is really in our best interests" (p. 96). Here Lezcano pleads for willing suffering and rejoicing at this pain and urges prayer as the only proper remedy. Moreover, if a petition is not realized, this should be accepted as God's will; an individual should not seek to change the course of events.[7] Lezcano, who had earlier participated in urging Sandino and his followers to turn themselves in to the occupying forces, thus counseled a policy of humility, resignation, and suffering to Nicaragua's Catholics. (Women, he noted, should also set an example by not becoming "the leaders of mobs demanding the right to vote.") The proper behavior for the country's Catholics, then, was to be docile, for, as he counseled, "This form of docility, prompt, punctual and generous, is very necessary for the true Christian who really wants to serve and love God for eternal life. It is because some bad Christians do not possess this quality—in this period of rebellion and poorly understood liberty—that society is in such disorder, almost in complete ruin."[8] Needless to say, Somoza García was delighted with these pleas for "docility," since such passivity ensured a solid foundation for his personal enrichment and the dynasty he headed.

Elsewhere in his collection of sermons, Lezcano lists the social ills laying siege to contemporary Nicaraguan society. It is noteworthy that miserable socioeconomic conditions, brutality, the abuse of human rights, corruption, and the like are simply not listed; instead he outlines what he sees as more "significant" social ills. All these problems have come about, the bishop claims, as a direct result of Nicaraguans' ignoring the true message of Jesus. Among the profound ills afflicting Nicaraguan society he lists "the dreadful shows, corrupting novels, the lack of modesty in women's clothing and their customs, the dangerous relationships between young people, forced marriages, children's insubordination, drunkenness among women, sacrilegious bigamy, and, above all else, the wave of bloodshed caused by hatred, resentment, and vengeance among men."[9] One hardly needs to add that this "wave of bloodshed" had stemmed from what for Lezcano was clearly a cardinal sin, namely, the lack of "docility" by people opposed to the corruption and brutality of Somoza, about which Lezcano deliberately said nothing.

The twin enemies of Catholicism during the early decades of Somocismo were the same as they had been in the 1920s—namely, Protestantism and communism—the difference being that in more recent times both had grown in importance and represented more of a challenge to Catholicism, so they were now criticized even more ferociously. Making a somewhat illogical leap of faith, Lezcano sought

A Protestant church on Corn Island, on the Atlantic Coast.

to convince Nicaragua's Catholics that both were inherently linked and had to be avoided at all costs: "It has been totally proven that Protestantism, with its free interpretation of the Bible and its spirit of rebellion against all teaching authority, has engendered rationalism, which in turn has produced materialism. And it is this process which has produced communism and the Bolshevik ideas of those who do not know God, nor any kind of moral, or law. They are only interested in destruction and the ruin of the family unit, and society."[10]

Clearly, the archbishop was delivering a consistent sociopolitical commentary that—whether he meant it to or not—was encouraging Catholics to refrain from changing their lot in life. This implicit (and at times explicit) support for the Somozas' control can be seen from the press coverage of a rather pathetic, if illustrative, ceremony in 1942 at the National Stadium. There Archbishop Lezcano crowned Somoza's daughter Lillian "Queen of the Army" and placed on her head the crown of the statue of the Virgen de la Candelaria. (He also described the National Guard, not renowned for its respect for the law, as a "magnificent institution . . . fundamental to the social order and well-being of the country.")[11] Nothing serves as a better symbol of the deliberate subordination of the Church to Somocismo than this example of the archbishop's conduct. When Somoza was assassinated in 1956, official condolences and blessings were sent by Pope Pius XII (and Cardinal Spellman), while Archbishop González y Robleto of Managua (of a similar ideological position as Lezcano) ordered a full two hundred days of indulgence to all who attended the funeral ceremonies. Needless to say, the dictator was buried with all the pomp and ceremony afforded by the Church to a person befitting his rank—a full "Prince of the Church." (It is worth noting that Msgr. Calderón y Padilla showed his disdain for these events, preferring to participate in a rural mission campaign than to attend the official requiem mass. His position, however, was clearly the exception rather than the rule.)

Given this legitimization of the dictatorship by Church leadership and the deliberate inculcation among the faithful of a conservative ideology of docility and resignation, the salient features of the Catholic Church that developed between the 1930s and the 1950s come as no surprise. Admittedly this condition was in part due to the fact that, on a worldwide scale, an aggiornamento was badly needed by the Church universal. In the Nicaraguan case, however, decades of accommodation with Somocismo (and of receiving benefits and rewards from the dictator) had stultified whatever desire for change had previously existed and made the Church particularly outdated in its view of social priorities. This can be clearly seen in a series of representative Church publications that serve as a useful supplement to the equally conservative pastoral letters and constitute an important reflection of offical policy at the grass-roots level.

Accommodating Somoza García

A common preoccupation of the Church during this period was the fear of the two great social ills communism and Protestantism. For example, at the Primer Congreso Catequístico Nacional de Nicaragua (celebrated in León from December 28, 1938, to January 1, 1939), Archbishop Lezcano apparently forgot the central purpose of the conference (namely, to devise improved techniques for teaching the official catechism) and focused instead on what he presented as the major problems facing the Church: "We are in the midst of evil times. A frightful wave of Paganism is advancing, invading the Christian world. . . . On the international front the hate of the vanquished against the victor is bringing about new wars. Within society the struggle between classes is growing, and likewise the appetite for earthly goods, as well as the breakup of the family, the shamelessness of women, unbridled luxury. And there is a marked shift back toward the barbarous ways of Paganism."[12]

It is also significant that a telegram from Somoza to Nicaragua's bishops, wishing them success in their deliberations ("which I consider to be of great momentousness for the people of Nicaragua" [p. 28]), should be printed in the official record of the Church conference. Two years later, at the Magno Congreso Nacional del Apostolado de la Oración y de las Juventudes Marianas de la República de Nicaragua, (Major National Congress of the Apostolate of Prayer and of the Young Followers of Mary in the Republic of Nicaragua), a photograph of Somoza was prominently displayed at the front of the souvenir album published after the conference, and his congratulatory letter to Archbishop Lezcano concerning the conference was reprinted.[13] The president obviously took great pride that the Nicaraguan population "exercised their religious devotion within the broadest freedom guaranteed by my government." In 1944 Somoza showed that he was not above taking more blatant advantage of religious ceremonies for his own political ends. The occasion was the 1944 Eucharistic Congress in León, at which—for a price—Somoza García did some rather crude stage-managing: "[He] contributed 10,000 córdobas (U.S. $2,000) toward the expenses of the Congress on the one condition that the Bishops would meet his train at the León Station and march with him on foot to the Cathedral. . . . The bishops did await the President at the Station and marched with him in procession to the Cathedral followed by an enormous crowd."[14]

Some six years later, at the Congreso Eucarístico de Cultura Católica (held in Masaya on January 3–8, 1950), further evidence can be located to show just how totally the Church hierarchy had been co-opted by Somocismo. In addition to the photographs of Pope Pius XII, the papal nuncio, and Archbishop Lezcano, one finds in the conference record a photograph of Somoza—now elevated to the lofty status of "Honorary President of the Congress of Christian Eucharist and Culture." (A further note is added that "in order to celebrate the Major Procession he sent along the band of the National Guard"—the same institution responsible for a series of bloody massacres of opponents of the regime.) Once again the objective of the hierarchy was to avoid "rocking the boat" at all costs, since to do so would be to the detriment of the Church's interests. It was a policy that, with few exceptions, the hierarchy followed consistently during this period.

Among the themes espoused by the conference was the need for Christian charity, patience, and resignation (but not justice), and once again the concern over the spread of Protestantism was omnipresent. Antonio Barquero, a magistrate of the Supreme Court, advised participants: "Suffer all adversity with patience. . . . One has to live one's life (and even death) with patience, in order to live life more fully—and die a little less every day."[15] This particular piece of counsel is strikingly consistent with the official Church position outlined earlier, as is the reaction to the Protestant menace: "Some twenty years ago the Protestants were stoned by our people. . . . They were a handful of foreigners who held different religious beliefs from Nicaraguans. Nowadays we are infested with them. They have come to destroy that religious unity which we inherited from the nation's founders and, encouraged by the indifference of our laws, they continue to grow like a cancer."[16]

In January 1953, a major conference of Catholic men took place in Managua. Some of the presentations given at this conference are particularly noteworthy. One participant, Sr. J. Alberdi, noted that "in 'social' matters we should seek harmony among the different classes, especially between capital and labor." But how was this class harmony to be realized? Simply by good Christian example, counseled Sr. Alberdi, confident that this would be more than sufficient stimulus for Nicaraguan businessmen to promote its imitation among their workers ("In every workshop, factory or business, our men will conduct themselves with Christian exemplariness, holding aloft the torch of truth . . ."). More practical, if indeed more bigoted, were the numerous suggestions of L. Lacayo Swan on ways to organize Nicaraguan Catholic men and to aid the development of Nicaraguan society along Catholic lines.

These suggestions fall into three basic categories: religious matters, broad social concerns, and petty frustrations. Dealing with the first grouping (which one would expect to form the nucleus of his presentation), Lacayo Swan advises all Nicaraguans to respect the Commandments, say the Rosary on a daily basis, provide the Sacraments to those who are sick, and encourage couples living together to marry in the Church. The second group of suggestions—related to social concerns—is particularly revealing, emphasizing as it does official Church policy on some of these problems: to encourage all Catholics to treat each other with fraternity (seeking "a treatment of fraternal equality"); to assist the needy ("depending upon the economic possibilities of the parish"); to encourage, in line with Pope Leo XIII's encyclical, a meaningful dialogue between workers and their employers ("let them deal on a Christian basis with each other, since we are all children of Our Lord Jesus Christ; *it would be a major form of avoiding communism*" [emphasis added]); and "to consider communism as the number one enemy of humanity." The third grouping included such ideas as the need to censor films and imported books; to encourage parents "to pay closer attention to their daughters' dresses, which at present leave a great deal to be desired"; to find an alternative form of taxation so that the lucrative returns from the sale of liquor would not be required and alcohol would be prohibited; to encourage the government to outlaw Freemasonry; to encourage Nicaraguans not to rent their premises to Protestants; and "to publicly condemn indecent dances such as rumbas, mambos, etc."[17] This catalog of suggestions can hardly be said to represent a profound understanding of Nicaragua's pressing problems, but it speaks volumes about the major concerns faced by Catholic lay representatives, who in turn were merely reflecting the ideology and preoccupations of the hierarchy.

It is clear from the publications resulting from these official Church conferences and Catholic gatherings (many of which were organized by the hierarchy itself) that Catholic social thinking in Nicaragua at this time was conservative, to say the least. Social justice concerns were rarely—if ever—addressed, and in their place the value of Christian charity was encouraged; the major enemies were the twin cancers of Protestantism and international communism; and the trinity of humility, resignation, and suffering was constantly emphasized by both the Church hierarchy and Catholic lay leaders as necessary facets of the human condition. This recipe for allegedly "apolitical" action on the part of Catholic Nicaraguans shored up the sociopolitical status quo since in effect it emasculated any movement for social change; to do otherwise was clearly against divine will, or so the hierarchy implied to Nicaraguan Catholics. During the twenty years of Anastasio Somoza García's rule, then, the Church leadership clearly made an accommodation with the dictator, who was in turn grateful for the hierarchy's subservience and rewarded the bishops accordingly. Occasionally a priest such as Azarías Pallais or a bishop like Calderón y Padilla would speak out about the need for social justice, but inevitably they would be quieted or merely ignored by the reactionary Church leaders, who were eager for the Church to continue its role of supporting the dictator.

This relationship of accommodation lasted for several decades and brought material benefits, authority, and real (temporal) power to all concerned. From the Church's perspective, however, it also ensured that any constitutional change enacted by the Somozas exercised as minimal an impact as possible on the Church—something that, in the light of actions of earlier Liberal administrations, was always a major concern. The new constitution in 1950, for instance, did continue the Liberal tradition of separating Church and state, of promoting civil wedding ceremonies (as *the* legal form), and encouraging lay education. Yet given the well-publicized attitude of the various Somoza presidencies, the friendship and support of the Somozas, and the tangible rewards given to the Church, Catholicism continued as the de facto "official" religion—despite the letter of the law—and the impact of such legislation was deliberately minimized by the government. In comparison with other Central American nations at this time (particularly Guatemala), the Church was thus let off remarkably lightly—and the Church hierarchy knew it.

In Search of Church Social Doctrine

By the 1950s, after substantial economic growth in the wake of World War II, a feeling developed in Central America that a modern era had arrived and that economic progress was finally possible in the region. Increased demand and higher prices stimulated rapid growth of the cotton industry: between 1949 and 1955 Nicaragua's cotton crop grew a staggering 120-fold. The rewards for this economic growth were poorly distributed, however, and in developing the market there were major social casualties—some 180,000 Nicaraguan peasants, for example, were forced to leave their traditional small plots of land to work on the seasonal crop.[18] The few trade unions that existed were either bought off or severely repressed; there was no attempt at meaningful agrarian reform; and wages were kept remarkably low. From the government's perspective, though, a hint of political problems could be discerned on the political horizon: the social democratic governments of Arévalo and Arbenz in nearby Guatemala from 1944 to 1954 (the year of the CIA-sponsored overthrow of the Arbenz regime), Fidel Castro's attempted overthrow of the Batista dictatorship in Cuba in 1953, and the incipient guerrilla movement throughout Latin America all indicated that a wind of change was in the air.

Within the Church itself this desire for change was addressed by a deliberately modified approach to social concerns. Catholic Action groups were developed as the result of official policy throughout the region in the 1940s and 1950s, and Catholic doctrine on social and political matters was refined to reflect the changing realities. The central objective of this strategy was to ensure that communist ideology did not gain a foothold in Latin American society; in essence these lay Catholic groups were organized to show the relevance of the Church as an agent for change, an alternative to those social groups that might find a left-wing message attractive. In pursuing this policy of modernizing social and political structures in response to changing world circumstances, the Church thus counseled the (willing) introduction of minor social reforms—before far greater social change was demanded by the exploited sectors of society. Other initiatives taken by the Nicaraguan Church to ensure that its message was widely spread include the founding by the Jesuits in various cities of the Asociación de San José Obrero in the 1940s, as well as the creation of Radio Católica in 1957 and of the social assistance organization Caritas in 1959.[19] All these initiatives were designed to support more effectively the official Church position espoused by Catholic Action groups.

To a certain extent the spiritual concerns emphasized in the 1920s and 1930s were now downplayed, and in their place concerns for workers' rights and for a fair distribution of land surfaced—albeit in a somewhat superficial manner. But a number of preoccupations—such as the need for film censorship, campaigns against gambling and prostitution, and, of course, the spread of Protestantism—were still commonplace. Above all, the Church remained vehemently opposed to the possibility of communism reaching the region. Indeed, the bishops of Central America, meeting in May 1956, called the threat of communism "the major political and religious conflict in our time."[20] Thus the social doctrine now espoused by the Church called for moderate social change while warning of the grave dangers of communism, usually accompanied by the epithet "atheistic." Meanwhile, despite initiatives for social change found in papal encyclicals such as *Quadragesimo Anno* and the impressive *Rerum Novarum,* for most of Nicaragua's Church hierarchy support from the Somozas was a continuing temptation and the pew remained as comfortable as ever. In short, the hierarchy paid lip service to the new official position stemming from Rome (soon to unleash the major reforms of Vatican II) but preferred a minimal tinkering with Nicaragua's current socioeconomic model, a model that struck most Church leaders as essentially sound.

From the 1930s until the 1960s, church leaders in Nicaragua showed a remarkably consistent, two-pronged approach to social problems, one that could well be criticized for its opportunistic tactics. Not only did Church leaders deliberately seek to legitimize the Somoza dictatorship (in return for generous treatment from the various caudillos in the family), but also—when the need for change was indicated by the Holy See—they attempted to promote the resultant "social doctrine." At the heart of both these strategies, however, there remained the central objective of protecting the Church as an institution from whatever difficulties might befall it—and in the Latin America of the time the major problems looming on the horizon could be reduced to one word, revolution. By any reasonable standard, social conditions in Nicaragua throughout the four decades of the Somozas' reign were atrocious, and the level of repression was deep and widespread. The bishops knew this, of course, but deliberately subordinated their social criticisms to the desire to retain their influence in Somoza's Nicaragua. The possibility of violent political upheaval—as had happened earlier in Mexico, Russia, and Cuba—did become a pressing concern of the hierarchy, particularly after the violent death of Anastasio Somoza García in 1956.

Yet while revolution was a major preoccupation for the bishops, they seem never to have conceived that it actually could arrive in Nicaragua—perhaps because the control of the Somozas (particularly through the National Guard) was so pervasive. Accordingly, their pastoral letters—even when they sought to be sensitive to social concerns—always tended to support the status quo. This is readily apparent in a crucially important pastoral letter of Archbishop González y Robleto issued on August 3, 1959. In the same year as the revolutionary victory of Fidel Castro in Cuba and the sprouting of guerrilla groups throughout Latin America (and just three years before the winds of change would begin to blow throughout the Church with the advent of Vatican II), the archbishop chose to cling tenaciously to a way of governing that was clearly outdated. His opposition to radical change came just two months after a failed incursion headed by Pedro Joaquín Chamorro.

In his pastoral letter González y Robleto ("after meditating about the gravity of sociopolitical developments of Nicaragua, events which place the nation's tranquillity in grave danger")[21] takes great pains to indicate that his observations are not based on personal opinions but rather are official Church doctrine ("It is the Popes who are speaking," he notes authoritatively [p. 9]). Then, judiciously choosing his quotations from encyclicals of various pontiffs, he seeks to advise the faithful that even if they do not agree with his analysis, they are *morally obliged to obey* the papal pronouncements ("even if what the Church officially orders does not convince Catholics for whatever reason, nevertheless they are obliged to obey the Church's ruling" [p. 9]).

This central theme of the nature of legitimate authority and the proper response of Catholics to that authority is skillfully developed throughout the pastoral. The initial part of the communiqué (perhaps due to the archbishop's sensing a mood of frustration with his approach among younger clergy) is taken up with a warning that priests should not become involved in politics, either by identifying with a political party or by taking part in the political struggle against the government. Given the nature of the relationship between the Church hierarchy and the Liberal administrations of Somoza García and then Luis Somoza Debayle (who had assumed power following the assassination of his father in 1956), the first part of the message rings quite false: while strictly speaking the members of the hierarchy were almost certainly not card-carrying Liberals, they had clearly gone out of their way to show institutional support of Somocismo for nearly a quarter century.

The archbishop's warning to the clergy is supported by references to two priests who did become involved in politics with, it is implied, tragic consequences: Morelos in Mexico (who "was humiliated and then executed") and Matías Delgado in El Salvador ("a troublemaker, he was excommunicated") (p. 10). Clearly priests were not expected to ignore constitutional or ecclesiastical authority—hence the official warning. At a time when younger clergy were starting to question the continuing acquiescence of the hierarchy, González y Robleto and other senior clergy moved swiftly to reduce the level of polarization within the Church.

The body of the pastoral is directed at Nicaragua's Catholics and is a clear attempt to convince them to accept unquestioningly the Somoza administration as the legitimate constitutional government. Citing a letter of Leo III from 1892, the archbishop notes that "when new governments have been duly installed, respecting them is not only permitted—it is also demanded and even required in order to protect the common social good" (p. 11). Power and authority, he takes great pains to show, stem directly from God's divine plan for the universe and are therefore to be respected. He explicitly acknowledges that in the context of Nicaragua this means that the Somoza government must be respected—to do otherwise is to deliberately ignore God's will.

In what is perhaps the most important section of the pastoral letter, the archbishop raises the issue of the role of Catholics in the case where a leader becomes a despot or a tyrant ("something which is not the case here," he notes [p. 13], despite abundant evidence to the contrary). The answer is that *even in those circumstances* Church magisterium officially prohibits seeking the overthrow of the dictator, or even of "resisting such acts of the tyrant in question" (p. 12).[22] Preaching the need for the appropriate "fidelity and submission owed to our Rulers," he warns Catholics not to seek to overturn the divine plan for Nicaragua: "You should all know that, as the Apostle says, all Authority comes from God, and all things are arranged by that same God. Therefore he who resists that Authority, resists God, the arrangement undertaken by God, and in so doing condemns himself (Romans 13:21). As a result, those who—through dishonest meddling in rebellion—ignore the fidelity which they owe to their Rulers, and seek to wrest away their authority, should listen how every divine and human right cries out against them" (p. 13). To resist this divinely bestowed authority would thus be an act of "lese-majesty that is not only against society, but also against God" (pp. 13–14). In the event that a tyrant should ever resort to a form of unacceptable repression, what does the prelate counsel Nicaragua's Catholics? "The solution to these problems can be accelerated with the merits of Christian patience and fervent pleas to God" (p. 13). Once again, then, patience and prayer, resignation and humility were proposed as the good Catholic's appropriate response to the government—which in turn was counseled to practice Christian charity toward the less fortunate.

After establishing, by means of a variety of papal encyclicals, that authority must be respected at all costs, this extraordinary document then passes from the general to the specific as González y Robleto analyzes the contemporary situation in Nicaragua and praises lavishly the Somoza government. Ignoring the institutionalized violence that existed in the patently lopsided landholding patterns, the litany of shocking statistics related to socioeconomic conditions, and the repression by the National Guard (still active, despite the comparatively benevolent reign of Somoza García's son Luis), the prelate roundly condemns the fundamental use of violence when used against the established, constitutional rule of the Somozas. The government in Nicaragua is, he claims, a fair one and only pursues enemies of the common good: "It is a clear fact that, on the Government's side, nobody is punished or persecuted unless they are involved in revolutionary conspiracies, or acts of disloyalty against public order. . . . This is a fact which every sensible person knows" (p. 14). Finally, in a telling aside that reveals more about his own hierarchy than he probably intended, he bestows official institutional praise on the Somozas, showing to what degree the erstwhile Liberal enemy has been fervently embraced by the Church hierarchy: "we should state that our government is not an ungodly one; rather it is a benefactor of the Church" (p. 14).[23]

I have quoted extensively from this important document because it reveals quite clearly the level to which this policy of accommodation and complicity with the Somoza regime had become entrenched in the institutional Church of the time. Authority, however arbitrarily it may be administered, had to be respected—whether in Church or in government circles; patience and prayer were the only solutions approved by the Church for problems of social injustice—to resort to other tactics was to reject divine will. The Nicaraguan bishops had gone out of their way to bestow the seal of official approval on the dictator. Just three years before the momentous Second Vatican Council, the institutional Church in Nicaragua represented all that the modernizing trends later emanating from Rome sought to overturn. It was a Church that was self-satisfied, extremely conservative, fairly secure (after earlier scares at the hands of anticlerical Liberalism), and remarkably inward- and backward-looking. True, it had encouraged the development of a series of projects designed to inhibit radical politics from taking root in Nicaragua, but this had been done in a haphazard way and, as was the case with all social justice–oriented projects, had not been a priority for the hierarchy. (Furthermore it had, in part, been undertaken as a means of providing a social safety valve, thereby inhibiting the development of communism, and thus had not been pursued out of a deep-seated concern for social justice or meaningful reform.) Instead, the Church hierarchy had continued to worry about Protestantism, communism, declining social standards of comportment—and how to establish the

Church in the Somozas' Nicaragua as firmly as possible. Perhaps initially they had felt uncomfortable with their firm shoring up of the regime, but by the late 1950s that was no longer an issue: together with the Liberal party, the small oligarchy, the National Guard, and the United States, the Church leadership (with some important exceptions) had consciously aligned itself with the dictatorship. The spirit of openness and dialogue, of seeking social justice, of aggiornamento that would result from Vatican II (1962–65), and later from the CELAM meetings at Medellín (1968) and Puebla (1979), would certainly act as a veritable bombshell in this complacent Church body. Change was badly needed—but was slow to come.

The Church in 1969: A Profile

The death of Archbishop González y Robleto in 1968 gave the Church an opportunity to choose as archbishop of Managua a prelate more attuned to the magisterium emanating from Vatican II. Certainly the tasks facing the new appointee were daunting indeed: not only would he have to minister to an impoverished Catholic flock, but he would also have to decide what path to take with regard to the increasing repression by the National Guard (which was responsible for the massacre of more than three hundred people during a much-publicized Conservative party rally in 1967). Not the least of his responsibilities would be the pressing need to revitalize a despondent, complacent clergy (for decades dependent on Somoza largess) and to encourage their own aggiornamento within the Nicaraguan Church. It was a formidable task indeed, one that was accentuated by the burgeoning polarization within the Church.

Just how dire the situation facing the clergy was can be seen from an important Encuentro Pastoral (Pastoral Encounter) that took place in Managua in January and February of 1969. Significantly subtitled "Facing the Future of the Church in Nicaragua," the meeting brought together some 250 priests and religious (and three of Nicaragua's nine bishops) to analyze the situation of the Church in the light of Vatican II and the recent CELAM meetings at Medellín, Colombia. The event was particularly important in Nicaragua, not just because of the national context (including increasing sociopolitical polarization, the patently fraudulent election of Anastasio Somoza Debayle as president following the January 1967 massacre, and growing economic difficulties of the masses), but also because it was the first time that the Nicaraguan Church as an institution had attempted to engage in such a serious soul-searching process.

There were three central foci to the deliberations at the Encuentro Pastoral: one centering on the actual nature of the Church in Nicaragua, another examining what its role could (or should) be, and the third analyzing the sociopolitical reality of contemporary Nicaragua.[24] In all, the twelve days of meetings provided the best analysis to date of the reality of the Nicaraguan Church—bringing despair and concern to some and a sense of challenge to others. Perhaps even more important was the opportunity to vent these emotions in public for the first time and to commit the Church (or a section of it) to coming to terms with its mission in a post-Vatican II world.

What the participants discovered was hardly encouraging. Referring to a widespread polling of Catholic clergy and laity, the Jesuit priest Noel García provided the most damning indictment of the contemporary Nicaraguan Church. He reserved some of his most pointed comments for the hierarchy, a body of elderly clergy (the average age was over sixty) who were widely perceived as being far removed from the reality of Nicaragua: "[The hierarchy is] decrepit, conservative, stationary, advanced in age, apathetic, negative, disunited, hardly accessible to the public, some of whom have no idea about—or interest in—the hierarchy. It represents the desire to do nothing, merely repeating coldly and compulsively timeworn positions. . . . The Church in Nicaragua is sorely lacking true spiritual leadership from its pastors."[25] García makes an impassioned and articulate plea for a basic democracy in the Church, stating the need for the hierarchy to listen to the voices of the faithful. The traditional scheme of things, according to which dictates from the prelates are passed unquestioningly down the line to the laity, is no longer feasible in the light of Vatican reforms, he claims. At the same time, however, he ponders whether the teachings of Vatican II have even been considered by Nicaragua's bishops. "Can this form of democracy exist here when in this very gathering we have bishops who refused to participate simply because they refuse to allow dialogue, and consider it an impairment of their authority?" he asks with some bitterness (p. 43).

The diocesan clergy and those belonging to religious orders fared only marginally better in the surveys undertaken by García and his team. The former were criticized for their "lack of dialogue" and personal distance from concerns of the faithful: "There are complaints that a goodly number of them are only interested in their own economic welfare. By contrast, there is very little sensitivity to the social problems of the faithful" (p. 39). They were seen as having little understanding of, or interest in, the Vatican II spirit and as lacking in "authentic priestly witness" (p. 39), although several respondents referred to the emergence of a new group of young, politically progressive priests. Members of religious orders were less harshly treated, although it was widely felt that since the vast majority of them worked as teachers in Catholic schools, they tended to be quite individualistic and certainly removed from Nicaraguan reality. They were also criticized for their lack of cooperation with diocesan clergy and for living "an extremely comfortable existence in their spacious colleges and official residences" (p. 40). Nuns were treated in much the same way, essentially because of their isolation from the "real world" and because they were perceived as living in and for their schools—and with little concern for the community at large. At the same time, the Catholic schools themselves were criticized, both for the limited and poor-quality religious education they gave their students and for their preoccupation with expensive uniforms. In sum, the clergy and religious seemed dramatically removed from the central thrust of reforms emanating from Vatican II and, most recently, from the 1968 CELAM meeting in Medellín.

The center of religious life, the parishes, also received some harsh criticism. Very few of them had social justice committees (hardly surprising given the portrayal of clergy noted above) despite the fact that a full 70 percent of parishes were located in extremely poor areas. Monotonous sermons, ineffectual religious associations (usually consisting of "pious individuals and devout old ladies"), the rejection in conservative dioceses of the few progressive courses designed to show the Church's position on social justice concerns, a formalistic and ritualized approach to Catholic catechism, excessive fees charged by parish priests for religious services ("There should be a study of the fees charged by Church representatives—so that we understand how an image of priests and parishes interested for so long only in money has arisen" [p. 41]), and a class-based approach to religion (as typified by three different ranks of wedding ceremonies tied to the social status of the couple)—all are widely criticized. In general, then, the level of parish life leaves a great deal to be desired, largely because of the deficient approach of the parish priest: "The parish priest has little to do with the

A religious procession in the town of Masaya.

faithful, and any form of community life is sorely lacking. The priest is only seen at the Sunday mass, which is attended by very few people. The spirit of Vatican II has not reached the majority of parishes—whether that influence be on the level of the liturgy, preaching, or apostolate" (p. 41).

The conservative response to these criticisms was given by Msgr. Pablo Antonio Vega (who would later be expelled from Nicaragua by the Sandinista government for his lack of patriotism and support of the Reagan administration's belligerent policy toward Nicaragua). Vega cautioned against the approach of social involvement being counseled by younger colleagues. The Church's mission, he noted, was "to participate in daily matters without losing its spiritual mission"—to provide a pragmatic approach to Nicaragua's problems but with the proviso that spiritual and pastoral elements always take precedence. Obviously concerned by the more radical approaches proposed, Vega followed the more traditional model—not of changing the social structure itself, but of attempting to influence morally those in authority so that *they* would undertake such a mission: "Hence the importance of 'discerning' without dividing the flock: to encourage some without antagonizing others. To seek not the death, but rather the conversion, of the sinner: this is indeed a difficult task—but one which, as a pastor, it is impossible to forget" (p. 214). In short, Vega sought first the conversion of the individual, who, it was hoped, would then seek to remedy society's ills.

This milder reformist approach was clearly different from the general sentiment expressed at the Encuentro Pastoral. In the minds of most participants, Vega's suggestions must have closely resembled the hierarchy's traditional approach of accommodation with the same social structures the progressive clergy regarded as unjust and which they desired to overturn. (The position of Vega, on the one hand, and the frustration faced by many of the more politically progressive clergy, on the other, also reflected the religious polarization that was already evident among the clergy—a trend that would continue, and indeed increase significantly, when Miguel Obando y Bravo became archbisop of Managua in 1970.) More typical were the conclusions reached at an earlier gathering—the "First Course of Liturgical Pastoral Concerns" held at the National Seminary in July 1968—and reprinted in *Facing the Future*. There, the forty-nine priests who attended criticized the limitations of rich and poor alike but reserved their harshest criticism for the very nature of religious life being followed in the Nicaraguan Church: not only was there a total lack of guidance on the part of the hierarchy in regard to social policy of any meaningful kind, but there was also a lack of maturity in socioreligious matters, and little sensitivity to social demands of the Catholic faith.

Summing up the myriad criticisms of the contemporary Church that resulted from the Encuentro Pastoral, Noel García noted succinctly that "the Nicaraguan Church possesses a considerable deficit, and badly needs a speedy revitalization that will allow it to fulfill its apostolic mission" (p. 42). At that time such a prospect must have seemed daunting indeed, particularly in light of the Church's established accommodation with the Somoza dynasty, not to mention a tradition of religious life that was in essence totally antithetical to the spirit of Vatican II. Perhaps echoing this widely felt concern about the difficulties of devising a new approach to escape from this inherent logjam, Noel García noted with some apprehension: "Nobody can be visualized as 'the person' who can take over as the visible, aggressive head of the Church, with a diocesan or national plan, and with a clear, constructive outline for the future. The Church in Nicaragua is lacking true spiritual leadership for its pastors" (pp. 38–39).

Precisely to fill that leadership void, the Vatican appointed a relatively young Nicaraguan, Miguel Obando y Bravo, as archbishop of Managua in 1970. Obando was in many ways an unlikely candidate for the post, for besides his two-year stint as auxiliary bishop of Matagalpa his only other administrative experience had been as rector of a Salesian school in El Salvador. Unfortunately, the pool of potential candidates was quite small—a telling reflection of the Church's condition. The Vatican had clearly decided, however, that it was time to install a leader without close ties to the Somozas and thereby revive sagging Church morale.

✝

3   FROM DICTATORSHIP

TO REVOLUTION

The Church's Response (1970–1979)

In our opinion it is both
strange and ridiculous to see
the interpretation of the
Church's role assigned to it by
the old capitalism. According
to this interpretation, the
Church should be content
with its role in the sacristy,
exercising its influence through
individual conscience and in
private life. Its mission is to
warn the faithful against the
dangers of this world, recom-
mending a lack of concern with
worldly affairs, preaching
resignation, patience, and
hope in the next world, and
assisting—out of charity—
those poor souls who are
victims of alcoholism,
prostitution, abandonment,
and delinquency. However, in
social and economic matters,
the Church's mission is to
declare itself incompetent. It
is both to abstain from these
problems and to declare that
the established order, existing
social classes and structures,
as well as the government's
current policies all come
directly from God.

Archbishop Miguel Obando y
Bravo, 1974

IN HIS ARTICLE ENTITLED "Should the Church Get Involved in Politics?" (*Boletín de la Arquidiócesis de Managua,* April 1974), Managua's new archbishop (appointed in late 1970) spoke out strongly for a new approach by the Church toward social and political concerns—much to the chagrin of the last of the Somozas. Having served for two years as the assistant to the most outspoken bishop of the Nicaraguan Episcopal Conference, Msgr. Octavio Calderón y Padilla, the incoming prelate had learned firsthand the need for an independent Church. In comparison with his complacent predecessors who quietly accepted the excesses of Somocismo, Miguel Obando y Bravo was quite striking: of mixed Indian and mulatto background and sensitive to socioeconomic disparities, he rejected Somoza's attempts to co-opt him, and during his tenure as bishop he became the most outspoken opponent of the appalling human rights record of the dictatorship. His pastoral letters and regular columns in the *Boletín de la Arquidiócesis de Managua* reveal a man determined to steer the Nicaraguan Church on a very different course from that followed by his predecessors.

He also served—at the request of the Sandinistas—as an intermediary between the FSLN and the government on the two occasions when the insurgents staged spectacular hostage-taking incidents. For this he received increasingly harsh treatment in the Somoza-dominated publication *Novedades* (particularly in the late 1970s), and he was even referred to by the dictator as "Comandante Miguel"—as if he were another Sandinista leader. His refusal to accept a Mercedes as a gift from Somoza (who among his dozens of business interests owned the Nicaraguan franchise), his public rejection of invitations to attend official state functions (thereby delegitimizing them in the eyes of many), and his criticism of the excesses of Somocismo—particularly as the decade continued—earned him the reputation of a liberal Church leader greatly influenced by the modernizing trends resulting from Vatican II and CELAM. In many ways, then, he was a logical ally of the FSLN and its reform program for an independent Nicaragua.

Indeed, in the seminal November 1979 pastoral letter (analyzed in detail in the next chapter), the Nicaraguan bishops explained their careful optimism about the liberating experience that had recently swept through the country and urged Catholics not to fear socialism needlessly. Within two months, however, the relationship between the FSLN and Obando y Bravo had soured, and subsequently the archbishop became the harshest critic of the Sandinistas. What caused this dramatic change? The answer is complex, but its origins lie in this crucial decade as the people rose against a bloody tyranny that had lasted more than four decades. The Nicaraguans struggled to find their identity in the ruins of their war-ravaged country, a development in which the FSLN and the Church hierarchy participated—often in competition for the people's support. This chapter seeks to shed some light on this process, which has dominated the political scenario for the revolutionary government's decade in power. Through an analysis of political events and alliances at the time (including the Church's overtly political stance hinted at by the archbishop in the chapter-opening quotation) and an examination of official Church documents, I seek to chart the troubled development of the Church during this crucial decade—an era in which the Church came of age, as it were, but fell victim to its own polarized political views. Without a balanced understanding of this decade, it is impossible to grasp the essential dynamics of the subsequent developments within the Nicaraguan Church.

The Historical Background

When Luis Somoza's term of office expired in February 1963, he and his brother Anastasio handpicked René Schick to be Nicaragua's puppet-president. Four years later, after another fraudulent election, Anastasio himself took up the reins of power. The tone of his corrupt and brutal reign could be seen even before the election took place—in January 1967 several hundred opponents were coldly gunned down by the National Guard. Afterwards, during the few years when Somoza was not officially in power, he carefully controlled national political affairs from the sidelines. His power was virtually absolute—probably even more so than in the case of his father or of his brother Luis. The opposition was easy to deal with: the Conservatives were no match for Anastasio's political machinations (indeed, their leaders were often co-opted by the Somozas, as in the case of Fernando Agüero); the legal system was inherently corrupt, controlled as it was by the "first family" of the republic (who also owned several radio stations and print media to ensure that their message was spread throughout the country); and the Sandinistas, still few in number, offered little direct challenge.[1] The seven-thousand-member National Guard, buoyed by extensive military aid from Washington between 1967 and 1975, was always there to lend its support to Anastasio, who remained as their director—virtually a power unto himself, untouchable and omnipotent, despite the occasional election when for constitutional reasons he could not legally stand as a candidate.

During the 1970s, three basic factors combined to show that this apparent omnipotence could be shaken. (This is an important point to bear in mind because most Nicaraguans knew no other political system, having lived already for some thirty-five years under the extremes of Somocismo.) The first factor was the popular reaction to the devastating earthquake of 1972, which leveled downtown Managua and killed some 10,000 people (20,000 others were injured and approximately three-quarters of Managua's 400,000 inhabitants were left homeless). The second factor was the gradual development of a broad opposition composed of groups that had either been co-opted by Somoza in the past or had discovered fresh interest in deposing the dictator. This unusual mixture of opposing forces ran the gamut from peasant groups to the bourgeoisie (increasingly disgruntled with the Somozas' near-absolute control of business matters), from the Conservative party—led by the courageous editor of *La Prensa*, Pedro Joaquín Chamorro—to the Catholic Church hierarchy, now led by Archbishop Obando y Bravo. The third factor was the popular revulsion at the widespread abuse of human rights that resulted from the legalized brutality and absolute power of the National Guard. Put quite simply, as a result of this blend of factors, the Nicaraguan people finally lost their fear of Somoza—or rather, their loathing and disgust at the excesses of Somocismo, combined with a freshly discovered sense of empowerment, finally convinced them to participate in the widespread popular uprisings against the dictator.

The earthquake and its aftermath were an important catalyst for Nicaraguan society as a whole. When the earthquake struck in December 1972, Somoza thrust aside the governing triumvirate and took absolute control himself—ruling then by decree until 1974, when he again took constitutional control of the nation. The chaos that resulted from the earthquake's devastation was exacerbated by the National Guard's activities: initially the guardsmen simply walked away from their military obligations to look after their own families and interests. After millions of dollars' worth of relief supplies flooded into the country, they were finally encouraged by Somoza to return to the lucrative field of (essentially legalized) pillage of the incoming goods, many of which the guardsmen then sold on the black market. The example of callous corruption was set by Somoza, who simply pocketed much of the financial aid sent by the United States.[2] Middle-class alienation also resulted from the earthquake, not only because a prior decade of sustained economic growth was snuffed out in one blow, but also because it became immediately clear that the "new Managua" that was to rise from the ashes was to be built for the exclusive benefit of Somoza and his cronies. The bourgeoisie, which had formed an uneasy alliance with the dictatorship, soon found that their socioeconomic privileges were being steadily eroded as Somoza's greed developed apace. Whereas before they had supported the ruling family out of both a fear of communism and, more important, the desire to take commercial advantage of the regime, they now saw that the advantages of wealth were being increasingly concentrated in the family and among a small coterie of followers—from which they were excluded. Their steady economic marginalization thus bred a growing aversion to the excesses of Somocismo, which a few years later developed into a broad opposition movement.

The main beneficiary of the reconstruction boom following the earthquake was Somoza himself, whose extensive business interests included control of the construction industry. Horror stories abound as to how Somoza and his cronies took advantage of their knowledge of proposed reconstruction sites to buy land cheaply and then sell it for vast profits. Phillip Berryman, for example, tells of the purchase of 93.6 acres for $71,428 in July 1975 and the reselling (to the government) of 56.8 acres of it for $1.7 million just two months later.[3] While Somoza's personal wealth grew rapidly (most estimates of his wealth at this time claim that he was worth some $300 million and that he owned some 5 million acres of land), it increased largely at the expense of the middle class—who saw the dictator steamroller his way over their own business interests. Their nascent opposition, then, was born out of their deep-seated frustration with the unfair business practices resulting from the Somozas' virtual control of the nation—and after the earthquake the fiefdom was even more deeply entrenched.

The second factor in the growth of the anti-Somoza movement was the variety of groups who began to express their opposition to the dictator's control of the economy. Perhaps the most surprising of these was the alliance of bourgeois interests, who formerly had seen their fortunes develop—due largely to the benign wishes of Somoza. Of course they had been obliged to show their gratitude by financial contributions to his political campaigns—as well as through less subtle bribes and gratuities—but there had been a general understanding that "order" and "progress" were beneficial to both the government and the business class. In the wake of the earthquake, however, as it became increasingly clear that Somoza—who already owned the top twenty-six corporations in the country—meant to exploit the tragic situation of Managua to his own advantage, the bourgeoisie became increasingly alienated. By the time of the 1974 elections, a broad, middle-class-centered movement known as the Unión Democrática de Liberación, or UDEL, already constituted the main political opposition.

Another significant political development at this time was the growth of the Sandinista movement. The FSLN, which had experienced mixed fortunes since its inception in 1961, had been slowly regrouping in the 1960s but was never perceived as a real political actor. That changed dramatically, however, in the wake of a daring raid on December 27, 1974, on the house of "Chema" Castillo, a close associate of Somoza. The occasion was a Christmas party attended by a coterie of Somoza intimates, including U.S. ambassador Turner Shelton (who had just left the party), Somoza's brother-in-law Guillermo Sevilla-Sacasa, the mayor of Managua, the country's foreign minister, and other prominent officials. The Sandinistas held the guests as hostages until the following demands were met: the release of prominent political prisoners (including Daniel Ortega), the publication on national media of an FSLN communiqué condemning the Somoza dictatorship, a sum of money, and free passage to Cuba for the guerrillas. Archbishop Obando y Bravo acted as mediator in all the negotiations, and the Sandinistas were considered heroes.

If this spectacular incident served to show the Nicaraguan people that Somoza was not invulnerable, a more gradual—if equally convincing—process was already underway through Church activities. The steady growth of Christian base communities, the training of lay leaders known as Delegates of the Word, the development of new activist clergy, and a more progressive Church hierarchy all contributed to the rupture of the traditionally cozy (and mutually beneficial) relationship between

Somoza and the Church. This factor—as will be detailed below—was a major force for change starting in the late 1960s. Together with the nascent opposition of the middle-class business sector and the revival of FSLN fortunes, it contributed to a growing discontent with Somocismo.

The final factor that contributed to the opposition movement's rapid development was the eventual overcoming of a deep-seated and quite understandable fear of the violence that was used so brutally to keep Somoza in power. Anyone who has seen the film of the cold-blooded murder of ABC newsman Bill Stewart on June 20, 1979, by the National Guard can understand the mentality that drove the guard corps. If one magnifies that incident by some 50,000 (the approximate number of people killed in the struggle to overthrow the dictator), it is easy to see what the population, which numbered only 2.5 million, was afraid of. If one adds to that the dozens of reports and international commissions on the widespread torture, lawlessness of the "security forces," and countless disappearances that plagued the country, one can begin to comprehend the nature of the terror that had kept the Somozas in power. In particular the escalation of brutal repression by Somoza Debayle in the mid-1970s shocked the world community and served to galvanize the popular opposition to the dictator. Moreover, in the final months of the 1979 offensive, Somoza resorted to bombing his own cities—the first time that this tactic had been used to keep a ruler in power.

The three factors just outlined formed a volatile combination that acted as a catalyst, propelling people to take to the streets behind makeshift barricades. For the first time in many decades there was now an alternative opposition consisting of a middle-class commercial and political coalition, on the one hand, and "los muchachos," the youth of the FSLN, on the other. Perhaps most important of all, the level of repression had touched virtually every family in the country, and so much blood had been shed in the struggle for freedom that to return to the earlier status quo would have shown disrespect for the dead. In sum, during this decade the previously unthinkable happened: Somoza's power base that had stood so firmly for so long was rapidly crumbling.

The Church faced a critical question during this important decade: What role should it play in the upheaval that was sweeping through the country? The response was both muddled and inconsistent (paralleling the divided and polarized nature of the Church noted earlier), but one constant note was sounded: the Church finally had to recognize that times had changed drastically and that it had to participate in the developments convulsing the country. The responses to the Nicaraguan context, as we will see in the next two sections of this chapter, seemed to stem from the same pastoral concerns, but already there were fundamental differences between the grass-roots Church and the hierarchy.

The Church Response at the Grass-roots Level

Too often we tend to believe that "the Church" is limited to its hierarchy and that its stance is that put forward in official declarations. The Catholic Church has traditionally relied on a vertical and patriarchal structure, authoritarianism, exclusion of women from most positions of power, insistence on the faithful accepting the Church position, and papal infallibility on matters of doctrine; this relatively rigid approach is well documented and is deeply rooted in popular Catholic consciousness. Such a perspective is, by its very nature, limited and one-dimensional—and fails to take into account, as Vatican II and Medellín clearly indicated, that in actual fact "the Church" should comprise far more than these factors. Indeed, one could argue—as is implied in the central thrust of both Vatican II and the CELAM meetings of 1968 and 1979—that *the people are the Church*. At the very least, then, it became necessary for the hierarchy to take into account like never before the grass-roots Church, which quickly became one of the central forces of the opposition to the Somocista dictatorship.

In the case of Nicaragua we have seen how the hierarchy had traditionally intervened in political matters, willingly seeking to shore up the status quo, while at the base of the Church priests and religious attempted to share the lot of the exploited laity. After this latter form of conduct was legitimized by Vatican II, and Medellín pledged the Church to pursue actively the "preferential option for the poor," Church renovation developed apace in Latin America, particularly at the grass-roots level. With its new generation of Vatican II–influenced clergy, Nicaragua was no exception, and indeed innovative pastoral programs and approaches began to flourish in the late 1960s. (It should be noted, however, that the Nicaraguan hierarchy was slow to appreciate this new dynamic—as was sadly noticeable at the Encuentro Pastoral of 1969.)

The impact of Vatican II (which Edward Cleary called "the most important event in the life of the Latin American Church in almost five hundred years of existence")[4] was of crucial importance for Nicaragua. Among the many developments that would result from the conference—particularly at the base level—were a revitalization of religious life and of the Christian message, a refocusing of the pastoral duties of the Church, and a new attention given to the poorest and most exploited members of the Church. "Rediscovery" of the Bible, saying of the mass in the vernacular, and emphasis on ecumenism were all new and complementary facets of this revitalization process, yet it was this "preferential option for the poor" that seemed particularly pertinent in the Latin American context. Also important was the new emphasis on the role of the laity in the Church, which, although subordinate to the influence of the bishops, nevertheless constituted a "co-responsibility."[5]

These major substantive changes were taken one step further in the CELAM meeting held in Medellín in 1968. As Dodson and Nuzzi O'Shaughnessy have correctly noted, this conference was "a rereading of Vatican II in the light of Latin American reality."[6] It reaffirmed the innovations resulting from Vatican II, encouraged the role of the laity and of grass-roots activities, and commented eloquently on the many socioeconomic ills of Latin America. The institutionalized violence that resulted from political and economic monopolies made the need for true liberation starkly clear, and the bishops pointed an accusing finger at both international capitalism and internal domination by rapacious elites.

Perhaps most significant of all was the decision that the Church must pay for its traditional sins of omission and pledge its solidarity with the marginalized and the oppressed in order to bring about true liberation. This invocation to the Church to put aside past privileges and join the struggle with the poor in an effort to transform Latin American society was heady stuff indeed. In the case of Nicaragua, it represented a veritable bombshell, particularly at the base level, where for decades Catholics had been bearing the brunt of all that Medellín had signaled as being evil. Not unexpectedly, the lower clergy and the laity now looked to the hierarchy to help in harnessing this approach to their context. The Nicaraguan Church has never been the same since.

That this sweeping change within the Nicaraguan Church should start at grass-roots level and not at the top was certainly no accident: while the bishops generally lived well, had definite material benefits, and mixed with the privileged sector of society, the priests and religious (particularly those not teaching in private Catholic schools) lived alongside the impoverished masses and saw firsthand just how desperate socioeconomic conditions were for most Nicaraguans. In the wake of the Vatican II reforms they seized the opportunity to take advantage of the ecclesial "green light" to support the masses in their search for a better life. Senior religious leaders, older and more conservative, might well look askance at their innovative ideas and programs, but many activists were determined to continue the badly needed renovation of Church activities. Aided by the comparatively progressive stance of Archbishop Obando y Bravo, the grass-roots Church movement seized the moment and sought to shape the future direction of the Church. The distinctive historical moment, and in particular the steadily declining force of Somoza, combined with the momentous changes within the Latin American Church and the leadership of John XXIII provided an invaluable backdrop for the evolution of the Nicaraguan Church, yet the contribution of the grass-roots sector in shaping the agenda for change should not be underestimated.

This resulting renovation, initially a relatively small-scale phenomenon, started at the grass-roots level in the mid-1960s and constitutes the base of what the bishops would later disparagingly call the "Iglesia Popular" (People's Church). In fact, these initially isolated pastoral experiences, largely directed by foreign priests and religious, were only marginally involved in political activities and sought merely to activate parishioners' religious life and make it more relevant to their daily lives. (Indeed, many members would later withdraw for fear of government repression.) The seeds of the ensuing bitter dispute between the conservative and progressive sectors can thus be found in these two vastly different interpretations of the Gospel message and the Church mission in a post–Vatican II world—interpretations that came to the fore in the late 1960s and hinted at future religious and political polarization.

Perhaps the best-known example of the radicalization of parish activity is the religious community founded by priest (and minister of culture in the Sandinista government) Ernesto Cardenal. In 1966 he founded the isolated community of Solentiname on Lake Nicaragua in the south of the country, encouraging the campesinos living on the island to reflect on their living conditions in the light of the Christian message. The extent to which Cardenal was successful can be seen in his

María Guerrero of the Solentiname community.

anthology of religious-political reflections and observations by the members of this community.[7] The level of religious and political commitment espoused by these campesinos and the love and respect for the broader community that stemmed from their religious faith are quite noticeable to any who read their testimony. Several members eventually decided that the logical conclusion of their reflections on the relationship between the Gospel and Nicaraguan reality would be to oppose "un-Christian" conditions by taking up arms against Somoza: as a result, the military garrison at San Carlos was attacked and routed, after which the National Guard invaded Solentiname, killing all suspected of sympathizing with the FSLN and destroying the community. While on one level the Solentiname experiment failed, nevertheless it was successful in illustrating how practicing Christians could incorporate their religion and their daily lives in a more meaningful, satisfactory, and essentially Christian fashion.

A more successful approach—on which, in part at least, the central concept of Solentiname was based—can be seen in the community of San Pablo Apóstol (in the "14 de septiembre" district of Managua), founded by the Spanish priest José de la Jara. This project, which began in 1966 in a poor squatter barrio, was to have a major effect throughout the country. By encouraging Catholics to question their reality in the light of the New Testament and to dialogue with the priest and with each other (indeed, for the first time the priest was now merely the catalyst for multilateral dialogue rather than the fount of erudition he had previously been presumed to be), the parish consistently urged members to view themselves as equal members of a *community*. These were all revolutionary concepts at the time. Just as unusual was the fact that Father de la Jara, unlike any of his predecessors, decided to live in this poor squatter district, causing tremendous surprise in the barrio: "When we learned about his decision to stay, we became suspicious and concerned. We had lost faith. We knew that on Sundays, when we managed to get a priest to say mass, he did so reluctantly, and that we had to both pay for a taxi and give him 75 córdobas. This procedure didn't fill our spiritual vacuum, and so once the mass was over things went on exactly as before."[8]

At the time that the experiment at San Pablo began, José de la Jara was teaching at the national seminary. He was joined by several Maryknoll sisters (including Maura Clark, one of four U.S. religious workers savagely killed in El Salvador by the National Guard). Two other Spanish priests and several other religious were also attracted to the "pilot project," and word of its success spread throughout the country. The activities of the parish, which served a large community of some sixty thousand people, were extremely varied: meetings were held with women parishioners to reflect on their needs and cares; Bible study classes (typical of Protestant missions but quite unusual for Catholics at that time), courses for young couples seeking to get married, and study groups on the essence of Christianity were held; a local credit union that was managed as a cooperative was formed—all with the support of the parish. As one member of the community noted, this teamwork approach involving all interested members of San Pablo was crucial: "The secret of San Pablo's success was that we gave the lay people in the parish the responsibility which they deserve in the Church. Lay people thus began to participate in classes to interpret the Bible, participating in the Sunday homilies, and helping to evangelize by means of the various classes we gave in people's houses."[9] It was a concept with which most Nicaraguans, long accustomed to "vertical communication" (from their religious superiors downward), were simply not familiar.

Spurning the traditional use of Latin, the community celebrated the mass in Spanish, and the sermons (unlike the normal pattern of the priest preaching down to the people) were based on the concept of dialogue between priest and parishioners. The community's desire for a more relevant form of religious life also led them to "rediscover" the Bible in a variety of classes (usually held in informal settings in parishioners' homes). In February 1968 members of the community also composed the Misa Popular (Popular Mass), which sought to show that Christ was—like them—a poor worker. This mass (based on Nicaraguan rhythms and using a variety of local instruments, including guitars) spread to other base communities seeking to modernize religious celebrations and make them more relevant; however, the Misa Popular was banned by the hierarchy, for whom its intent to "humanize" Christ was almost sacrilegious. This example of religious polarization—precisely at a time when opposition groups were uniting against the dictator—clearly augured ill for the future possibilities of intraecclesial dialogue.

Another innovative feature of life in San Pablo was the need felt by many to harness this enriched religious life in order to serve better the community at large. The basic concept was simple: to build on this community spirit and improve the physical conditions of people in the barrio. A number of programs were instituted to sweep the streets and repair the roads, establish literacy programs for the many adults who could not read or write, organize activities for the youth of the parish through the Christian Youth Movement (Movimiento Juvenil Cristiano) that originated in the parish in 1969, and provide a weekly newsletter. Such efforts helped to unite the community, creating a sense of identity and belonging, mutual support and trust.[10] According to the members of San Pablo themselves, by 1969 they had felt the need to direct their community-related gaze further afield, still based on their Christian faith but now examining how the excesses of Somocismo affected their life. Inspired by the teachings of Medellín, and after much soul-searching and some difficulties, they concentrated their attention on the need to raise their collective awareness of the Nicaraguan context. The end result of this process of *concientización* was their decision to have their voices heard when they, inspired by their Catholic social teachings, saw abuses occur. San Pablo residents spoke out forcefully against price increases for basic foods, transportation, and the like. (In a well-known incident, several thousand residents participated in a campaign to prevent bus fares from being increased from thirty to forty cents.)

The logical outcome of this collective involvement in seeking greater social justice and—in the light of this radical rereading of the Gospels—of questioning the nature of the Somocista dictatorship was to oppose what was clearly a repressive, corrupt, and unjust tyranny. In just a few years a number of political stands were taken and activities engaged in that show how deeply involved the community had become in the anti-Somoza struggle: demonstrations, occupations of churches to protest government brutality, and campaigns of solidarity with the victims of National Guard atrocities (particularly relevant in 1977 after the Guard unleashed a campaign of terror on the Atlantic coast). One result of this process was the increase in young parishioners who joined the ranks of the FSLN. Moreover, when the final round of the insurrection started the churches were used as safe houses, with food and medicine being gathered by the community for Sandinista combatants.

Similar progressive, community-oriented Church groups sprang up in several parts of Nicaragua—in part because of the many representatives of San Pablo who were invited by progressive priests and religious to spread the word about the successes of their community, but also because of the need felt by an outspoken minority of clergy at the base level to modernize the Church's function and make it more relevant to the Nicaraguan context. In the archdiocese of Matagalpa, for instance, Father Pedro Vílchez was responsible for a particularly successful program of training peasant leaders and developing rural communities. In the northeast of the country, in the area bordering Honduras, campaigns were made (using Bibles translated into Miskito) to spread the message of the "new Church." Given the lack of priests for such an immense area, the need for lay Catholic leaders to evangelize was clear: in Waspán, to take one important example, the number of lay leaders increased from 16 in 1967 to 120 in 1970.[11] The Capuchins on the Atlantic coast were particularly successful in promoting this new form of pastoral activity, giving one course on political involvement to more than three hundred Church workers. It was also the Capuchins who in 1976 presented a letter of denunciation to Somoza, accompanied by a list of some 170 campesinos who had been killed, tortured, or disappeared at the hands of the National Guard. (Significantly, all of the Capuchins in the area signed the document.)

The Capuchins had been active in the area for several decades, organizing rural communities and training Delegates of the Word to undertake priestly functions in those areas with limited numbers of priests. Later these training programs took on other obligations, developing the "Delegados" as community leaders with rudimentary knowledge of health care, education, agriculture, and literacy. Agricultural cooperatives were set up, campaigns of preventive health care were organized, and the seeds of consciousness-raising were sown. Later, when the National Guard expropriated much of the land owned by the Miskitos and conducted a campaign of terror against them, the firmest backers of the campesinos were the Capuchins. Gradually, they too came to see that opposition to the Somoza dictatorship (which was ruthlessly destroying their programs of much-needed social development) was the logical extension of their commitment to the peasants. Common to all these projects was a yearning by the Capuchins to atone for the sins of omission in the past and to channel their deeply rooted religious feelings into the struggle for a newer and, as they saw it, more Christian society.

A very different, if equally significant, development was also taking place in the working-class Barrio Riguero in eastern Managua, where a young Franciscan priest, Uriel Molina, was involved in an experiment similar to that of José de la Jara. Molina, who had been a theology student in Rome at the time of the momentous reforms of Vatican II, was keen to encourage the necessary modernization in his own parish.[12] Molina, who was also a highly regarded professor at the Jesuit-run Universidad Centroamericana (UCA) in Managua, was approached in the early 1970s by some university students who invited him to organize a base community in his parish and to involve them in its functioning. Some forty people participated in this community, most coming from the UCA and a few from the National University (also in Managua). Reflecting on those days, Molina explains the community's continual focus on religion and political activity: "My only training was from the point of view of faith, of the Bible. We would analyze the Gospels and also learn from them. We lived in continual reflection, but this was never separate from our political activities on issues that concerned the community."[13]

Many of the university students who participated in Molina's community were from privileged social backgrounds but were disenchanted with the Nicaraguan leadership. Also disillusioned with the role of the Church hierarchy, they turned to Molina—already known as an outspoken and progressive priest who spoke highly of the theology of liberation beginning to spread throughout Latin America. He was assisted by the Jesuit priest Fernando Cardenal, later minister of education during the Sandinista tenure, who had been vice-rector of the UCA until he was fired for supporting a student strike. In the priests' approach to both organized religion and Nicaragua's glaring social inequities, these young people found an avenue for reconciling their own political frustrations and taking corrective potential action. (One of the early members of this community, Roberto Gutiérrez, explained their position in the following way: "We wanted to be with the people, with the oppressed, in the struggle for justice. We found we couldn't really tackle these questions in the family and university environment in which we lived and got the idea of building a living and working community. At the same time this meant we also changed our understanding of religion. We saw the need to regard faith not as an individual question but a collective one. We came to see that one's faith could not be authentic except around those who are poor and exploited.")[14] The Riguero community thus became a focal point for the activities of this group, drawing the ire of the National Guard and of many of the (wealthy) families of the students, who could not understand their children's actions.

Crucial to the activities of Molina's group was the blend of politics and religion that was the lifeblood of the community. And, just as many members of Jara's parish had discovered the need to shift their focus from their own community to the larger community of Nicaraguan society, so too did the people in the Barrio Riguero. The question raised by this change in focus was whether the base communities spontaneously joined the anti-Somoza struggle or whether their leaders were duped by the Sandinistas. One proponent of the latter view is Humberto Belli, currently minister of education in the Chamorro government, who reflected on what he viewed as the manipulation of the Church by the FSLN: "We had no fears of the revolutionary Christians converting Sandinista militants to Christian faith—nor did we need to. There was no reciprocal process of conversion. Sandinista atheists were not becoming believers."[15] Certainly there was growing communication—usually at the initiative of FSLN leaders—between the Sandinistas and the progressive clergy. The opposing interpretation is expressed articulately by members of the base communities themselves, for whom a revived and relevant form of religious life, combined with grossly unacceptable socioeconomic conditions for the vast majority of Nicaraguans, increased repression by the National Guard, and an ineffective traditional opposition, meant that the Sandinistas constituted the most promising alternative for restructuring Nicaragua along fairer and—for many—more Christian lines.

This conscious decision to live out the Christian faith in a radically new, community-related fashion later led to the formation of the Movimiento Cristiano Revolucionario, closely allied with the FSLN. Inspired by the Riguero experience, students from several Catholic schools took up the challenge to direct their faith toward changing radically the corrupt Somocista society. Many of their leaders later assumed high responsibilities with the FSLN, including Luis Carrión (vice-minister in the Ministry of the Interior and member of the Sandinista national leadership), Joaquín Cuadra (vice-minister in the Ministry of Defense and head of the chiefs of staff of the Sandinista People's Army), Alvaro Baltodano (head of the military training center of the Sandinista army), Fernando Guzmán (minister of industry), Roberto Gutiérrez (vice-minister in the Ministry of Agriculture and

Agrarian Reform), Salvador Mayorga (vice-minister in the same ministry), Mónica Baltodano (*comandante* and head of the mass organizations of the FSLN), and many others also active in the government.[16] Common to all was a desire to encourage Christians to recognize that the kind of society then in existence was not what Christ had preordained and that the role of the Christian sector was to seek to restructure society so that a more just socioeconomic structure could be created.

For many Christian activists, this meant urging people to reflect on contemporary Nicaraguan reality—and then to join the struggle against the dictatorship by supporting the group deemed by them most likely to change society in a way that reflected their Christian conscience, namely, the Sandinista Front. This was a general strategy agreed upon by many of the progressive priests opposed to Somoza, and it was, of course, well received by leaders of the FSLN. (Indeed, many of the *comandantes* became firm friends of the priests in this process.) For the Sandinistas, this was essentially a policy of common sense, given the overwhelming Catholic nature of the Nicaraguan people; for the progressive clergy, such an alliance with the Sandinista Front was in many ways merely the logical extension of the magisterium of Medellín. Critics of the Sandinistas see this as calculated manipulation of the Christian sector and point—correctly—to the tactic of the FSLN to infiltrate Christian groups at the time of the insurrection and convince them of their shared cause. Others would argue, however, that such actions clearly constituted supporting the "preferential option for the poor." Whichever interpretation one takes, it is clear that for this sector of the Church political activity and religion were inseparable and that the role of Christians was absolutely crucial if the dictatorship were to be overthrown. Indeed, as one activist pointed out, there were many basic similarities among all those seeking to overthrow Somoza:

> Whether there was a God or not, wasn't the concern. The concern was the practical politics we were involved in and how our Christianity got expressed. For us to be Christian meant to work with those who were poorest and at that time it meant working with the Sandinista Front. That gave us the possibility of helping liberate the people and working towards a different world, the kind of world that the Bible talks about. We read the Bible, studied liberation theology and discovered that if you really read

the Bible with your eyes open you find that the history of the Hebrew people is a history of their fight for liberation. When you read about the life of Jesus Christ you realize that whether he was or wasn't God, he was a man who was with the poor and who fought for the freedom of the poor.[17]

A final example of this form of radicalized community development in an urban setting can be seen in Barrio OPEN 3 ("Operación Permanente de Emergencia Nacional"), particularly in the wake of the 1972 earthquake. Maryknoll sisters had worked in the district since 1969, but it was after the earthquake that the shantytown swelled to an unmanageable size. It was then too that the corruption of the National Guard (who helped themselves to relief supplies) was noted, angering many of the local residents. The barrio was in desperate shape, as Manzar Foroohar has pointed out: the infant mortality rate was approximately one in three children, more than 50 percent of the working-age population was unemployed, there was not a single paved road in the barrio (indeed, communication with Managua, some 12 kilometers to the east, was also by dirt road), no houses had potable water, and few had electricity.[18] Anger and frustration were key sentiments among local residents—particularly when protests against living conditions were met with repression by the guard. In December 1976, as the struggle against Somoza intensified, priests and sisters working in OPEN 3 were also beaten by the military as they sought to intervene against the violent treatment meted out to local young people. With little to look forward to in Somoza's Nicaragua, the local residents had little to lose by joining the FSLN; at the same time, it was also very difficult for the clergy ministering to the needs of the poor not to be affected and angered by their living conditions.

A final key element needs to be mentioned in order to appreciate the fundamental approach of the grass-roots Church: the intellectual leadership that stemmed from two short-lived publications, *Testimonio,* published by progressive Catholics at the UCA between 1969 and 1970, and *SID* (Information and Documentation Service), edited by the Jesuits in the mid-1970s. Both journals presented an innovative, dynamic approach to social and political problems of Nicaragua as seen from the base, and both became increasingly critical of the dictatorship's repressive measures. They also criticized the Church hierarchy for ignoring the fundamental messages of Medellín and for tempering denunciations of Somoza out of self-interest and lack of historical vision. Typical of the central thrust of *SID* was one incisive article from the March–April 1976 issue, "The Impact of Medellín on the Nicaraguan Church," which explained how the Church under Archbishop Obando y Bravo had indeed overcome the traditional complicity with the dictatorship yet still lacked the courage to pursue the Church's prophetic mission to its logical conclusions:

> Denunciations of torture, exploitation, and injustice found in the country are beginning to multiply. . . . The Church began to take the initiative in these accusations. A new side of Christianity was slowly emerging: priests left the sacristy to go out into the street. . . . A new assessment of the prophetic dimension of religion took place: a new form of living one's faith was initiated. Certain Christian sectors were now seen as dangerous for civil and ecclesial "order." There then resulted a time of falling back to defensive positions. Medellín was now seen in a somewhat suspicious and subversive light. Some Nicaraguan bishops have an abysmal ignorance of Medellín, and large sectors of the Church— deliberately or unconsciously—ignore its conclusions.[19]

Only eighteen issues of *Testimonio* were published (in 1969 and 1970), yet their impact was significant among young clergy and religious who were eager to see articulated their own frustrations and anger at Somoza's Nicaragua and at a hierarchy that was struggling, without apparent success, to discover the spirit of post–Vatican II Catholicism. The journal published a variety of material to reveal not only the problems of Nicaragua but also the way in which progressive Church groups were tackling them. The very subtitle of *Testimonio* ("in favor of an authentic Christianity") indicated the scope of its objectives, and the editors were tireless in publicizing how pockets of Church workers *were* harnessing the spirit of Medellín to their mission. It was also a useful forum for these Church workers to express their concerns and report their successes—a forum that was lacking within the mainstream of the Church, which was still grappling with the implications of accepting the full scope of Medellín's conclusions.

To give a fuller understanding of the role and contribution of *Testimonio,* a brief thematic synthesis of the articles published is in order. Studies on rural development programs were featured alongside official communiqués on the nature of charitable actions. Interviews with Nicaraguan bishops, base community workers, foreign and national clergy—commenting on a diversity of topics dealing with political and religious life in the country—were also common. The dated nature of Church activity is seen in a spirited series of articles in a circular released by Msgr. Julián Barni on the proper use of clerical garb, which drew a storm of protest. Typical of these reactions was Roberto Sánchez, director of the John XXIII Institute for social development, who, in an article titled "Whether or Not to Wear a Cassock: Major Problem," drew some ironic conclusions at the expense of his colleagues who were concerned about the issue:

> To pray standing up, and with an empty stomach, is a problem. To travel to mass, barefoot, from the farm is also a problem. To try and refrain from drinking and from committing adultery, when you know that others who, because of their position should not, are in fact doing so, is a problem. To try and leave a common-law arrangement, only to have to pay too much for a priest to marry you, is also a problem. To take over lands at the expense of our brothers. To lend money . . . at extortionate rates. To drive about in luxurious automobiles. To slander and libel. To charge excessive rates for serving God—these are all serious problems.[20]

As can be imagined, a common theme of the issues published concerned the appropriate political role of the clergy in Somoza's Nicaragua. The *Testimonio* editors were understandably opposed to the dictatorship, but at the time there were still members of the hierarchy opposed to any stance against Somoza, and their sentiments were expressed in reprints of articles—generally published first in Somoza-controlled media. These articles were published to remind readers of the journal precisely why they subscribed to *Testimonio* and how great was the historical burden of the pre–Vatican II approach within the Church. In part this support for Somoza was due to the outmoded concept that, in the words of one veteran bishop, "the Church was only responsible for the spiritual welfare of the faithful, leaving to one side all material concerns."[21] But there was also a feeling shared by elder clergy that Somoza had treated the Church well and that it was therefore wise not to antagonize him.[22] Others—clearly of a conservative bent—waxed poetic at the dictator's benevolence and urged all Nicaraguans to obey and respect him. This stand reflected the traditional position of the Nicaraguan hierarchy concerning the need to respect legitimate governments—but was clearly out of date by this time:

> The president receives this power from God because, according to Saint Paul, all authority comes from God; and so all who resist legitimate authority are therefore opposing God.
>
> For good Christians, then, obeying God means respecting the authorities, and obeying their orders. . . .
>
> It is not through organizing conspiracies or violent revolutions, nor making agreements with subversive parties, that one serves God. Those revolutions merely wrest away from the poor all their good qualities. . . .
>
> Many people sow hatred and preach violence as a means of reaching this goal. Yet here we have Somoza, who has come to inform us that we are not forgotten.[23]

Understandably, the *Testimonio* staff had few admirers among the hierarchy at this time. The activist politics espoused by the contributing priests, their scorn of what they saw as outdated Catholic social doctrine and concerns that had little to do with "the real world"—all alienated the supporters of *Testimonio,* who felt betrayed by the lack of interest in the magisterium of Vatican II and Medellín shown by their bishops. Reflecting one year after the 1969 Encuentro Pastoral, *Testimonio* editors asked why virtually nothing had been done to resolve the manifest problems facing the Church as they had been outlined at the meeting. Their conclusions were quite simple: "There is just one reason: the influential members of the hierarchy. . . . They have built a wall of authority in order to prevent the message of Vatican II from reaching Nicaragua. . . . Until the bishops change their attitude (or until the bishops are replaced), all steps taken to modernize the Church will be seen as being of a temporary, dispersive—and subversive—nature."[24] The importance of this observation should not be underestimated, for it reveals precisely how divided the Church was more than a decade before the Sandinista revolution.

The controversial nature of the publication and its articulate criticism of so many facets of contemporary Nicaraguan society created many enemies for the editorial team. *Testimonio* simply spoke too plainly, raised too many pointed arguments at the expense of the powerful (in both political and religious spheres), and was considered too dangerous by the Nicaraguan elite. As a result, the editors needed to defend themselves, while probably knowing that their enemies were too powerful and would not rest until the journal ceased publications.[25] In the spring of 1970 (in the journal's penultimate issue), the editorial team advised their readers that *Testimonio* would soon exist no more. With great poignancy they expressed their original vision for the publication, their somewhat naive expectations, and the manner in which their hopes had been dashed. It was a message filled with sadness at the way in which the many positive developments at the base level had not received the necessary support at the level of the hierarchy—whose leaders had then attempted to pressure *Testimonio* to close its doors:

> *Testimonio* was born believing in the good faith of those who claimed to want for our Church a renewal influenced by Vatican II. . . .
>
> When *Testimonio* was born our Church was in an extremely weak, semidormant stage. We therefore decided that the immediate task was to seek to shake out this drowsiness by denouncing those elements which oppress our Church. In error we believed that this stage would soon pass and that—as a first step in that process of renovation—the results of the Pastoral Encounter would soon be put into practice. Today, more than a year later, we feel even more alone than at the beginning. We therefore believe it to be our duty to express these feelings to those people whom we tried to serve.[26]

Significantly, another article in the same issue explains the nature of the opposition to the journal within the Church itself: "In most parishes they even prohibited the sale of *Testimonio*. . . . In some clerical circles it was practically an underground publication, and publicly almost nobody had the bravery to associate themselves with *Testimonio* (as so many had done in private)" (p. 3). In November 1970 the last issue rolled off the presses. A meaningful voice for change had been silenced.

Yet this is a superficial conclusion, for while indeed the journal was closed down, what had been lost was merely the public forum that stimulated debate on the need for a Church more attuned to the modern era. The same innovative desires, the same small-scale local development projects, the same spirit and commitment, and the same support among the generation that had been touched by Vatican II and saw the possibility of meaningful change—all these remained. Throughout the 1970s this commitment to Church renovation grew, and it would be ignored with great difficulty by the hierarchy. Therefore, while *Testimonio* would disappear, in its place a variety of programs and institutions would spring up, all seeking to implement the postconciliar spirit.

There are simply too many of these developments initiated in the late 1960s and continuing in the 1970s to name in detail, but a rough listing of the most important features of this program of renovation will give some indication both of the range of activities and of the depth of commitment. Of key importance was the concept of the Christian base community, which, despite opposition from members of the hierarchy, continued to thrive (indeed, by 1979 there were some three hundred base communities in Nicaragua). The "pilot project" of José de la Jara had thus spread rapidly to urban and rural areas alike and was avidly imitated. The leading influence of other communities, such as Uriel Molina's Barrio Riguero experiment and that of the Maryknoll sisters in OPEN 3 (now renamed Ciudad Sandino), continued throughout this decade too—and the influence of the work of Molina and Fernando Cardenal with the university students in Managua was also seminal. Extremely important was the work done among the campesino sector, both by the Capuchins in the northeast and by members of CEPA (Center for Rural Education and Development)—both groups had trained Delegates of the Word in Christian community leadership and practical agricultural and social development skills. The many "courses in basic Christianity," work by the John XXIII Institute, the moral support by many faculty members at the Universidad Centroamericana, growing ties with CEPAD (the coalition of mainstream Protestant Churches, formed after the 1972 earthquake, which adopted an increasingly political stance toward Somoza during the 1970s), and—most important of all—the ongoing radicalization of faith—all are worth emphasizing.

Common to all these initiatives was a series of factors that motivated and indeed inspired Christians in this prerevolutionary decade to live out their faith. Chief among them was an acute awareness of the need to combat the "un-Christian" nature of Nicaraguan society. The hierarchy's traditional ignoring of sociopolitical matters that went against the status quo was a further concern. The glimmer of light sparked by the

Vatican II meetings in 1962–65 and the Medellín conference of 1968 revealed to these concerned Church people that this situation did not have to continue, that there was indeed an alternative—and one that was justified by the Church itself (regardless of whether or not that message had yet reached the conservative hierarchy in Nicaragua). The sense of community was of course essential to all of these developments. One participant at the San Pablo Apóstol base community emphasized the nature of lay involvement as being crucial to that community's success, an element that could apply to all the programs examined in this chapter. It was time to turn away from the earlier vertical and closed structure of the Church, according to which the bishops ordered, the priests transmitted the command, and priests and lay people alike followed the "party line" as specified by the hierarchy. Enlightened by Vatican II and Medellín, the grass-roots Church underscored the nature of dialogue, a "horizontal" approach, and the need for lay people to participate in both analyzing their spiritual and community needs and devising strategies to fulfill those goals.

These were powerful initiatives facing Archbishop Miguel Obando y Bravo as he took up his position as the head of the Nicaraguan Church. The grass-roots Church had grown dramatically in strength throughout the early 1970s, and in the following decade it would deepen its support. The increasing repression by the National Guard would encourage the hierarchy to assume a more critical role (and Archbishop Obando y Bravo had already made it clear that he would not follow the example set by his predecessors in acquiescing to the Somoza dictatorship), but the gap between the progressive base and the leadership would continue throughout this decade. The hierarchy would eventually seek to follow a more prophetic role, but for many at the grass-roots level it would prove too little too late.

The Hierarchy's Response to the Crisis

Upon assuming the position of archbishop of Managua in 1970, Obando y Bravo was faced with two basic problems, both of which would prove extremely difficult to resolve. On the one hand was the question of what role the Church as an institution should play in a country like Nicaragua, where there were massive imbalances in socioeconomic conditions, where corruption was imbedded in all aspects of life (from the sham elections held periodically to the bribes required to obtain business contracts), and where all attempts to change these manifest injustices were met by repression at the hands of the National Guard. In such circumstances, what should the mission of the Church be? On the other hand was the issue of what to do about the existence of an invigorated, enthusiastic, and committed "Church of the poor," which was driven by a zealous missionary spirit to change radically the nature of the Church itself while encouraging Catholics to rise up and oppose the injustices so apparent in Nicaragua. The incoming archbishop thus faced major difficulties in this rapidly polarizing, contentious Church.

During the course of the next decade, Obando y Bravo struggled to improve the situation of the Nicaraguan people and, in a firm and uncompromising fashion, to prevent polarization within the Church. Deeply troubled by the nature of the Somocista dictatorship, he dismissed Somoza's clumsy attempts to buy his support and voiced his criticism in pastoral letters and in the *Boletín de la Arquidiócesis de Managua*. As Somoza consistently ignored Obando's criticisms, the archbishop retaliated by gradually withdrawing the Church's legitimization of the government (by, for example, refusing to participate in elections or to inaugurate political ceremonies). More difficult, however, was his attempt to resolve problems within his own Church where, as noted above, an activist progressive movement was pushing hard for a revitalized presence. Fearful of continued polarization, Obando y Bravo preferred to pursue a cautious policy of publicly criticizing the dictatorship while reminding his rebellious flock that they owed respect to the authority of the archbishop—a theme to which he often returned after the Sandinista victory. It was clearly the wrong tack to take with the grass-roots Church, which was fundamentally opposed to the traditional authoritarian role of the bishops. Indeed, it can be argued that the archbishop's heavy-handed approach at this critical juncture laid the foundations for the antagonism and distrust that has persisted to the present day.

Even so, Obando y Bravo's stance against the dictatorship was both courageous and consistently maintained throughout the decade. It stands in sharp contrast to the slavish pandering of a colleague just a few years earlier. Msgr. Buitrago, at a public ceremony, said that he trusted Somoza "because Somoza's word translates into roads, schools, peace, progress, well-being. . . . Continue on, Sr. President, along the roads of Nicaragua. Onward, onward, always with Somoza!"[27] For his part,

Obando y Bravo sold the Mercedes Somoza gave him as a gift (distributing the proceeds among the poor) and, more significantly, announced that he would not attend the ceremony to celebrate the pact signed by Somoza and the Conservative Fernando Agüero that established a corrupt bipartisan triumvirate that would rule until 1974, in essence because the archbishop opposed the flagrant manipulation by Somoza. His widely reported decision to abstain from voting because of the lack of political choice sent an unequivocal message to Anastasio Somoza, who was left with no doubts that Obando y Bravo would not be co-opted by him.

An analysis of the archbishop's public speeches and articles during this decade reveals three distinct phases in his opposition to the Somoza dictatorship. The first begins with his appointment in 1970 and continues through 1974, including his mediation at the hostage-taking incident at "Chema" Castillo's Christmas party. During this time—particularly after the 1972 earthquake—the archbishop's tone was critical, but he still seemed convinced that if the democratic rights of citizens were respected, then Nicaragua could develop to its potential. The second period, from 1975 to 1977, reveals a Church leader who had lost some faith in the formal concept of democratic procedures (as practiced in Nicaragua) and was increasingly appalled by the rampant abuses of human rights at the hands of the National Guard. The final period, 1978–79, is in many ways the logical conclusion of the preceding one, particularly as the repression increased: it reveals Obando y Bravo as a person convinced that Somoza had to be overthrown, and in fact he denounced the dictator constantly. (Significantly, however, he refused to accept the FSLN as an alternative to Somoza, preferring instead to throw his moral support behind a middle-class coalition of traditional political foes of the dictator.)

This decade represents the coming of age of the Nicaraguan Church as it finally stepped out of the shadows and sought to find its postconciliar identity. No longer justifying the excesses of Somocismo, 'the Church bravely took on the dictator and condemned his brutality. Helped by a relatively young hierarchy (only three of the nine bishops in 1968 still held their positions in 1972), Obando y Bravo carefully laid out his plans for Nicaraguan society. If Somoza as well as the members of the progressive Church had analyzed carefully the archbishop's plans, both sides would have been displeased by his prescription for the national ills—particularly in the first phase of his opposition.

The essence of Obando's worldview was spelled out in several official documents. On March 19, 1972, for example, the Nicaraguan Bishops' Conference published an important pastoral letter ("On the Principles That Govern Political Activities of the Entire Church as Such") that was intended as a warning shot, not only against the growing number of priests and religious becoming involved in politics (a problem that would again become extremely difficult to resolve when the Sandinistas took power), but also—and in particular—against Somoza.[28] The document was long and in it the bishops seemed a little insecure (there are more references to Church magisterium than is normal, possibly indicating their desire to show that they based each step of their analysis on established teaching). Nonetheless it represented a courageous decision for them—as well as a totally new direction. In the pastoral letter the priests and religious were advised of the need to respect their bishops as well as of the unquestioned necessity of "unity around the bishops" (p. 7). They were also reminded that they were "obliged to abstain from involvement in the struggle between political parties" (p. 8).

Turning to the national situation in Nicaragua (where, they note, "it is evident that, beneath an appearance of stability, political and social tensions are beating with growing intensity" [p. 4]), the bishops talked of a moment of crisis in Nicaragua. One could sense, they claimed, "the cry, no longer restrained, of a people who are aware of their situation, and are seeking a means of breaking the ties that imprison them" (p. 12). It was a time for new structures ("It is necessary for the people not to seek merely simple adjustments to their situation, but rather to pursue an authentic social transformation that will incorporate the entire nation in forging their own destiny" [p. 18]) and for greater freedom in the country. Veiled criticisms were leveled at Somoza's expulsion of priests from Nicaragua and at the repression against social justice projects organized by Church workers, but at this stage of the Church's political awakening there was no open denunciation. Instead the central focus was on the need for all Nicaraguans to take an active part in political life; revive the nation's flagging democracy; and form associations, unions, and cooperatives in order to pool their collective talents. The government, for its part, had to ensure that these essential rights are respected:

Within the same line is the right of our citizens to pursue a plurality of political options. Yet such a right is worthless unless it is guaranteed by an open legislation which will allow all who seek to labor for the common good access to government office. . . .

Let the government officials understand their tremendous responsibility at this moment which is so decisive for our political development, when there are so many possibilities to act nobly. Let them not fall into the temptation of using force and repression to impose solutions that will return us to the sad, and painful, past. (pp. 14–15)

Two years later, on May 27, 1974, in the "Declaration of the Nicaraguan Episcopal Conference Meeting in an Extraordinary Session",[29] the stance of the bishops was much the same: they warned of the increase of social tension; stated that the military's functions had to be subordinated to the nation's defense and not to the dictates of Somoza ("Their functions cannot be defined in an arbitrary fashion, nor can they act merely for any private service" [p. 87]); and continued to appear extremely ingenuous as they spoke of "the need for people to seek a new approach which will allow justice to shine forth and political rights to be exercised with civic liberty" (p. 87).[30]

It was laudable that the bishops' concern about the deteriorating national situation should be expressed, but the resolution to the crisis would surely not be solved by appealing to Somoza's better nature or conscience. Similarly doomed to failure were their appeals to all Nicaraguans for "a greater calmness and good sense in order to avoid chaos and repression, which only increase feelings of hatred" (p. 88). But the hierarchy in this first phase seemed to believe, rather ingenuously, that appeals to Somoza's generosity would suffice for him to improve dramatically national socioeconomic conditions and to order an end to the repression. For those aligned with the progressive Church, such documents only served to emphasize differences between their approach and that of the hierarchy, about whose naïveté they felt grave concern. For while they agreed in principle that there were inherently unjust socioeconomic structures in the country, their view was that the appeals of the bishops to Somoza, their vague aspirations for greater equity, and their failure to condemn the National Guard for a reign of increasing terror were doomed to failure. The progressives intimated that a radical reform program of sweeping redistribution would be the only way to rectify Nicaragua's quasi-medieval landholding patterns. These fundamental differences, in addition to the bishops' demands for respect of episcopal authority, augured poorly for any kind of understanding or cooperation at a later stage.

Reading through Obando y Bravo's monthly column in the *Boletín de la Arquidiócesis de Managua* during the early 1970s, one is struck by two aspects—this same naïveté and his rather authoritarian spirit. On the one hand, he is deeply aware of the grave disparities in Nicaraguan society: "We can see in our country *excessive inequalities* between the social classes. A tiny minority is fabulously wealthy at the expense of the impoverishment and misery of the masses of Nicaraguans," he noted in August 1973.[31] Yet on the other hand, he seemed to believe that Somoza and his cronies would willingly give up their wealth if a sufficiently articulate appeal could be made. He consistently referred to the need for fraternity, social harmony, mutual understanding, and love as the only meaningful solution for Nicaragua's ills, and he apparently believed that his message would be accepted: "We demand from all their support for a crusade of love, justice, and—no doubt—sacrifice in order to overcome the present difficulties. This is to be done as a gesture of solidarity with the sacred heritage left to us by Christ: the poor who, in His name, we should assist and shelter: 'I was hungry and you gave me food. . . . ' "[32]

At this stage, then, the Nicaraguan bishops felt alienated from Somoza and were disturbed at the rise in human rights abuses. They were not, however, prepared to go one step further and call for a radical restructuring of Nicaraguan society. Moreover, they were concerned at some of the initiatives stemming from the progressive wing of the Church—largely because such programs were independent of their central authority and could potentially lead to parallel structures of control. As a result, while many members of the Episcopal Conference were increasingly disturbed by the actions of the government, they were unable either to call for a radical restructuring or to support the ideas of the grass-roots Church. Instead they leaned heavily toward the bourgeois opposition, who wanted comparatively minor social and economic reforms under a new leader and who would also be a valuable counterweight to any Sandinista incursions. This political alignment—which in essence called for minor social restructuring along lines traced by these middle-class opposition parties and organizations—would continue during the last years of the Somoza dictatorship, with bourgeois opposition politicians becoming the major allies of the Church. Throughout the eleven and a half years of the Sandinista government, the hierarchy would turn to this political grouping for support and would identify their own interests with the UNO-COSEP coalition that would win the 1990 elections. While harboring little sympathy for the FSLN, the Catholic hierarchy felt extremely comfortable with the bourgeois opposition.

In the wake of his public humiliation following the hostage-taking incident in December 1974, when the FSLN showed how powerless he was, Somoza declared a state of emergency and initiated a fresh campaign of brutality to eliminate the guerrilla movement. In doing so, however, he gave the National Guard carte blanche, thus unleashing a savage bloodletting that terrorized the nation and shocked the hierarchy into taking a more focused stand. Between 1975 and the FSLN victory on July 19, 1979, it became increasingly clear that Archbishop Obando y Bravo now pursued two goals: the overthrow of Somoza and the installation of a bourgeois Christian Democratic government.

The archbishop's pastoral letters, communiqués, monthly column in the *Boletín de la Arquidiócesis de Managua,* and published interviews reveal that during 1976 the Church hierarchy gradually, and perhaps somewhat reluctantly, decided to take a collective stance against Somoza. The bishops had finally come to agree that the dictator simply had gone too far and must leave office if anything resembling normalcy was to return to Nicaraguan political life. Their tone was measured and reflective, but by the end of the year most of the bishops saw no other alternative but for Somoza to leave political office.

This conclusion was reached quite slowly, much to the frustration of the progressive Church sector. Indeed, a careful reading of official communiqués during 1975 and throughout most of 1976 supports this slow realization of the full extent of Somocismo on the part of Archbishop Obando y Bravo. In 1975, for example, it was clear that Somoza would brook no dissent, and repression against the campesino sector in Zelaya was already well documented. Yet in his official Christmas and New Year's message (published in January 1975), the archbishop ignored the manifest abuses of human rights. Instead he expressed concern with three different problems facing society: sexual morals, the high rate of traffic accidents, and the inflation rate.[33] Repression might well be widespread, the country in the initial stage of a civil war, and the dictator ruthlessly quashing all dissent—yet for the archbishop the solution to Nicaragua's most pressing problems was to be found in a time-honored appeal for selfless conduct: "The most basic aspect of these rules is love for one's neighbors. Only by overcoming all kinds of egoism or love for oneself, and only by emphasizing the concept of love for our fellow man, is it possible to keep one's hands firmly on the steering wheel, and one's heart open—and thus avoid the majority of dangers that can occur" (p. 7).

Throughout 1975 the archbishop's communications reveal a similar lack of understanding of what was really happening in the country. Appeals for love, understanding, and social harmony can be found along with statements defending the role of the journalist and the need for a "Christian culture" and for Church renovation—but renovation on terms outlined by the hierarchy. An analysis of these observations reveals a man who was clearly out of touch with his country. Undoubtedly possessing the best of intentions, Obando y Bravo called for facile solutions to Nicaragua's complex problems. For example, he underscored the need to "seek a greater equality for all in life's opportunities, so that all with the appropriate aptitude can further their studies and thereafter assume social responsibilities and positions."[34] Similarly ingenuous was his plea for all to "do everything possible to improve living conditions for the workers. For many of them, especially for the masses of manual workers and peasants, these conditions make any dignified cultural development virtually impossible" (p. 6). Such an appeal not only betrayed ignorance of Nicaragua's current socioeconomic conditions but was also insulting to the intelligence of those on whose behalf Obando y Bravo was appealing. The government obviously had no intention whatever of improving conditions to ensure greater access to higher education for peasants, nor did it have the slightest interest in encouraging a "dignified cultural development." Nonetheless the archbishop continued with this parallel tack of appealing to the government while circling around the thorny issue of whether or not the Church should become directly involved in political matters.

Examples of the archbishop's lack of appreciation of events in Nicaragua abound. In a speech to members of the media he urged them to show "truth, the common good, honesty, good customs, professional honesty, fidelity in all contracts, healthy friendship,"[35] while in an address to Nicaraguan legislators he reminded them that the laws that they passed "should bring true joy for all Nicaraguans."[36] Speaking to the Chamber of Commerce, he urged members to develop two fundamental virtues— justice and charity. Warning them that property speculation was "one of the greatest offenses against the people of God,"[37] he advised them that "whoever appropriates goods that are superfluous to their needs—when at the same time another social class, which also participated in the production process, does not have sufficient to carry on a dignified human existence—is guilty of a great injustice" (p. 8). The next month the archbishop turned his moral suasion against advertising, criticizing the commercialization of Christmas as well as the sponsoring of cultural and sporting events by "business companies whose products are not always morally laudable."[38]

These communiqués—along with the numerous invocations to various professional associations, benedictions at the inauguration of several buildings, and comments at other official functions—reveal some of the principal concerns for Nicaraguan society as perceived by Archbishop Obando y Bravo as late as mid-1976. They reveal a man who felt the need to speak out often on a wide range of topics, seeking to strengthen the Church's influence and at the same time help his nation. Yet the archbishop was not reading the signs of the times (or if he were doing so, he preferred not to speak openly about them). His outlook was conservative, and he apparently believed that merely appealing to a common Christian conscience would lead to a resolution of Nicaragua's problems. The broader social concerns and the rapidly increasing level of repression seemed—in the mid-1970s—to go unheeded.

The juxtaposition of two articles in the archdiocesan publication of December 1976 speaks volumes about the Church hierarchy's approach to the "Nicaraguan question." The bishops had decided, albeit reluctantly in some cases, that Somoza should leave political office—but they were still very much in favor of maintaining a similar political system and were opposed to any radical solutions. In a message to priests and Delegates of the Word, the archbishop urged them to subordinate struggles for sociopolitical liberation to spiritual concerns—and reminded them that they should strive to convert individuals to the real meaning of Catholic social teaching: "We will never be prophets of violence or of the class struggle; rather, we will support fraternal dialogue, based upon conversion and love. We should insist on the conversion of man's heart. . . . There will be no new continent without new men."[39] On the following page, an official communiqué from the Nicaraguan Episcopal Conference was published, forbidding—in an exceptionally harsh, authoritarian manner—the singing of the Misa Popular, which by now had become widely used in the grass-roots Church. While the Archbishop had to design a strategy that would be more pertinent to Nicaragua's pressing problems, he also had an equally grave problem within the Church that badly needed to be addressed.

So what does this analysis of Obando y Bravo's communiqués and pastoral letters show? First, despite ample evidence to the contrary, the archbishop continued to hope that appeals for fraternal love and harmony, together with adherence to traditional Church teaching on social questions, would suffice to eradicate the most abhorrent features of Somocismo. Second, many features of preconciliar teaching (especially concerning the need for Church unity and for unquestioning respect for Church authority) remained deeply ingrained. These aspects would continue until the present day, but a new feature would slowly emerge during 1976 as the repression of the National Guard would gradually affect the Church's own work. At that point the hierarchy began to raise its objections with Somoza and to become attuned to the problems facing Nicaraguan society as a whole. Even then, however, the hierarchy seemed unaware of the level of popular opposition to Somoza, was inconsistent in the nature of its political stances, and continued to lag far behind the determination of the people to bring down the dictatorship.

The initial catalyst for the political awakening of the Nicaraguan hierarchy came as a result of the level of repression encountered by Church workers in Zelaya, where the Capuchins had been particularly active since 1971. As a result of increasing military incursions into the area, the order prepared a list of killed and disappeared, and three high-ranking Church spokespersons (Msgrs. Salvador Schlaefer, Julián Barni, and Clemente Carranza) presented the list to Somoza. There was incontrovertible evidence regarding the role of the National Guard in these acts, yet the respectful tone of Msgr. Schlaefer in a subsequent pastoral letter reveals how—in May 1975—the Church was not prepared to take the matter any further: "We left the presidential office, thankful to the president and his officials, but with a fervent prayer in our heart and on our lips: 'May the Holy Spirit illuminate the mind and soften the heart of those who are causing so much suffering among the campesinos of Matagalpa, Estelí, and Zelaya.' I beg all faithful brethren to continue with our prayers in favor of justice and the evangelical message: 'Love each other as your brothers.' "[40]

Schlaefer's advice notwithstanding, the level of repression increased quite quickly, and in June 1976 all the Capuchins living in Zelaya sent Somoza a detailed list of some 170 campesinos who had been tortured or killed or had disappeared at the hands of the National Guard. Subsequently the grass-roots Church took it upon itself to publicize these atrocities abroad, particularly in the United States. Fernando Cardenal was especially active in this campaign, denouncing the abuses of human rights before the U.S. House of Representatives and traveling to several countries to seek support for the struggle against Somoza, while in April 1977 Miguel D'Escoto presented a full list of human rights abuses to another subcommittee of the House. To a certain extent, it was this process of denouncing Somoza abroad (so that external pressure, particularly from the United States, the dictator's major international backer, could embarrass him) that awakened the Nicaraguan hierarchy and forced it to take a more active stance.

The best evidence of the hierarchy's rapidly awakening opposition to Somoza came in their January 1977 pastoral letter, which denounced in no uncertain terms a litany of deeply rooted problems in Nicaragua. An eloquent statement of fundamental democratic principles, it reveals a new stage in the Church's understanding of the nation's crisis. The problems referred to by the bishops can be broken down into two groups—those dealing with inherent socioeconomic injustice in the country, and others dealing with brutal repression by the National Guard. The more striking criticisms were directed against the corrupt judicial system: "Many crimes have been committed, yet sentences have not been given, nor punishment sought. . . . The number of people arrested, but not accused of any crime, continues to grow—yet it is not possible to begin legal proceedings."[41] Increasingly, Church activity was becoming the target of repression, and in the pastoral the bishops told of a series of problems encountered by Church workers: official permission was often demanded by military authorities for Church meetings to take place; in Zelaya and Matagalpa, military patrols had taken over church buildings as military barracks; some Delegates of the Word had been pressured to suspend cooperation with priests; and many Catholics had been captured and tortured and had disappeared.

The bishops presented three basic demands: respect for constitutional guarantees, a proper and fair legal process for all prisoners, and freedom to seek a more just social order. This document was the most focused of the hierarchy's communiqués to date, and it was also the first in which the bishops referred so directly to the pathetic socioeconomic conditions faced by many. From this time on, the hierarchy's opposition to the dictatorship was firmly entrenched. (Considering that in the Church's official New Year's message exactly two years earlier one of the major concerns had been the country's high rate of traffic accidents, one can measure how far the hierarchy's interpretation of events had developed.)

Even more critical, however, was the bishops' 1978 message in which they passed from sharp criticism to outright denunciation, condemning "the state of terror . . . the arbitrary, indefinite detentions . . . the inhumane methods of investigation; the lack of respect for life; the accumulation of wealth in the hands of a few; the lack of sentences for many crimes; interference in religious matters, which at times results in the open or underhanded persecution of priests or Catholic lay leaders."[42] The bishops then announced dramatically, "We simply cannot keep quiet" (p. 101) and produced a lengthy list of abuses by Somoza. Significantly, they noted: "We cannot reduce our pastoral mission to simply the sacramental and catechistic aspects. Even Christmas tells us about God-made-flesh, who assumes our problems" (p. 102). It should be pointed out, however, that the problems they referred to had long been in evidence and that for many years the hierarchy had responded according to traditional Church doctrine of appealing to individual conscience. A dramatically new level of political involvement in support of the people's rights was now being initiated, but it was the hierarchy that had changed, not the people.

The Church leadership—to a large extent following the lead of the "Church of the poor"—had rapidly radicalized its faith. True, there were still glaring inconsistencies (such as in July 1977, when Somoza was suffering from heart problems and three bishops sent letters wishing him a speedy recovery and 233 masses were offered to pray for his improved health), and the Church leadership had reacted extremely slowly to the national crisis. Nevertheless the hierarchy, headed by Obando y Bravo, had indeed come to appreciate the evils of Somocismo and to denounce courageously its continuation. The abuses of human rights (particularly as they affected the delivery of Church work), the awareness of rapidly increasing popular unrest throughout society as a whole, and the determination not to have the progressive wing of the Church dominate the proceedings—all finally coalesced to galvanize the Church into action. By January 1978 the Church leadership was in the forefront of the opposition to Somoza's rule. The political assassination of the Conservative leader and *La Prensa* editor Pedro Joaquín Chamorro on January 10 was the final straw—and the Church leadership rapidly joined the escalating struggle.

From January 1978 to July 19, 1979, the Church leadership continued to preach reconciliation and love among all Nicaraguans while knowing full well that such a policy was doomed to failure. Seeking to stave off the inevitable bloodbath, the bishops issued a pastoral letter on January 28, 1978, calling for "caminos civilizados" and reminding all Nicaraguans of the need for love and mutual understanding.[43] The silence at these suggestions was deafening, indicating that the bishops' pleas were built on wishful thinking rather than a solid appreciation of contemporary Nicaraguan reality.

In August of that year a more substantive document was published by the Episcopal Conference. Its message was far more blunt: "Fidelity to Christ's message imposes upon the Church (upon all its members) the duty of struggling to create a more humane and more just society, denouncing all forms of oppression. The Gospels should be translated concretely into our personal and social life."[44] The bishops called for "a new sociopolitical order" and demanded specific reforms in matters of political organizing, distribution of wealth and benefits, reorganization of the National Guard, freedom of expression, and legal reform. Significantly, however, they refrained from calling for Somoza's resignation and intimated that the FSLN should not be considered a potential replacement for him: "Today the nation demands radical positions (yet not precisely extremist ones), to be applied with generosity and patriotism" (p. 109).

The following day another message was released by the archbishop and his council of advisers, which went further in suggesting that Somoza should consider stepping down, although the message was couched in extremely diplomatic terms (Nicaraguan leaders were invited to "reflect upon the feasibility and urgency of a temporary national solution, based upon a common agreement and mutual concessions by all").[45] The bishops again spoke of the need for justice and the end to institutionalized violence and concluded with a special appeal to the youth of Nicaragua, urging them to pray and work for peace. This concluding message was especially directed to "los muchachos," the Nicaraguan teenagers who constituted the basis of the Sandinista ranks. Once again, while gradually accepting the premise that

Somoza had to go, the bishops were quite clear in their opposition to the "extremist" position of the Sandinistas.

The most outspoken document issued during this time was a letter representing the diocesan clergy, executive of the National Conference of Religious, and all religious orders and congregations in Nicaragua sent to President Jimmy Carter on September 15, 1978. Far more direct than any pastoral letter, it urged the U.S. president to cut off all aid to Nicaragua. It condemned the institutionalized violence of Somoza's Nicaragua, gave numerous examples of the abuses of human rights, talked of the impossibility of bringing about change while the dictator (whose leadership was termed a "regime that sowed death in its wake") clung to power, criticized the rampant corruption of the dictatorship, and stated a stark conclusion: "We cannot continue in this state of suffering, uncertainty, and anguish."[46]

While one can question why it took the Church hierarchy so long to understand fully the message of the CELAM conference at Medellín in 1968 (or rather, to ignore its conclusions), it is undeniable that the Church—and in particular the "Church of the poor"—had become a major target for government repression. Newspaper accounts throughout 1978 and 1979 show how the National Guard deliberately sought to terrorize the Church sector. In September 1978, for example, thirty-five priests from the archdiocese of Managua protested against the level of repression; Father Pedro Belzunegui had been expelled from the country; Father Donald García had been beaten by the National Guard in Masaya; an old priest, Father José María González, had also suffered at their hands; armored cars had driven into the María Auxiliadora church, where soldiers had sprayed the walls with machine-gun fire; the church of Nuestra Señora de los Angeles (the parish church of Father Uriel Molina) and that of San José in Diriamba had also been fired upon; San Antonio in Jinotepe and San José in Matagalpa had been invaded by the National Guard—who had also invaded the cathedral in Matagalpa; the Salesian College in Masaya had been shot up by National Guardsmen (for the fourth time), and the priests teaching there had been roughed up.[47] Three days later, after Archbishop Obando y Bravo went to the main police station in Managua to arrange the release of several priests from the Colegio Calasanz, he too was the victim of insults and threatening gestures.[48]

Throughout the remainder of 1978 and during 1979 until Somoza fled, the population took up the struggle against the dictatorship. In many ways despite itself, the Church saw itself drawn into the vortex, particularly as repression against the Church continued. Even the decision of two priests, Gaspar García Laviana and José Antonio Sanjines, to take up arms and fight alongside the guerrillas did not cause the hierarchy to back down—it was already too late for that. In late September 1978 the body of José Francisco Sandoval, a priest in Estelí, was found. In Jinotepe Father Baltodano was dragged out of bed and beaten with rifle butts by National Guardsmen, who then aimed their weapons and pretended to shoot him.[49] Rockets and heavy artillery shells were fired against the Church of San Juan Bautista in León, while in Jinotepe Father Sediles was beaten by the military.

By February 1979 the situation had deteriorated further, not only for the Church but also for the people as a whole. An important article in *La Prensa* on February 17 ("The Church Clamors for Justice") told of the murder by the National Guard of five young people in a church in León. The same article referred to a complaint lodged with the government by the executive of Christian schools in the country, who denounced the invasion of the La Salle College campus by the National Guard on February 15, as well as the subsequent machine-gunning of the school building. Most serious was the way in which soldiers had beaten up two Brothers teaching at the school (José María Miguel and Basilio); a third, Brother Agustín Díaz, had been seriously wounded and was in an intensive care ward. That same month a large mass was held to pray for all those who had fallen at the hands of the National Guard, especially two priests, Gaspar García Laviana and Francisco Luis Espinoza. Finally on June 2, 1979, as repression at the hands of the hated guard continued and as the final offensive rapidly gained ground throughout Nicaragua, the bishops finally recognized that armed resistance could be legitimized by Church teaching: "All of us are hurt and affected by the extremes of revolutionary insurrections, but its moral and juridical legitimacy cannot be denied in the case of evident and prolonged tyranny, which seriously threatens the fundamental rights of the individual and undermines the common good of the country."[50]

The Church Takes Sides

Reading through the pages of popular newspapers and magazines from Managua at that time, one cannot help but be struck by the degree to which the Church participated in the popular struggle against the dictatorship—and how it suffered, particularly at the base level, at the hands of the National Guard for its solidarity with the people. This solidarity should be emphasized, for it must surely represent the fundamental goal of Church pastoral action—namely, to "be with" the people. In the Nicaraguan case, however, it was a goal that was not evenly pursued, even when it was obvious that ordinary Catholics were being repressed by the National Guard—and were increasingly participating in the direct resistance against the dictatorship. Nevertheless, even among members of the hierarchy it gradually became clear that the people would continue the struggle against the dictatorship, and as a result the leadership somewhat belatedly followed suit.

This decade in Church history was ushered in by the appointment of Obando y Bravo as archbishop of Managua. He was a man with remarkably new ideas and an innovative approach for the Nicaraguan Church. At the level of the hierarchy, he almost single-handedly brought his colleagues in line with a more modern postconciliar interpretation. This was no mean achievement, given the nature of the traditional Church. He also recognized—albeit belatedly—that Somoza had to leave the presidency, and he made his feelings known. His voice, then, was an important weapon among traditional Catholics.

There is absolutely no doubt that Obando refused all attempts by Somoza to co-opt him, and he is to be commended for escaping from the pattern established by his predecessors. One can argue, however, that he was slow to read the "signs of the times," since many of his junior clergy had shown the way for constructive engagement in Nicaraguan society many years before he did. (Indeed, a criticism can also be leveled against him for being somewhat dictatorial in his dealings with junior colleagues engaged in these projects.) Moreover, he can be criticized for taking so long to encourage the development of a pastoral action program along the lines encouraged by Vatican II and Medellín. Perhaps one can claim that his tardiness to justify the armed struggle against the dictator also smacked somewhat of political opportunism, since by June 1979 (only six weeks before the overthrow of the dictator) it was obvious that Somoza would not last long.

Three characteristics of Archbishop Obando y Bravo's leadership stand out from the first decade of his tenure—aspects that would continue to dominate his leadership for the following eleven years. He was determined to ensure that a uniform message on Church matters be the norm and was prepared to brook no dissent on that matter. The existence of what he clearly interpreted as a parallel magisterium, which he referred to as the Popular, or People's, Church ("la Iglesia popular"), was thus wholly unacceptable, in no small part because it threatened Church unity—whose parameters *he* reserved the right to define. Closely allied with this visceral rejection of political grass-roots activity (in July 1982 he noted that Church base communities "have absolutely nothing religious about them: they are a façade to breed Marxism-Leninism") was his determination that uniformity on Church matters had to be shepherded cautiously by episcopal authority. A pre–Vatican II structure with a downward-flowing chain of command was essential to this approach, and all decisions of import were to be made in consultation with one's superiors. As a result, when the Misa Campesina was composed, or when the decision was taken to occupy church buildings in order to draw attention to human rights abuses, the archbishop condemned these tactics. Authority was thus a key component of his approach, as members of the "Church of the poor" would learn at great personal cost following the victory over Somoza. The third factor that deserves attention is the archbishop's stubbornly conservative streak. By no stretch of the imagination can he be considered a liberal Churchman, prepared to seek compromises and to understand the perspective of other Church representatives; rather, he is an authoritarian, courageous, and obstinate man who in 1979 was determined to ensure that the Church would speak with one voice, on terms drawn up by him. While the Church as a body moved to the left in the wake of the repression unleashed by the National Guard, Obando y Bravo at all times retained his uncompromising conservatism—which guides him still as he charts what he believes to be the only true course available to the Church. His innovative spirit of the early 1970s has thus been steadily replaced with an authoritarian determination to keep the Church traveling along a traditional and remarkably orthodox path from which no deviations are permitted.

The story of the Church in Nicaragua during this decade was one in which the hierarchy finally came to terms with its temporal role in that country and in which the grass-roots Church discovered its own identity. The hierarchy and the grass-roots wing held two opposing views of the role of the Church, with fundamental differences in everything from magisterium to approach and from ceremonies to philosophical leanings. Indeed, there was little of substance binding them together other than the fact that both wings professed to constitute the authentic voice of Catholic religious expression. Throughout this decade of self-discovery they largely ignored each other, preferring instead to carve out a niche for themselves in Nicaraguan society—and, toward the end of the 1970s, to survive in the face of increased repression. There was no time to argue with each other over philosophical matters during this stage, since survival was paramount. After the success of the final offensive and with Somoza in exile, however, it was time to take stock and determine whether such different Church approaches could coexist. As Archbishop Obando y Bravo celebrated a victory mass shortly after the revolutionary triumph, observers could be forgiven for thinking that perhaps these two radically differing interpretations could in fact be reconciled and that the hierarchical and grass-roots styles could be accommodated in the same Church. Unfortunately this would not prove to be the case, for despite efforts to the contrary religious polarization could not be avoided.

✝

4   FROM JUBILATION TO DESPAIR

(1979–1982)

[My work with the FSLN]
helped me a lot because,
whatever else may be said
abroad, it personally signified
a way in which I could better
live out my faith, my love, my
Christian service for the
poorest people in my country.

Father Fernando Cardenal,
1980

Nicaragua has gone in search
of its historical liberation. Not
in search of new Pharaohs.

Nicaraguan Episcopal
Conference, 1980

THE POLITICAL DISAGREEMENTS and tension within the Church that had clouded the struggle against the Somoza dictatorship resurfaced soon after the revolutionary victory. Indeed, tension increased noticeably beginning in late 1979, reaching a fever pitch three years later as preparations were made for the March 1983 visit by Pope John Paul II. This chapter analyzes the major developments that contributed to this spiraling antagonism and mutual recriminations. The quotations above give some indication of the imminent collision course on which both sectors of the Church—each with its own distinctive vision of the meaning of bearing Christian witness in society—were bound. The clash was inevitable; the question was merely how long it would take before the ecclesial explosion occurred.

At the time of Somoza's overthrow, religious tension to this degree seemed inconceivable, largely because of the role of virtually all sectors of the Church in opposing the Somocista dictatorship. The traditionally conservative hierarchy, as noted in chapter 3, had gradually become more outspoken in their criticisms (and eventual denunciation) of Somoza under the brave and tenacious leadership of Archbishop Obando y Bravo. Church divisions had been temporarily shelved as all sectors of society (including the dictator's former supporters in the bourgeoisie) contributed significantly to toppling Somoza. Apparently inspired by the teachings of Medellín (and recognizing that popular support for the armed struggle against the dictator was almost universal), the Catholic hierarchy issued a pastoral letter on June 2, 1979, that justified armed resistance in Nicaragua's situation—the first time that a Latin American episcopal conference had legitimized such a step. When the hated National Guard surrendered, Obando y Bravo was a major protagonist in the ceremony marking the transfer of power to the revolutionary junta. In the days immediately following Somoza's flight in July and the entry into Managua of "los muchachos," dozens of masses of thanksgiving were offered, as were many more for the tens of thousands of Somoza's victims—the "héroes y mártires" as they are termed in Nicaragua. Religious music figured prominently on radio and television broadcasts, especially the "Misa Campesina Nicaragüense" of

FSLN supporter Carlos Mejía Godoy that was so disliked by the hierarchy.

Rejoicing and harmony continued for several months, although it must have been obvious to all the main actors that this was only a temporary respite. The presence of Obando y Bravo in Caracas, where he was trying to tack together a right-of-center coalition to prevent the FSLN from taking power, on the eve of the popular victory augured ill for future developments. For behind the mood of jubilation and gratitude there were grave concerns in many circles about the kind of society that would emerge in Nicaragua and who would hold power after the smoke had cleared. The ensuing struggle to establish control, impose the official development model, and assure hegemony was analyzed throughout the country and at all levels of the Church. And what members of the Church hierarchy saw during the three crucial years following Somoza's downfall was not to their liking.

The Early Church Documents

Just twelve days after the fall of Somoza, the Nicaraguan Episcopal Conference published its first pastoral letter of the revolutionary period. The bishops used this pastoral to issue a warning, not a call for jubilation. They voiced two basic concerns: on the one hand, they made veiled allusions to Marxist ("foreign") influence; on the other, they emphasized the need to seek God's divine inspiration. The first of these concerns was stated firmly and unequivocally: "Man's greatness *does not stem from any foreign system or theory*. It comes from the very fact (and from a profound awareness of that fact) that man was created as a living image of God" (emphasis added).[1] To underscore the need for a Nicaraguan approach, and perhaps to reject the Marxist influence, the bishops emphasized once again that "raising sociopolitical awareness (*concientizar*) does not mean imposing foreign ideas" (p. 70).

The second facet of this pastoral revolved around the need for the new Junta of National Reconstruction to seek divine inspiration. The bishops specifically advised the government not to forget the inherent Catholic nature of Nicaragua, for to do otherwise would be to betray the *patria:* "Without God, political awareness becomes merely the repetition of alienating slogans, void of all critical sense and human transcendence. If one marginalizes God, the very principles of national self-determination and self-control are thereby destroyed" (p. 71). The bishops were obviously concerned about the direction being taken by the revolutionary process and felt the need to have their voices heard.

The bishops were particularly troubled by the strong leftist tilt of the Sandinistas, a concern that Archbishop Obando y Bravo had personally experienced for many years. They were also worried about the potential loss of influence in political, social, and moral terms—which until this time the Church had enjoyed. Faced with an ever-growing popular identity with "los muchachos" of the FSLN, the hierarchy understandably feared a decline in its role, both spiritually and politically. (The division within the Church, with an outspoken minority enthusiastically embracing the Sandinista cause and urging the hierarchy to overcome its prejudices, did little to assuage the bishops' fears.) The danger of an atheistic philosophy was also a grave threat in the eyes of many, particularly in light of the ties between the FSLN and the Cuban government. Finally, the bishops had always preferred the idea of a more traditional, middle-class alliance heading the new Nicaragua. Members of the bourgeoisie were naturally more attuned to the weltanschauung of the bishops: most had been educated at private Catholic schools and were active in their parishes, many were personal friends of individual bishops, and they possessed a similar ideological disposition. Moreover, the hierarchy and the bourgeoisie shared a basic belief that the Nicaraguan political system did not require the major revamping that the Sandinistas promised—and they knew they stood to lose from such a radical restructuring. In sum, the bourgeoisie and the Catholic hierarchy in Nicaragua were natural allies who shared a similar outlook and vested interests, and both faced potentially severe losses if the FSLN program were to be implemented.

Given the potential alliance of the bourgeois sector and the Catholic hierarchy, the July 1979 pastoral is noteworthy both because it fails to mention the people on whose behalf the revolution was made (the poor) and because of the concerns expressed at the "confusion" felt by the middle-class sectors of the country: "We cannot help sharing too the anguish and fear during this time of transition. We understand that there is serious confusion, regarding both ideological aspects and the new state structures" (p. 70). At a time when the vast majority of the population was rejoicing at the popular victory over Somoza (and worrying little about the direction being taken by the country), the bishops (undoubtedly reflecting the concern of their greatest and most influential supporters, the leaders of the bourgeoisie) were desperately seeking to emphasize to the Sandinistas the need for their inclusion in the decision-making process. Also significant was the "anguish and fear" they expressed, representing a warning shot across the bows of the FSLN. To say the least, the message of this pastoral was hardly an encouraging or auspicious sign for a unified approach to Nicaragua's daunting problems.

But in November 1979, just four months after the victory over Somoza, the bishops published a truly extraordinary pastoral letter ("Christian Commitment for a New Nicaragua"), unique in the annals of Nicaraguan Church history. Indeed, this document is so unlike anything previously written by the Nicaraguan hierarchy that observers can be forgiven for asking who helped the bishops compose it. In content and style it was the absolute opposite of the letter written scarcely four months earlier—its tone is warm, encouraging, confident, and supportive of the FSLN-led revolution. To date, no thorough analysis of the reasons behind the hierarchy's about-face has been provided—which serves to emphasize even more the extraordinary nature of the November document. This pastoral was also self-critical of the Church's limitations—another first: "We are convinced that, for the Church, there is much to do and that we have not always been able to fulfill what the needs of our people required from us."[2] Perhaps most important, there was a symbolic olive branch extended to members of the Christian base communities. There was, for instance, a call to continue the dialogue with these communities—an urgent need, given the differing interpretations of the Church's role by the hierarchy and the grass-roots Church. Toward the end of this impressive document the bishops expressed their respect for the contribution of the base communities with words that can only have caused great surprise in that sector: "The people of God should renew their vitality by means of the Christian base communities, increasingly fraternal. The Church should both learn and teach the faithful to see things from the perspective of the poor, whose cause is that of Christ" (p. 82).

There were many other surprises in this document. The references in the July pastoral to the "alien" qualities of the revolution were replaced by a conviction of "the originality of the historical experience that we are living" (p. 75). The strong influence of Sandino was noted approvingly ("something which accentuates the originality of the Nicaraguan revolution, giving it its own style" [p. 76]), and the bishops made it clear that they harbored no doubts as to the originality of the revolutionary process: "We are confident that the revolutionary process will be something creative, profoundly original, and in no way imitative" (p. 79). This is quite remarkable, given the accentuated warnings sounded in the earlier publication, and leads one to question how and why this sudden conversion had taken place. Some may argue that the November pastoral was intended as a form of conditional support for the new government, but this position is undermined by the document's tone of openness, fulsome praise, unabashed optimism, and express desire to cooperate with the FSLN—even in the construction of a socialist society.

The two most prominent features of the pastoral were the bishops' emphasis on respecting the "preferential option for the poor" and their urging that the Nicaraguan socialist experiment not be rejected out of hand. The bishops spoke of the need to do all in their power to help the poor, to support the laws that protected the people from becoming marginalized, and to ensure that all members of society had the opportunity to develop. They were convinced that the influence of the Gospels could be authentic only "if we listen with humility and discernment to the call that the Lord is making to us through such signs of the times" (p. 82). They emphasized the exceptional nature of the Nicaraguan experiment, urged their faithful not to be afraid to venture along new paths, and, in two paragraphs that seemed to have been taken directly from Medellín, insisted on the need to pursue at all costs the necessary "preferential option for the poor":

> Today we are living in our country an exceptional occasion to witness and to announce the kingdom of God. It would be a grave betrayal of the Gospels if through fear and distrust, the insecurity that every radical process of social change creates in some, or through the defense of individual interests, we were to allow this crucial moment to pass by. It is a moment that would allow us to turn into practice that preferential option for the poor that both Pope John Paul II and the Bishops' Conference of Puebla demand of us. (p. 81)

With words that have come back to haunt them many times (because they had never before or after expressed anything similar), the bishops developed their argument: "This option assumes the rejection of old-fashioned forms of thinking and acting, and the profound conversion of ourselves as the Church. . . . Unlike the situation now in Nicaragua, never before has it been so imperative for us to ratify in convincing fashion this preferential option for the poor" (p. 81).

This public acceptance of the "preferential option for the poor" as the prime focus of the Church, as well as the self-criticism of "old-fashioned forms of thinking and acting," was truly exceptional—and quite opposed to the sentiments expressed by the hierarchy both before and after this pastoral was issued. (Indeed, in July 1982 Father Bismarck Carballo, the archdiocese spokesman and secretary of Archbishop Obando y Bravo, noted in a personal interview that one should also not discount the preferential option for the rich, since they too had souls.) Yet the importance of this newfound missionary zeal pales in comparison to what the bishops had to say about the viability of the socialist model being implemented in Nicaragua.

The significance of this can be gauged by reflecting on what they had traditionally stated—most recently as four months earlier—on the dangers of "alien ideologies" (read Marxism). The bishops now approached the potential implementation of socialism with great equanimity and indeed some support. With perspicacity they criticized the idea of class hatred, but they supported the potential advantages that would accrue from a genuine restructuring of Nicaraguan society: "In regard to class struggle, we believe that there are two forms: one is based on the dynamic fact of struggle, which should lead to a just structural transformation; the other is based on class hatred, which is directed against people and contradicts radically the Christian duty of love toward one's fellow man" (p. 79). The bishops expressed their faith in the revolution's ability to distinguish between the two and pursue the "dynamic fact" of class struggle.

The bishops analyzed in some detail the advantages of "good" and "bad" socialism (the latter being the subjugation to "the manipulation and dictates of people who would arbitrarily hang on to power" [p. 78]), yet refused to be cowed by the idea of socialist doctrine being implemented in Nicaragua. Indeed, they proclaimed, in this "middle way" there were undoubtedly many positive elements that the Church could not only live with but would also support:

If, on the other hand, socialism means, as it should mean, the superiority of the interests of the majority of Nicaraguans and a planned economy model in which all can participate, then we have no objections. A social project that guarantees the common destiny of the wealth and resources of the country and seeks on this basis, to satisfy the fundamental needs of all Nicaraguans and improve the human quality of life seems just to us. If socialism means the growing diminution of injustice and traditional inequality between the cities and the countryside, and between remuneration paid for intellectual and manual work; if it means the participation of workers in the products of their work, overcoming in this way economic alienation, then there is nothing in Christianity to contradict this process. . . .

If socialism is based on a concept of power exercised from the perspective of the masses and shared increasingly by an organized people, so that it leads to a true transferal of power to the popular classes, then once again it will find in the Catholic faith only encouragement and support. (p. 78)

This was all quite new and went dramatically against all that the bishops had traditionally said on the subject. Even allowing for divisions within the Episcopal Conference, this pastoral was seen by the government and the progressive wing of the Church alike as an extraordinary document. They could, of course, be excused for believing that this mixture of self-criticism, acceptance of the class struggle and socialism, praise of the Sandinistas, and emphasis on the "preferential option for the poor" constituted an excellent base for cooperation. Indeed, on paper these goals outlined so articulately by the bishops seemed to resemble remarkably closely the broad planks of the reform programs put forward by the FSLN. But this potential cooperation—unique in the annals of Church history had it been nurtured and maintained—was stillborn. Within Nicaraguan society the social polarization that accompanied revolutionary change continued apace, the Sandinistas engaged in the speedy introduction of sweeping reforms (usually enacted in favor of the poor social sectors at the expense of the bourgeoisie), and revolutionary rhetoric was widespread. This was a heady mixture, one that was made worse by a parallel process of radicalization within the Church itself—as some priests and religious (mainly foreign) identified solidly with the Sandinista program, while others (mainly Nicaraguan diocesan clergy) reacted with some fear at the proposed reforms. The election of Ronald Reagan in late 1980, with his hawkish rhetoric on the need for a far more aggressive U.S. foreign policy, also became a factor in Nicaragua's revolutionary process. The honeymoon phase between the hierarchy and the Sandinistas was soon to end, and by mid-1980 the FSLN leadership and the hierarchy were bound on a collision course.

Early Irritants in Church-FSLN Relations

The best illustration of this dramatic cooling off of relations is the Church's attitude toward the literacy campaign of 1980. Using techniques refined by the successful Cuban literacy program of 1961, and with the advice of the renowned Brazilian educator Paulo Freire, the revolutionary government attacked the problem of illiteracy with remarkable enthusiasm. More than 95,000 volunteers formed the Ejército Alfabetizador, charged with reducing the illiteracy rate of 50.35 percent. From March to August of 1980 the literary *brigadistas* went out to the most remote areas of the country, in the end teaching the rudiments of reading and writing to more than 406,000 Nicaraguans and reducing the illiteracy rate to 12.96 percent—a remarkable achievement that was greeted around the world as a major success. The campaign was headed by a Jesuit priest, Fernando Cardenal, who later would become minister of education.

The initial Church reaction to the program was one of pride, and pleasure, that a priest was in charge of this project—one who was as concerned with political consciousness-raising as with literacy. It was both a remarkable achievement and a noteworthy sign of respect for the Church's influence that such a highly regarded Jesuit should be chosen for this vital undertaking. More than three hundred religious participated in the literacy project, ensuring a major Church influence on the crusade. In March 1980, when John Paul II met junta delegates Daniel Ortega, Violeta Chamorro, and Father Miguel D'Escoto in Rome, he commended the project and encouraged young Nicaraguans to participate. The hierarchy also asked volunteers to become involved, praising the objectives and the approach of the project.

Soon after the campaign started, however, complaints began to surface. The principal target of criticism was the Cuban teachers who had come to work alongside the Nicaraguans; many traditionalists condemned their Marxist influence, despite claims to the contrary by Fernando Cardenal.[3] From this point on, the hierarchy's criticism of the program was a commonplace occurrence.

By the end of the crusade the educational issue had become mired in controversy. Claims and counterclaims about the "materialist ideology" surrounding the literacy campaign abounded—despite the claims by Cardenal and Minister of Education Carlos Tünnermann (a respected Catholic layperson) about the program's Nicaraguan and Christian nature. Cardenal's assertion that in light of the emergency situation in Nicaragua (not to mention four decades of Somocismo which had hardly fostered cultural or educational development) it was necessary to develop speedily a popular awareness of the country's problems by means of the campaign was rejected by the hierarchy. Thanksgiving masses for the success of the project were interrupted by demonstrations both against and in favor of the Sandinistas' reforms, and what should have been a unifying factor and source of pride for all Nicaraguans became a matter of bitter debate.

The issue of education continued to be a source of conflict between the Church hierarchy and the FSLN. By 1982 (after Violeta Chamorro and Alfonso Robelo resigned from the governing junta, claiming that constitutional changes were undemocratic) the educational reforms brought in by the Sandinistas were rapidly alienating the middle-class and conservative sectors of Nicaragua. In particular, what was seen as the increasingly Marxist and atheistic nature of teaching materials being used in public schools and the determination to politicize educational and cultural matters were roundly condemned by the Church hierarchy. The release of a document, "Ends and Goals of the New Education," by the Ministry of Education in September 1982 merely added fuel to the flames from the conservative perspective: its talk of creating a "new man," influenced by the principles of Sandino and the revolution, and its scientific, anti-imperialist view of the world were anathema to the bishops. (For their part, the Sandinistas can be criticized for their lack of sensitivity to the hierarchy's concerns—for it should have been obvious that education had long been regarded as the bailiwick of Church leaders. This political insensitivity of the FSLN—particularly among the middle-level cadres—exacerbated the increasingly problematic relationship between the FSLN and the Church hierarchy.) The bishops' conference lost little time in raising its voice to condemn "the tendency to treat some aspects of the formation of youth from a purely materialist perspective . . . a gradual loss of criticalness [reasoned analysis] in the education . . . the fostering and fueling of hatred between brothers . . . the propaganda in behalf of a literature which is alien to our people and which is in disagreement with its values and Christian beliefs [an oblique reference to Marxism-Leninism]."[4] Thus, as early promise gave way to growing tension, the fate of the literacy campaign in many ways constitutes a microcosm of FSLN-hierarchy relations during this early period of the revolutionary process. Subsequent educational reforms introduced by the government (even during the later tenure of Fernando Cardenal as minister of education) were treated in the same fashion.

The hierarchy was particularly disturbed by what it saw as an attempt by militant Marxist elements of the FSLN to marginalize the Church, appropriating symbols regarded as being purely "Christian," censoring Church avenues of communication, and in general seeking to move in and diminish traditional Church elements. For Church leaders, sensitive to the threat of a "Marxist takeover," it was a challenge that had to be confronted head-on. For many, cognizant of the marginalization of the Church in Cuba in the wake of the 1959 revolution and fortified by a dogmatic, anti-Marxist pontiff, this was literally a struggle of spiritual life and death.

There were several specific decisions taken by the FSLN Directorate that accentuated this process of alienation and convinced Church leaders that they had to take a stand in order to prevent the government from exploiting traditional Catholic symbols and festivities. Humberto Belli, formerly a journalist with *La Prensa* and subsequently a Vatican adviser and leader at the Puebla Institute in Michigan (until the Chamorro electoral victory, when he became minister of education), outlines examples of the Sandinistas' appropriation of traditional Catholic symbols—a process that, in his opinion, was a deliberate attempt by the FSLN to manipulate the religious question and ultimately divide the Church. These examples include the presence of Sandinista leaders at religious ceremonies; aid from the Sandinistas for progressive institutes supporting the government, such as the Instituto Histórico Centro-Americano (publisher of the book *Fe Cristiana y Revolución Sandinista en Nicaragua* [*Christian Faith and Sandinista Revolution in Nicaragua*], on whose cover a drawing of Christ is superimposed on the image of a guerrilla fighter), the Centro Ecuménico Antonio Valdivieso, and CEPA; the publication of a series of pamphlets (by the Centro Valdivieso, the Instituto Histórico, and the John XXIII Institute), complete with cartoons, encouraging Catholics to participate fully in the revolutionary process and not to be afraid of socialism; praise for the

Misa (which presents Christ as standing in solidarity with the oppressed); the use of slogans ("Sandino Ayer, Sandino Hoy, Sandino Siempre") based on the Christian faith; and frequent media references to the "martyrs" of the revolutionary struggle. For Belli, this appropriation of Christian mythology was morally unacceptable and represented a deliberate attempt to exploit Church symbols. Critics would argue, however, that in a country as fervently Christian as Nicaragua these symbols were part of the public domain.

To the Church authorities, Sandinista designs were patently clear in the official FSLN communiqué of August 18, 1980, on the desirable nature of Christmas celebrations—which in essence called for a sober, reflective appreciation of the religious feast day and a decrease in the drunken revelry that traditionally accompanied the festivities. Surely there was no more Christian celebration than the birth of Christ—and here were the Sandinistas imposing guidelines on how to honor the feast day! Whether the FSLN suggestions were valid or not was immaterial; what mattered to the hierarchy was the Sandinistas' audacity to become involved in something that fell squarely within the Church's domain. This was ironic because, as was shown in the preamble to the Sandinista document, the basic objective was to emphasize that "the Christian festivities should recover their true popular and Christian meaning."[5] The intent was to reduce the excessively commercial nature of Christmas and to promote what the FSLN regarded as "authentic" Christian values. In no way can the communiqué itself be viewed as interfering with the nature of Church celebrations. Instead it emphasized the need to "spiritualize" the celebration: "All advertisements and commercial offers that utilize or make reference to Christmas and everything related to the birth of Christ in order to encourage the sale of goods or services are forbidden" (p. 101). Regardless of these aims, the hierarchy was afraid that the government would preempt the religious aspects of the festivities, and the bishops made their feelings known both within Nicaragua and at the level of CELAM.

The communications with CELAM were particularly important, for in them the hierarchy—feeling itself in desperate straits against the increasingly materialist, atheistic influence of the Sandinistas—called for ecclesial reinforcements to shore up its position. The Spanish priest Teófilo Cabestrero noted in January 1981 how shortly before his arrival in Nicaragua he had met with CELAM representatives in Panama. They had warned him that "Nicaragua is heading for atheism, and that the Sandinista Front was already suppressing Christmas and the feast of the Immaculate Conception."[6] Upon arriving in Nicaragua, he found much to his surprise that not only had these celebrations not been suppressed but they were actually encouraged by the revolutionary government and the Sandinista Front: festivities were held in various ministries, a program of celebrations was organized by the Ministry of Social Welfare, toys were provided to all children, commercialization of the religious feast was prohibited, and a national holiday was proclaimed. Cabestrero's conclusions were quite remarkable: "This revolution is not prohibiting or curbing religious activities, but rather is offering the churches a unique opportunity to re-evangelize themselves, and to evangelize the entire population with new evangelical vigor" (p. 137). Prophetically, he added: "For the present, the danger for religion and the Church is not with the Sandinista people's revolution, but rather is in the utilization of religion and the Church against the people's revolution" (p. 137). These comments, made in January 1981, were appropriate, for tension between the FSLN and the Church hierarchy continued to escalate. Misunderstanding and prejudice—clearly not restricted to the Sandinistas—thus destroyed the initial promise that resulted from the widespread and enthusiastic Christian support for the FSLN visible at the outset.

The Church hierarchy sought support from fellow bishops in CELAM (an organization that has become increasingly conservative since its momentous 1968 conference in Medellín), and in early 1980 a rather conservative program, known as the Plan de Ayuda (the Assistance Plan), was introduced in Nicaragua. Some of the stated objectives were to send CELAM specialists (that is, conservative theologians) to give religious courses in Nicaragua, distribute twenty-five thousand Bibles, reopen the National Seminary, and provide financial and moral support to the Nicaraguan bishops. More than anything, the CELAM leadership and the Nicaraguan hierarchy wanted to issue a warning to the "Church of the poor" throughout Latin America that it was the bishops, and not they, who held the keys of Church magisterium. Concerned by the rapid development of ecclesial base communities and the spread of liberation theology's influence, they focused their attention on the one place where conditions seemed most propitious for the development of what they derogatorily termed the Iglesia Popular. Nicaragua was thus perceived as being in the eye of this ecclesial storm—a storm that had to be quelled. According to some sources, part of the covert aspects of the Plan de Ayuda was to expel progressive foreign priests who supported the Sandinistas' program and to prohibit priests and religious from taking political posts. One source quotes Brazilian theologian Frei Betto: "This campaign of aid brought about by CELAM assumes that for Marxist political logic which is emerging in Nicaragua there is only one antidote, the Christian faith. Thus, faith in God reduces itself to mere political rationality, and in the last instance it ends up identifying Christian faith with middle-class ideology."[7]

The timing of the Plan de Ayuda was analyzed by many Nicaraguans—particularly since during the CELAM conference held in Puebla in 1979 (the last year of the Somoza dictatorship) the general secretary of CELAM, the conservative Colombian López Trujillo, refused to sign a letter of solidarity with the Nicaraguan bishops.[8] The plan's subsequent implementation (for a total cost of about $300,000) was suspicious, to say the least, and it was clearly designed to support the Nicaraguan hierarchy's ongoing struggle to bring the progressive wing of the Church back into line. The CELAM strategy was one that six base communities in Managua considered dangerous and hypocritical.[9] In his monumental work *The Religious Roots of Rebellion: Christians in Central American Revolutions,* Phillip Berryman concludes that the objective of CELAM was not so much an attack on the revolutionary government as an attempt to "spiritualize" religion and support the moral authority of the bishops. He is probably right, but the fact that powerful international organizations were stepping in to shore up an increasingly conservative hierarchy (and at the same time cast aspersions on the progressive wing of the Church, which favored the government reforms) could not have been lost on the Sandinistas.

At the same time that the CELAM plan was introduced into Nicaragua, the polarization of the Church was accentuated by heavy-handed measures taken by both the revolutionary government and the Church hierarchy. The basic objective of such measures was to show that each would not be cowed or intimidated by the other, and both engaged in ideological warfare that merely served to confuse Nicaraguan Catholics—who probably prayed that cooler minds would prevail. Each "hierarchy" felt threatened by the other, and accordingly each worked to shore up its own constituency and cast aspersions on the other. Caught in the middle, of course, were those Nicaraguans who regarded themselves as both faithful Catholics and loyal supporters of the revolutionary process.

As tension mounted around the religious question (which for all intents and purposes had passed from the religious realm and become a source of political friction), the government sought to reduce the impact of the hierarchy, and vice versa. The Sandinistas, increasingly preoccupied by the evolution of Obando y Bravo as the leading opposition spokesman, tried rather clumsily to silence him. In July 1981 they canceled the weekly televised broadcast of a mass traditionally celebrated by the archbishop, who refused their request that he share the weekly spot with other (more progressive) priests to comment—in a more favorable fashion, it was hoped—on the revolution's trajectory. When he refused to comply with their request, his mass was cut. The following year, in the wake of increasing contra attacks, the government decreed a state of emergency, which included a strict censorship law. Periodic closures of Radio Católica (and *La Prensa*) followed as the Church sought to disregard the law and the government retaliated in a rather arbitrary fashion.

In 1982 the revolutionary government also banned the publication of a letter from John Paul II to the Nicaraguan bishops in which the pontiff expressed the need for Church unity to be built around the bishops— clearly intended as a slap at the progressive Church sector. At first the government withheld publication of the letter but then allowed it to be circulated some six weeks later. Something similar happened to a second letter from John Paul II in 1985—such developments could only have strengthened the bishops' fears about a totalitarian Marxist state suppressing all freedom of thought and made them furious at government meddling in what they saw as an internal Church matter. A coolheaded approach to some very serious matters was no doubt sorely lacking on both sides.

For their part, the Sandinistas felt increasingly annoyed by what they saw—rightly or wrongly—as the Church's meddling in strictly political affairs. A case in point was the decision by the government in February 1982 to move the Miskito Indians living along the Honduran border. The previous year Steadman Fagoth, leader of the indigenous organization MISURASATA, had been arrested after attempting to lead an uprising against the Sandinistas. Upon his release he had moved to Honduras, taking some three thousand Miskitos with him, and from there he joined the contra forces fighting in the area. Since the official border between Honduras and Nicaragua is the River Coco (a boundary established in the mid-twentieth century and often disregarded by the Miskitos who hunt throughout that area), and since the Miskitos were spread alongside both sides of the river—traveling freely between settlements in both Honduras and Nicaragua—the alliance of the Miskitos with the contras was a major blow for the Nicaraguan government. Compounding the problem was the fact that during the years of the Somoza dictatorship the Miskitos (who are geographically and culturally removed from the mainstream of Nicaraguan society and still refer to the inhabitants of the rest of Nicaragua as "the Spanish") had not been actively involved in the fighting. As a result, they were not particularly supportive of the Sandinistas (who had behaved in a rather culturally insensitive fashion since the revolutionary victory of 1979). Instead they identified with their fellow Miskitos—on both sides of the rather tenuous border—thus representing a major political problem for the revolutionary government, which sought to bring them within the mainstream of Nicaraguan society. As a result, when Fagoth joined the Washington-supported contras, a large portion of the Miskitos either followed suit or were prepared to provide moral support to their fellow Miskitos. The revolutionary government thus encountered a major political problem on the Atlantic coast, one that could only be resolved by the forced removal of the Miskitos from the area.

Recognizing that the indigenous sector of the Atlantic coast was not particularly supportive of their policies, and in light of the increase in contra activity in the region (between December and January 1982 some sixty people were killed there in contra attacks), the Sandinistas decided to move the Nicaraguan Miskitos fifty miles south, away from the border. Belli estimates that approximately 10,000 people were moved. The army also razed their villages and crops, creating in effect a free-fire zone, so that contras coming from Honduras would not be able to find food, shelter, or potential allies on their sorties into the area. It is interesting to note the different approaches to the "Miskito question" by Catholic and Protestant leaders. The Moravian Church, for example, which ministers to the spiritual needs of some 70 percent of the Miskitos, privately expressed their profound disagreement with this government policy, whereas the Catholic Church condemned the move in extremely forceful terms in a pastoral letter dated February 18, 1982. Significantly, the same criticisms had been made just one day earlier in an official bulletin published by the U.S. embassy, thus exacerbating the concern felt by many Sandinista leaders that the archbishop was working closely with the Reagan administration—whose foreign policy was wreaking such havoc in the region and killing so many Nicaraguans.[10] Such criticisms only fanned the growing flames of frustration and mutual hostility.

The Nicaraguan bishops criticized the "grave violations of human rights of individuals, families, and entire groups of people,"[11] condemning the forced march of the Miskitos and the destruction of their homes and livestock. "We state with sad surprise that in some concrete cases there have been serious violations of the human rights of individuals, families, and even entire villages," they concluded.[12] The reaction of the Nicaraguan government was swift and predictable: they rejected the bishops' criticisms and asked why they had turned down the government's invitation to inspect the resettlement camps. With the advantage of hindsight, it seems clear that the Sandinistas had indeed reacted with great cultural insensitivity both in their general dealings with the Miskitos and in the forced evacuation of nearly ten thousand of them from their traditional homeland. At the same time, however, the bishops should have been aware that the country was headed for war because of the increasingly ferocious contra attacks and the fact that dozens of people in the Miskito area had already been killed by marauding bands. In any event, from the perspective of Church-state relations the episode was a disaster, merely confirming previously held suspicions and prejudices for both sides. For the Church hierarchy, it confirmed their suspicion that the Sandinistas would go to any lengths to ensure the continuation of their militarized, totalitarian, and oppressive form of government. For members of the Sandinista leadership, the incident underscored the fact that despite the lofty-sounding rhetoric of the November 1979 pastoral letter, Archbishop Obando y Bravo was fundamentally opposed to the goals of the revolution—and, by criticizing the relocation of the Miskitos and not the contra massacres, he revealed himself as a contra supporter. The end result was a notable hardening of the position held by each camp and an emotional rejection of the other's point of view.

The Campaign against Progressive Clergy

If the Church leadership felt that the government was increasingly infringing on Church territory, a case can be made to show that the government also had reason to be disturbed at the encroachment of the hierarchy. Many government supporters were progressive clergy who felt the brunt of the archbishop's heavy-handed treatment and arrogance. The hierarchy doggedly pursued a dual policy of destroying organizations that empowered priests and religious at the grass-roots level and weeding out "pro-Sandinista" clergy by removing them from their parishes or work centers.

In the rush to criticize the antidemocratic measures of the revolutionary government (who indeed had expelled a handful of conservative priests), it is often forgotten that Archbishop Obando y Bravo himself engaged in a far-reaching campaign of relocating progressive priests and nuns from the archdiocese of Managua. In addition, he pressured the superiors of progressive foreign priests and religious who generally supported the Sandinistas' social reform program. This relocation effort was probably undertaken to preserve Church unity (or perhaps the archbishop's control of his Church), but it was carried out with a tremendous lack of sensitivity—and with a brutally authoritarian spirit. Examples abound of priests and nuns taken from their parish: Father Rafael Aragón Lucio was removed from the poor Managua neighborhood of San Judas, as were Sister Pilar Castellanos of Ciudad Sandino and Jesuit priests Luis Medrano and Otilio Miranda. In San Judas several sisters were removed from the parish house, and Father Pedro Belzunegui was replaced while he was abroad. In 1981, an attempt to remove Father Manuel Batalla from his Managua parish was averted only by the arrival of the Dominican superior, who negotiated a resolution of the crisis.[13] Philip Williams concludes that between 1980 and 1982 no less than fourteen priests and twenty-two sisters were "either removed from their parishes or had their official pastoral authorization suspended."[14] According to one source, by 1988 this number had risen to sixty, leading Italian priest Ubaldo Gervasani to comment: "There's religious persecution inside the Catholic Church itself. It's a persecution campaign against foreign religious in solidarity with the Nicaraguan people."[15] In an interview in July 1982, Father Bismarck Carballo (the archbishop's secretary) insisted that these moves were all "routine measures," part of an ongoing process of rotating priests and religious. However, the fact that all the priests removed were progressives and supporters of the revolution indicates that political considerations played a major role in these relocations.

One striking example will serve to illustrate this policy of ecclesial authoritarianism. In the summer of 1982, José Arias Caldera (an elderly priest who for many years had tended the Santa Rosa parish in a working-class district of Managua and was known as "the monsignor of the poor") was informed by Archbishop Obando y Bravo that he was to be transferred, despite his wishes to stay in the parish. When the archbishop insisted on the transfer, parishioners occupied the church in protest. On July 21, 1982, Arias Caldera—a sympathizer with the Sandinista government and a personal friend of several Sandinista *comandantes*—saw Auxiliary Bishop Bosco Vivas enter his church and spirit away the ciborium from the altar. The incident was significant for Bosco Vivas was removing the vessel containing the consecrated bread and wine—which Catholics believe have been transformed into the body and blood of Christ. In removing them, the auxiliary bishop was stripping the sanctuary of its essential religious significance—as well as showing his contempt for the parishioners. Accompanied by several supporters (including a photographer from *La Prensa*), Bosco Vivas went directly to the altar. When the parishioners sought to prevent him from taking the ciborium, Vivas fell.[16] According to *La Prensa,* he was brutally beaten about the face and needed medical attention—although the picture on the front page of the July 22 edition shows him pointing forlornly at his left arm ("indicating the inflammation on one of his arms as a result of the beating," the caption notes). Parishioners I interviewed the day after the beating claimed that Vivas had merely stumbled.

The day after the *La Prensa* story appeared, the archbishop announced that the parishioners who had occupied the church and sought to prevent the auxiliary bishop from taking away the ciborium would be automatically excommunicated from the Catholic faith—unless they asked for the archbishop's pardon.[17] (It is worth noting that the hierarchy refused to condemn, much less excommunicate, the contras—despite their undeniable record of atrocities—yet rushed to excommunicate the parishioners of Santa Rosa.) For his part, Arias Caldera—who had been a supporter of the FSLN since the early 1960s—stated in an interview that he was certain his parishioners would not have attacked Vivas. The lead story in the July 23 issue of *El Nuevo Diario* (titled "Acts of the Pharisees [*Fariseísmo*]" and showing discrepancies between Vivas's story and that of the parishioners) would appear to support the version of events told by the monsignor.

The significance of this incident goes far beyond the case of one priest who was removed from his parish. Its political impact is revealed by the fact that the story received front-page coverage in *La Prensa, El Nuevo Diario,* and *Barricada* for four days—and was also commented on frequently by the electronic media. The Caldera crisis was symptomatic of the growing schism and polarization within the Church, as two distinctive outlooks on the revolutionary process became more clearly defined. Moreover, the incident also revealed that just as the government was prepared to pursue a hard-line policy toward what it regarded as manipulation by the Church hierarchy, so too were the bishops prepared to ensure that their authority would be respected at all times and at all costs.

The Issue of Priests in the Government

One important facet of this rapidly escalating war of words within the Church had to do with the role of priests within the revolutionary government—and the hierarchy's reaction to this phenomenon. There were a handful of priests engaged in official government business: Ernesto Cardenal was appointed minister of culture; his brother Fernando (a Jesuit) directed the 1980 literacy campaign and then served as director of the Juventud Sandinista and finally as minister of education; Miguel D'Escoto (a Maryknoll missionary) became minister of external affairs; Edgar Parrales was minister of social welfare before becoming Nicaragua's ambassador to the OAS; and the Jesuit Alvaro Argüello became the delegate of ACLEN (the Association of Nicaraguan Clergy) to the Council of State. In addition, a number of clergy also took up advisory positions with a host of government institutions.

With the inauguration of the Council of State in May 1980 (and the subsequent resignation of Violeta Chamorro and Alfonso Robelo from the revolutionary junta), effective political power now resided with the FSLN. That same month the bishops officially requested the priests in government to resign their positions, claiming that "inasmuch as the circumstances constituting the exception now no longer obtain, Christian lay persons can just as efficiently discharge the public duties now being performed by certain priests."[18] When the priests involved requested an opportunity to dialogue with the bishops, they were met with a firm rejection.

In an extremely impassioned pastoral letter dated October 17, 1980, the Nicaraguan hierarchy showed that it would brook no dissent from the priests in question. While the pastoral contained several direct criticisms of the Frente Sandinista, the most pointed comments were directed against the priests directly involved in political or government matters:

> It is one thing for priests to participate practicing their own religious ministry, within political groups. Yet it is quite different for them to practice their religious ministry while they are acting to serve directly systems of power. We serve as priests when we evangelize, denounce, and collaborate in the Christian and human development of our historic situations; when we defend the poor, the oppressed, and the weak, those who have been unjustly deprived of their freedom by any system or abuse of power. Yet we cease to serve as priests, or we lose the freedom to do so, when we ally ourselves with others or seem to have "given ourselves up" to a particular regime.[19]

So that there would be no doubt concerning their absolute rejection of the priests' involvement in government, the Nicaraguan bishops dedicated several paragraphs to the danger of "the instrumentalization of the priest" (p. 121). Convinced that the priests in question were being cleverly manipulated by the FSLN to justify their policies, the bishops warned that such manipulation could divide the Church irreparably (" 'Wounding the shepherd in order to disperse the sheep' is a strategy that Christ himself denounced," they declared [p. 121]). They then proceeded to belittle the priests by intimating that they were being corrupted by flattery as part of a deliberate strategy to disrupt Church activity: "It is sufficient to introduce disorder and lack of discipline among the ministers, with flattery and sinecures, well-documented guile. It is sufficient to redirect the priest's actions to favor the interests of a party or group. Yet religion cannot serve those interests" (p. 121).

This pastoral reveals that the bishops were not prepared to countenance the continued role of their priests in any form of political action and that they were convinced that the "emergency situation" (which, by canon law, had allowed their political function) was now over. So that the message would be perfectly understood by all, they released an additional pastoral letter on October 22, 1980, "Jesucristo y la Unidad de Su Iglesia en Nicaragua" ("Jesus Christ and the Unity of His Church in Nicaragua"), which lamented the "wounds" and "perplexity" felt by many Catholics because of the lack of obedience shown to the bishops: "This is scandalous when the people involved are priests or religious. The Catholic people, who possess a true sense of faith, can clearly see the need for communion of religious and priests with their bishop and with the pope. . . . It is a grave act of indiscipline, and one that wounds the indispensable unity of the Church, to act without the support of the bishop, or without holding an attitude of communion and obedience toward him."[20] By this time there did not seem to be any room to maneuver from the perspective of the hierarchy: for the bishops it was a matter of retaining control over, and the obedience of, these priests, thereby avoiding any kind of fissure within the Church.

The reaction of the priests was a combination of desiring negotiation but politely rejecting the bishops' arguments. They based their position on a conviction that they were undertaking a more Christian mission by helping their fellow citizens than by submitting to the hierarchy's dictates. For as Fernando Cardenal noted, "I believe that at this moment in Nicaragua we are doing more in the name of God for the poor by supporting the revolutionary process than by merely naming him a lot."[21] They pointed out that they were not there, as the bishops had intimated, as mere ecclesial "window dressing," since their portfolios and responsibilities were extremely important. Fernando Cardenal, for instance, was responsible for the literacy campaign and later headed the entire Ministry of Education (it was, of course, difficult for the bishops to complain about an atheistic Marxist influence on the education system with a Jesuit priest heading the ministry); his brother Ernesto was in charge of all manifestations of culture in the country—books, television and radio, theatre, art; Edgar Parrales, as minister of social welfare—and later as Nicaragua's representative at the OAS—also had a key role to play in formulating government policy; and Miguel D'Escoto's responsibilities in establishing and representing Nicaragua's foreign policy were also extremely important.

The priests involved interpreted the bishops' demands that they resign their government posts as a power play to replace the post-Vatican II interpretation of the priestly vocation with a more conservative one. Given the dire situation of Nicaragua, the hierarchy's concern about the growing Marxist influence in government policy, and above all their fervent desire to contribute to the rebuilding of the nation, these priests were convinced of the validity and usefulness of their role in government and resented the misplaced zeal of their religious superiors in pressuring them to resign. Their most articulate spokesman was Fernando Cardenal, at that time head of Juventud Sandinista:

> In my work with these young people, I live with the same apostolic attitude as a missionary priest in a mission country where he's been sent and where he has to devote some years of his life to the work of pre-evangelization. During this stage he doesn't explicitly talk about Christ or the faith. He "speaks" by the witness of his life, by his presence, by his dedication to applying Christ's love present in his faith—by enhancing the humanity of this missionary world he's been sent to. He speaks via his commitment to teaching, educating, and human betterment. . . .
>
> There are Jesuit priests who spend their lives teaching algebra, and nobody goes running up to them to tell them that that's not priestly. I myself, before I joined the revolution full-time, was a professor of philosophy in the national university. I fulfilled my vocation by teaching the ideas of Plato, Aristotle, Descartes, and Kant, without its having any explicit relationship with my priesthood. And I never thought that this was somehow in contradiction with my priestly state. I never felt frustrated in my courses, I never had a guilt complex just because I devoted myself to something not explicitly "priestly." I saw that these courses, too, were part of the Church's whole effort to further the coming of the kingdom of God.[22]

After reading a variety of interviews with these priests (and after interviewing some of them personally), I am convinced that all remained committed Christians, torn between ecclesial obedience and following the dictates of their conscience. They were aware that for the first time in history a socialist revolution was being realized that was not anti-Christian—one on which Christians had the opportunity to impose their own seal. Conscious of the loss for the Church that their withdrawal from the revolution would mean, these priests decided to remain committed to the revolutionary process and true to themselves, regardless of pressures or threats from the Catholic hierarchy.[23]

The priests' determined opposition to calls from the hierarchy that they resign was based on two key premises. Fernando Cardenal has articulated the first premise, namely, that the priests involved were pursuing a far more "Christian" and "priestly" function in their present government roles than if they had been involved in other, more traditional aspects of the priesthood. Indeed, if the bishops' complaints about the creeping Marxism of the Sandinistas were true, what could be more effective in combating its atheistic influence than the presence of four Catholic priests in key government positions? The second premise had to do with the sociopolitical situation of Nicaragua at the time. Initially, Church authorities had permitted the priests to exercise their political prerogative, and they justified this by referring to the "exceptional" nature of the Nicaraguan context—one that, less than a year later, had apparently disappeared. In fact, however, with the election of the Reagan administration, the onset of the contra war, the exodus of talented technicians to the United States, and the monumental rebuilding necessary after more than four decades of Somocismo, a case can be made to show that truly exceptional circumstances still continued.

These priests thus rejected the rationale for the bishops' arguments; they considered these arguments that their continuing role in the government would be divisive to be false. Indeed they probably believed that in many ways they were being truer to the spirit of the Gospels than their religious superiors; they believed that they were indeed being faithful to their priestly vocation by bearing prophetic witness in their ravaged country; they were convinced that their role was useful both to the country and to the Church; and finally, they believed that their role was totally justifiable—despite whatever penalties were given them by the hierarchy and the Vatican.

There was an obvious political element to this entire situation that, as in the case of the removal of Arias Caldera, soon took precedence over the issue of the priests themselves. For conservatives, the presence of these "Marxists in priests' dress" was total anathema—and the claims of Ernesto Cardenal that Marxist social teachings were a useful tool for analyzing society, or his much-publicized praise of the Cuban revolution, only confirmed their worst fears about the rebel priests. It led them to conclude that the Church had somehow been co-opted by the Sandinista revolution (the same revolution that had reduced significantly their political clout and traditional privileges) while it also strengthened their resolve to fashion the image of Archbishop Obando y Bravo as the great opposition figure and voice of reason in an increasingly totalitarian society. Finally, the high profile of the

Cardenals, D'Escoto, and Parrales in the international media worked decidedly against the conservatives' claims that Nicaragua was in the grip of an atheistic Marxist dictatorship. For the hierarchy, then, all possible pressure had to be exerted in order to force the priests from power. Meanwhile, of course, the radical Christians were delighted at the contribution of the priests and felt that their socially constructive role was a welcome change from the position of the hierarchy.

Both sides in the dispute sent delegations to the Vatican in an attempt to resolve the issue in an amicable fashion, but to no avail. The complex issues of conflicting interpretations of priestly mission and of the exceptional nature of the Nicaraguan circumstances, as well as differing views of ecclesial authority and the alleged danger of Church disunity in the Nicaraguan context, were simply too volatile to be resolved. The Vatican preferred that the issue be handled by the principals involved and so shied away from any significant pronouncement.

Not so the Nicaraguan hierarchy, which by June 1981 had decided that the issue had to be resolved once and for all. On June 1, they issued a tersely worded communiqué, claiming "it is our responsibility to urge fraternally, but with firmness, that the laws of the Church are to be observed."[24] In the document they spoke in generalities about the need for harmony, unity, fulfilling Church responsibilities, faithfulness, and obedience, but then made it very clear that this master plan could not be realized in the Nicaraguan context, where certain priests clearly disagreed with the archbishop. Accordingly the priests were issued an ultimatum: "We declare that if those priests presently occupying public posts and undertaking activities to benefit a political party do not immediately leave those responsibilities and return wholly to their specific priestly functions, we will consider them to have adopted an attitude of open rebellion and formal disobedience of the legitimate authority of the Church; and they will receive the appropriate penalties as stipulated by Church law" (p. 167). The bishops concluded with a further broadside at other progressive priests engaged in work at a variety of research centers that supported the priests in question—and also supported the revolutionary government: "We take this opportunity (and beg your pardon since it is a little out of context) to add a clarification, since this has been asked of us by many of our faithful: the Instituto Histórico, the Valdivieso Ecumenical Center and CEPA are not official units of our Church—nor do they have the approval or support of this Episcopal Conference" (p. 167).

This was an extraordinary document that went out of its way to force the rebel priests to comply with the wishes of the hierarchy—despite being shrouded in traditional ecclesial language ("this present communication has as its only objective the strengthening of Church unity and effectiveness"). The shrill message of disapproval was compounded by the pointed aside about respected research institutes that had been critical of the bishops and possessed a vision of the Church's mission oriented along the lines of Medellín. This was clearly an issue of Church authority and of respect for the central thrust of Vatican II reforms. That there should be an alternative vision of the Church's role was difficult for this conservative hierarchy to accept. When this divergence of opinion was underscored by a clear-cut refusal by the priests in question to accede to the demands of their superiors, the bishops were convinced that their authority was waning and that decisive action was called for. There was no middle ground in this dispute: just as Ronald Reagan wanted the Sandinista government to "say uncle," so too did Archbishop Obando y Bravo demand that his priests accede to his view of ecclesiology.

Just one week later the four priests, perhaps foreseeing that this issue would prove to be a long, drawn-out affair, issued a response to the hierarchy's pastoral letter. It was an emotional creed based on the idea of service to the teachings of the Gospels as they interpreted them: "because our posts have given us the power to serve, and not to dominate; the power to strip ourselves of our comforts, and not to enrich ourselves; the power to resemble Christ by serving our brethren; the power to be ready to listen to, and obey, the voice of God."[25] However, the statement of principles ended on a controversial note, with an extremely pointed comment expressing support for the Sandinista revolution: "Finally we declare our unbreakable commitment with the Sandinista revolution, faithful to our people, which is the same as being faithful to the will of God" (p. 169).

Thus an impasse had been reached, one that could not be resolved in the political climate of the early 1980s. But a modus vivendi emerged as a result of a visit to the Vatican by delegations of the government and the Nicaraguan Episcopal Conference and meetings with Cardinal Agostino Casaroli (Vatican secretary of state). This compromise was made public on July 15, 1981, and in essence gave the priests a temporary breathing space. They would not be disciplined by the Church but would have to refrain from all priestly functions and keep in contact with their bishops during the course of this temporary dispensation. The bishops viewed this not as a truce, but rather as a period of "temporary toleration"—one that, unfortunately, was not to last. By late 1982 reports surfaced that demands were once again being voiced that the priests resign—only this time the bishops were apparently supported by the pope.[26] A new code of canon law, issued in 1983, further complicated the priests' situation. In 1984 the Society of Jesus expelled Fernando Cardenal, and in 1985 he, his brother, Parrales, and D'Escoto were suspended from the priesthood.[27]

There was, however, one final step for the hierarchy to take to ensure its political control over clergy and religious with opposing political views: to bring ACLEN under its influence. In 1982 the Sacred Congregation for Clergy reviewed the ACLEN guidelines and made sweeping recommendations for change that would have destroyed the very nature of the association. After an unsuccessful attempt to negotiate with the bishops, in 1982 ACLEN members decided to dissolve the association rather than submit to the recommendations. A parallel organization, CONFER (Conference for Religious Workers), had its statutes revised significantly by the Sacred Congregation for Religious in 1983, the end result of which was a major restructuring that clearly favored the conservative wing of the Church.[28] While the hierarchy would talk of Church unity being strengthened, members of the grass-roots Church saw the gains of Vatican II and Medellín slowly dissipate. Orthodoxy had clearly won this round.

The Battle of the Documents

An important dimension of the Church's struggle to establish its identity during this crucial period of Church-state relations is that which concerns the publication of official pastoral letters and communiqués, to which partial mention has already been made. Written statements of this kind are an invaluable source of information, for they reveal the specific goals and aspirations of the organization or group publishing it. During the period 1979–82, a flurry of official documents were published—by the Church hierarchy, the base communities, and even the Frente Sandinista. Since this was a period of growing polarization, it is to be expected that there would be a variety of emotionally charged and highly focused communications in which each side iterated its fundamental principles or responded to other communiqués.

The pastoral letters issued by the Nicaraguan Episcopal Conference in this period show an increasingly political tone. Reference was made earlier to the hierarchy's criticism of the forced removal of the Miskitos and of the human rights situation in the country. As we have just seen, the silencing of the progressive wing of the Church was also pursued tenaciously by Archbishop Obando y Bravo. (It should be noted, however, that the Catholic hierarchy did not approach the question of religious polarization with the same single-mindedness as did the archbishop and Bishop Vega. There was an attempt by some bishops— such as López Ardón, Schmitz, and Schlaefer—to develop amicable working relationships with progressive clergy. In general, however, the influence of the archdiocese made itself felt, seriously hampering intraecclesial dialogue.) An overarching concern in all these official communications was with Church unity—on terms specifically spelled out by the hierarchy. Another major preoccupation was the fear of atheism contaminating the faith, for as the bishops noted in October 1980: "We judge it to be our duty not to leave our faithful defenseless when faced with this attack by materialist ideologies that are in contrast to the Catholic faith, or not in agreement with it."[29] A final common theme, connected to the idea of Church unity, was that of obedience toward the bishops on the part of all Catholics—with special reference to the priests—an issue to which the hierarchy would return with frequency throughout the decade. (Indeed, in the October 1980 pastoral letter the bishops go off on a tangent, noting: "At times our families are suffering because of the lack of guidance about important aspects of family and social morals from those priests who have abandoned the doctrine of the pope and of the bishops" [p. 132]. Once again the theme of necessary *obedience* of the clergy to the hierarchy is emphasized without much subtlety.)

For their part, the grass-roots Church and the base communities released a series of documents seeking to explain their theological position and challenge that of the bishops. Critical of the pastoral plan of CELAM, of the charges made against progressive priests (who, like them, supported the reform program of the FSLN), and of what they saw as the increasing instrumentalization of religious matters by the hierarchy, they made their voices heard in several communiqués. Their approach can be summed up by their statement released on March 30, 1980, which explained their goals: "Preferential option in solidarity with the poor means in today's Nicaragua to work under the Sandinista

A cross on the hill of the Masaya volcano.

leadership to 'transform the earth and other productive resources' so that men and women from the popular masses can 'live and make this Nicaraguan land a place of justice, solidarity, peace, and freedom, where the Christian announcement about the kingdom of God can be fully realized.' "[30] Unfortunately, these lofty-sounding goals were incompatible with those of the bishops, and as a result the base communities were increasingly marginalized. In light of the hierarchy's position, a meaningful accommodation with the *comunidades eclesiales de base* could not realistically be expected.

For its part, in October 1980 the Frente Sandinista produced its own "Official Statement on Religion" to define its position and respond to what it saw as a campaign of misunderstanding about its religious intentions. The document is similar in tone and breadth to the expansive

November 1979 pastoral of the Episcopal Conference and, as was the case with that pastoral, seeks to be conciliatory. It begins, for example, with an expression of recognition of the valiant efforts of many Catholic priests and lay people who fought against the Somocista dictatorship (ironically, given the circumstances, it emphasizes the important role of Obando y Bravo), concluding: "Christians have been an integral part of our revolutionary history to an unprecedented degree in any other revolutionary movement in Latin America, and possibly in the world."[31]

The central text of the document ("The FSLN Positions on Religion") deals with some common misunderstandings. It begins by accepting the fundamental right of all citizens to profess a religious faith and then rejects outright the traditional Marxist dictum about religion being necessarily an alienating experience, noting: "Our experience shows that it is possible to be both a believer and a conscientious revolutionary, and that there is no irresoluble contradiction between the two" (p. 109). The document then emphasizes that all Nicaraguans are welcome to join the FSLN, regardless of their religious affiliation, but advises that in the name of the Frente's unity religious proselytism is not possible. The authors express respect for religious celebrations and traditions but also concern at the commercialization of the same. They also warn their fellow Sandinistas that religious matters are the proper purview of the Church and that no member of the FSLN speaking for the Frente is to give an opinion on them.

The issue of the politicization of the Church is dealt with openly in the communiqué: "Some reactionary ideologues have accused the FSLN of trying to divide the Church. This is a false and malevolent accusation. If there exists a division within various religions, this is something that is completely independent of the actions or the will of the FSLN" (p. 110). Noting that religious polarization and division have always been features of the Church's history, the authors provide several examples of Catholic priests who participated in the revolutionary struggle against Somoza—and of other priests who supported the dictator. They deal with the controversial issue of the priests holding government posts by outlining the right of all Nicaraguan citizens to hold government office, claiming that "exercising the right to participate and fulfill one's patriotic obligation is a matter of personal conscience" (p. 111). They conclude their document by claiming that the revolutionary state itself is of a lay nature and that citizens' religious preferences are private concerns.

Despite this incisive, thoughtful, and conciliatory document, the response of the bishops just seven days later left no doubt about the level of frustration in the Episcopal Conference regarding the FSLN plans for Nicaragua. In turn, this response could only fuel the despair felt by many Sandinistas at what they interpreted as the hierarchy's intransigence—and total disinterest in any form of dialogue. Once again, however, it is worth noting that despite the collective nature of pastorals issued by the Episcopal Conference, there was occasionally divergence of opinion among the bishops. When this occurred, the minority that sought a more conciliatory relationship with the Sandinista government and the progressive wing of the Church was almost unfailingly undermined by Archbishop Obando y Bravo and other ecclesial hard-liners. The end result was that the progressive minority, in the interests of episcopal collegiality, subordinated its position to that of the majority—giving the impression that all shared the views espoused by the archbishop.

The bishops' response was one of sharp and bitter polemic. Two examples from this long document indicate its general thrust: "Nicaragua has gone in search of its historical liberty. Not in search of new Pharaohs";[32] and "As Christians it is our duty to demand a conscientious, thoughtful form of political participation. Like free men, and not like slaves" (p. 119). The document expressed the bishops' concerns about "totalitarian systems," "materialistic atheism" ("Both atheism and materialism are examples of impiety against God" [p. 122]), and the "instrumentalization" of the people. The bishops again took issue with the role of priests in political life and condemned the "disintegrating parallelism" that could result if this phenomenon were not checked. They intimated that these priests were being exploited for political ends by the FSLN, noting: "When the priest is manipulated, the religion that he represents is also manipulated" (p. 121). This desperately angry pastoral concluded with an embittered warning: "The Church and Christians are not against the Nicaraguan revolution; rather the counterrevolutionaries are those who are turning it aside from the religious feelings of our people" (p. 124). Hence the bishops saw no possibility for achieving common ground with the FSLN directorate: the battle lines were firmly drawn.

This concluding note—embittered, confused, and frustrated—sums up the whole approach of the Nicaraguan Episcopal Conference at this time.[33] The hierarchy had determined that the path on which the country was being led was totally wrong and that nothing could be gained by a constructive relationship with the Sandinistas. Perhaps the issue of the "disobedient" priests, who had decided to retain their government offices despite extensive pressure from the hierarchy, constituted a filter through which the bishops saw everything. Or perhaps this open challenge to their previously unquestioned authority acted as the catalyst for their increasingly frustrated opposition. Whatever the underlying motive for their badly jaundiced interpretation, it was clear that their attitude was one of hostility and confrontation—and that the modus vivendi that the country so desperately needed was no longer feasible.

Strange But True: The Circus of Religious Polarization

Two incidents deserve examination as examples of the level of fanaticism that increasingly permeated the religious question. The stakes (both in political and religious terms) were already extremely high by late 1980—and emotions were charged and easily manipulated. Both incidents provide some light relief from the earnest approach of official documents noted above, but they also show the lengths that minor players in the unfolding political drama in Nicaragua were prepared to go in order to further their cause.

The first of these involves the unlikely case of the "sweating Virgin," a statue that was popularly venerated as a miracle shortly after the alleged appearance of the Virgin Mary to Bernardo Martínez, a sacristan in the town of Cuapa. The "sweating Virgin" became almost a cult figure among certain sectors in Nicaragua: it was featured with reverential respect on several occasions in *La Prensa,* and popular legend among conservatives had it that the statue of the Virgin was in fact crying for Nicaragua because of the communist path along which the Sandinistas were dragging the beloved *patria.* Archbishop Obando y Bravo even blessed the statue, and processions were organized by opponents of the revolutionary government to the location of the "shrine." In a country as fervently imbued with popular religiosity as Nicaragua, this phenomenon was taken extremely seriously by traditional Catholics. Soon, however, it was discovered that the "miracle" was a fraud: the owner had merely soaked the statue in water and then frozen it—bringing it out in the midst of a carefully orchestrated publicity campaign. As the statue was warmed by the air, the frozen water absorbed by the plaster melted—causing the appearance of a "sweating Virgin." Whether this stunt was done to obtain money or to discredit the Sandinistas is not clear, nor is it particularly important; the significance of this incident is that it reflects the ease with which increasing religious tensions could be magnified in the public domain. The support of influential members of the hierarchy also reveals the extent to which they were prepared to grasp at any straws in order to discredit the government.

The other case, that of the "naked priest" (involving Bismarck Carballo, the secretary of the archbishop and director of Radio Católica), was far more serious—yet it too showed the degree to which religious matters could become full-blown front-page political stories overnight. There are two versions of the incident in question, which took place in August 1982. According to Carballo, he had been visiting a female parishioner when a man armed with a pistol arrived at the house and ordered him to undress. At that moment he was dragged out to the street, where a crowd of people (including a crew from Sandinista television) were passing by, and the incident was filmed. Carballo claimed the incident was an obvious setup that showed, in exceptionally crude fashion, how far the revolutionary government was prepared to go to belittle the leading figures of the Church. The other version of the incident is quite different: Shots were heard from the house where Bismarck Carballo was engaged in a romantic liaison with a parishioner. Returning home, the woman's husband discovered the two in a compromising position; enraged, he chased them out of the house where a television crew, passing by after filming a demonstration at a nearby embassy, caught the melodrama in full swing.

Regardless of the actual events, the importance of the episode resides in its impact on the rapidly deteriorating relations between the Church and the FSLN leadership. Masses were said in support of Father Bismarck Carballo (who was publicly defended by Archbishop Obando y Bravo), and charges of entrapment were hurled at the Sandinistas. Photographs were then published of the event, offending many Nicaraguans and discrediting the government and the Church alike. In Masaya there was a large demonstration in favor of Carballo, after which shots were fired on a counterdemonstration in front of a local school run by the Salesian order. The government then asked the school's director to leave the country.

The "naked priest" episode goes far beyond making Bismarck

Carballo the butt of jokes or converting him into a martyr figure, for it shows clearly the volatile nature of Church-state relations as 1982 drew to a close. In many ways it was the symbolic straw that broke the camel's back, for it convinced the Church that depraved Sandinista leaders would stop at nothing in order to discredit the Church and plunge the country further into an orgy of atheistic communism. For the government, on the other hand, the incident showed that the Church leadership was prepared to do all in its power to incite conservative Catholics to violent protest, even after one of its members had been caught in nothing more serious than an ill-fated midday tryst. The episode could not help but fan the flames of discontent at a time when the U.S.-funded contras were escalating their war of destruction in the country.

The Political Context

It is crucially important to understand political developments that acted as a backdrop for all these events and that help to put them in a proper perspective. By late 1982, after three years of struggle, internal power had been consolidated by the Sandinistas. Approximately one-half of the population over the age of sixteen already belonged to mass organizations organized by the FSLN, and their influence was extremely strong.

The Sandinistas had sought to put in place that rarity in Latin American politics, a true social revolution, and a major social upheaval was to be expected—especially as new laws and reforms were implemented that favored the formerly dispossessed and exploited at the expense of the privileged minority. In the countryside, for example, an ambitious land-reform program had distributed land to some 45,000 campesinos by 1984.[34] Changes in education also benefited the population. Mention was made earlier of the vast improvement in the literacy rate as a result of the 1980 literacy campaign. Also important was the increase in preschool and special education facilities—both of which had seven times more students in 1984 than in 1978—and in adult education (virtually nonexistent in 1978), which had some 167,000 students enrolled by 1980.[35] In the field of health care, ten new hospitals and 300 health centers were built by the revolutionary government from 1979 to 1984, and the number of health consultations increased from 200,000 to 6 million by 1984.[36] Nicaragua's standard of living (as measured by GDP, and without examining redistribution of income and expansion of social services) rose a dramatic 7 percent between 1979 and 1983; in the rest of Central America, the standard of living actually fell 14.7 percent during the same period.[37]

While these reforms had been undertaken to benefit the formerly exploited sectors, it was obvious that the price paid by the bourgeoisie would be the gradual and steady removal of their political influence. The resignations of Alfonso Robelo and Violeta Chamorro in April 1980 and the increasing control of the parliamentary Council of State by pro-Sandinista elements showed the middle-class sectors that their influence was more symbolic than real. Formerly a fairly major political actor, the bourgeoisie now passed to a distinctly marginalized role, still powerful economically but dominated by a firmly established revolutionary regime. They might well still own vast tracts of land and direct factories, but their clout had been steadily reduced through a series of political and economic reforms. In the Council of State they exercised remarkably little power.

The April 1980 power struggle at *La Prensa* accentuated the rapidly polarizing nature of Nicaraguan society: a strike resulted after bitter infighting between Xavier Chamorro (the murdered editor's brother and publisher of the paper) and his sister-in-law Violeta, elected president in 1990. Put simply, Xavier supported the Sandinista revolution while Violeta opposed it, and after the family tried unsuccessfully to wrest control of the newspaper from him, most of the staff walked out and subsequently founded *El Nuevo Diario*. Finally, in November 1980, the killing of Jorge Salazar (vice-president of COSEP, the Superior Council of Private Enterprise) in a shoot-out with police, after he had been caught transporting arms for an alleged planned insurrection, showed that the increasingly rocky relationship between the Sandinistas and the bourgeoisie would only continue to deteriorate.

On the second anniversary of the revolution, a series of radical economic measures were introduced, including a broad agrarian reform law, the expropriation of thirteen major companies, a law against decapitalization, and another expropriating land of all absentee landowners. Several COSEP leaders protested in *La Prensa* against the clearly "Marxist-Leninist" nature of the Sandinista economic programs—and in October they were jailed. By 1982, the nine *comandantes* of the FSLN directorate were clearly in charge, having severely reduced the bourgeoisie's influence. The March 15, 1982, declaration of a state of emergency (due to stepped-up contra attacks) gave the revolutionary government even greater powers. They controlled the security forces, dominated the Council of State and the junta (through Daniel Ortega's presence), and held the major portfolios of Defense, Interior, Planning, and Agrarian Reform. With the influence of the bourgeoisie now virtually defunct, and with COSEP cowed, the mantle of the internal opposition needed to be taken up by someone else. It is not at all surprising that the hierarchy of the Catholic Church, energetically led by Archbishop Obando y Bravo (who was a personal friend of many bourgeois leaders), then became the focus of domestic opposition.

While this social and political polarization obviously had a major impact on the domestic climate, by far the most significant development on the Nicaraguan scene was the policy being enacted by the newly elected Reagan administration in Washington. Having been elected on a "make America strong" ticket, the incoming president sought to stop the "cancer of Marxism" in Central America and bring into play a hardline policy in the entire region. What followed was a campaign against Nicaragua waged on a variety of fronts and designed to destroy the Sandinistas' popularity. Bilateral aid from the United States was halted, and considerable pressure was placed on multilateral lending agencies (such as the World Bank, International Monetary Fund, and the Inter-American Development Bank) to deny all aid to "Marxist" Nicaragua. Later an economic embargo against Nicaragua was introduced.

By far the most effective pressure on the Sandinistas came from the covert war staged by CIA-backed Nicaraguan contra rebels based in neighboring Honduras. (Indeed, Honduras itself became the recipient of ever-increasing amounts of U.S. military aid: from $3.9 million in 1980 to a staggering $78.5 million in 1984. Another eleven military installations were built in that country by the United States at a cost of $87.85 million.)[38] In March 1981, just after Reagan took office, some $19 million was allocated to the CIA for operations against the Sandinista government. By July 1982 there were approximately 4,500 contras (and two years later some 10,000) divided into marauding bands that were based in Honduras but frequently conducted raids in northern Nicaragua. Equipped and funded by the CIA, they were remarkably successful in wreaking havoc and destruction in Nicaragua: from 1982 to 1986, for instance, over 20,000 Nicaraguans were killed, another 40,000 were either wounded or kidnapped, and some 250,000 were displaced by the fighting. Later the Honduras-based force, the

A disabled veteran in front of a Catholic church in León.

Nicaraguan Democratic Forces or FDN, would be supplemented by other contra groups, including Miskito groups headed by Steadman Fagoth (MISURA) and Brooklyn Rivera (MISURASATA), and a group in the south of Nicaragua (Edén Pastora's ARDE). The total cost of the war to the Nicaraguan government for this period was estimated at no less than $2.821 billion.[39]

The extensive gains made in the early years by Sandinista social programs soon dropped off in the face of this onslaught, especially as more and more funding was channeled into national defense. In addition, in regions where the contras were active, medical service often had to be curtailed. Finally, the contras deliberately targeted these same Sandinista achievements, killing some forty-two health care workers by the end of 1985, kidnapping twenty, wounding eleven, and destroying sixty-two health facilities. During the same period, some 800 schools had been closed because of the war, 170 teachers killed, and 133 kidnapped by the contras.[40]

The role of the Catholic hierarchy at this time was rather unusual, especially that of Archbishop Obando y Bravo. Unlike the closing years of the Somoza dictatorship when he spoke out courageously against the abuses of the National Guard, he now deliberately refrained from condemning the abuses of the contras—many of whose leaders were former National Guardsmen. This lack of consistency was not lost on the Sandinistas or on members of the grass-roots Church, who were appalled at his partisan political attitude. This apparent lack of appreciation for the suffering of many thousands of Nicaraguan families was accentuated by funding received by the archdiocese from the United States. Indeed, at a time when many of Nicaragua's much-vaunted reform programs could not be kept functioning because of a U.S.-directed campaign of unrelenting pressure, in 1981 the COPROSA commission of the archdiocese of Managua received $500,000 from USAID allegedly to train community leaders, but the objective of providing competition with government projects cannot be discounted.[41]

From Honeymoon to Divorce

As we have seen, the period 1979–82 began with apparently boundless promise for national unity, for developing a new model of Church participation in a totally different political structure—and ended up with a rapidly polarizing Church, mutual dislike and distrust, and the emergence of Archbishop Obando y Bravo as the de facto leader of the opposition in the country. The brave experiment in Church-state cooperation had failed miserably, and the dominant note as the Church prepared for the visit of Pope John Paul II in March 1983 was one of scarcely concealed hostility.

What caused this turn of events? This is a complex question, for which a complete answer is not yet available. Conservatives like Humberto Belli contend that the traditional Church was merely being true to its ecclesial mission: "demands for complete submission to the Sandinista party met a Catholic Church which had developed habits of independence during a decade of opposition to the Somoza dictatorship."[42] More liberal or radical observers would claim that the potential for Church-state cooperation was illusory, for Obando y Bravo—although painted as a "valiant and progressive leader" who had courageously battled Somoza's tyranny—in fact "had *never* supported the Frente Sandinista"[43] and indeed had tried consistently to undermine it.

While there are undoubtedly elements of truth in both arguments, a more dispassionate analysis shows that the situation is far more complex. The Sandinistas, for instance, undoubtedly had unrealistic expectations about the progressive nature of the Church hierarchy and about the support that could be expected from them. (The November 1979 pastoral letter accentuated this unrealistic appreciation of the hierarchy, which included individuals who were less critical of the FSLN than Obando y Bravo but were loath to differ from the archbishop.) For their part, the bishops apparently believed that their opposition to Somoza had earned them a far greater say regarding the country's political development than the Sandinistas were prepared to countenance. From the outset, then, there were unrealistic expectations on both sides that could not possibly be realized.

The lack of sensitivity on the part of the Sandinistas—ranging from their treatment of the Miskitos to some of the Marxist terminology used by the *comandantes,* from their praise of progressive clergy and scorn of conservative priests to their opinions on traditional religious celebrations—also aggravated the situation. To the bishops, it seemed that "los muchachos" (whom they believed, incorrectly, would prove more malleable) were closet Marxist-Leninists, prepared to turn Nicaragua into another Cuba. This fear became particularly acute after the education reforms introduced by the Sandinistas seemed to smack of leftist ideology. For the bishops, who came of age in pre–Vatican II times and fully believed that Marxism is necessarily "anti-Christian," this was totally unpalatable. Indeed it is quite possible that after having initially supported the literacy crusade, the bishops felt annoyed at themselves for not having seen its leftist bent.

This fear of "godless Communism," combined with an increasingly ferocious rejection of the "totalitarian" aims of the Sandinistas, came to represent a filter through which the hierarchy viewed all subsequent developments. The extremely cordial relationship that developed between the *comandantes* and Cuban president Fidel Castro must also have been a source of great concern to the bishops, who had already expressed their displeasure with the large number of voluntary teachers from Cuba involved in the literacy campaign. Remarks by "rebel clergy" like Ernesto Cardenal on the value of Marxism as an analytical tool for examining society[44] can only have hardened the bishops' resolve to battle communism with all their ecclesial might.

Another crucial element to bear in mind when assessing precisely what went wrong is the close connections between Archbishop Obando y Bravo and leading members of the bourgeoisie—the same social class whose traditional privileges were being steadily whittled away by the revolutionary government. An extremely important watershed, of course, was the resignation of Violeta Chamorro and Alfonso Robelo from the junta, since it signified that the bourgeoisie as a social class had consciously rejected the sociopolitical model being imposed. Moreover, it is important to remember that even before the revolutionary victory in 1979, Obando y Bravo had been in Caracas working to keep the Sandinistas from taking power (he preferred a far broader coalition, with middle-class hegemony). In just thirty months he had seen the political influence of his allies decimated and his country being drawn along a Marxist-influenced path. The treatment meted out to COSEP leaders, the infighting at *La Prensa,* and the marginalization of the bourgeoisie in the Council of State had convinced him that such dealings with traditional allies, and personal friends, was both reprehensible and unacceptable.

But the most important reason for this rapid souring of relations resides in the view held by Obando y Bravo about the necessary role and nature of the Catholic Church. The archbishop is clearly a conservative and traditionalist Church leader, suspicious of the sweeping reforms of Vatican II and Medellín. He felt threatened by the presence of four articulate and extremely powerful priests in key government positions— particularly because they espoused a view of the Church so radically different from his own. Undoubtedly he felt that their remaining in power undermined his own authority as the most influential Church leader, particularly because they were partial to the activities and beliefs of the progressive wing of the Church. Because religious orthodoxy had to be protected at all costs, a variety of disruptive tactics were implemented to ensure compliance with the archbishop's designs. Mexican priest Canuto Barreto, who resigned his position as the rector of the National Seminary in 1981, explained the determination of the archbishop to ensure orthodoxy at all costs:

In Nicaragua, of course, the hierarchy gives excessively open support to the reactionary forces. The archbishop loses no opportunity to show his sympathies for the bourgeoisie in both words and deeds. Using his power he seeks to curb all those movements of the Church that are open to the process of change, a tactic in which he succeeds. . . . The systematic persecution unleashed by the Curia against every priest or religious who collaborates with the revolution is well known. One after another those who wish to live out the spirit and the letter of the [November] 1979 pastoral letter of the bishops have either been expelled or forced out of their communities.[45]

This fear of Church disunity, with the resultant need to impose orthodoxy by means of the hierarchy's authority, is extremely important in understanding the fundamental dynamics at play in the Nicaraguan Church. By late 1982 division along political lines was deeply embedded in the Church. What accentuated the difficulties was the empowering nature of the revolutionary process, which had given hundreds of thousands of Nicaraguans the chance to begin an education and had encouraged them to question reality and their role in it. Within the progressive wing of the Church the influence of this process of *concientización* had already become firmly established, but it was greatly fortified by the sweeping societal changes taking place throughout the country.

In this context of wide-ranging sociopolitical change and the ensuing polarization of society, the Church as a corporate body merely came to reflect the inherent tensions found throughout Nicaraguan society. It was a time of great ideological ferment, of widespread questioning of values and systems that previously had been deemed beyond reproach. Perhaps most important of all, nobody seemed to know for sure in which direction the *patria* was headed—least of all the Church leadership. As a result, the hierarchy—profoundly concerned by the radical development plan of the revolutionary government, seeing the specter of atheistic communism looming on the horizon, and above all worried about the manifest lack of respect for Church influence (as personified in the archbishop)—desperately needed to protect its authority. Consequently, Church leaders awaited with great expectations the visit of John Paul II to rein in the errant wing of the Church, restore respect for the episcopal authority, and remind the faithful of the need to put Catholic orthodoxy and Church unity above all else. In the end, however, while orthodoxy and authority triumphed, the papal visit of March 1983 was to bring a profound wave of disunity in its wake and to leave the Church more polarized than when the pontiff had arrived.

✝

5   CHURCH-STATE RELATIONS AT THEIR NADIR (1983–1985)

It is very difficult to judge whether the United States is encouraging aggression against the Sandinista government from Honduras when the information on that matter comes from only one source. . . . We only know the Sandinista side of the story.

Archbishop Miguel Obando y Bravo, 1983

It is significant that President Reagan, at the moment when he feels so isolated (and at a time of growing congressional and public opposition to his policy in Central America), should resort to those who appear to be his last unreserved supporters—the members of the Catholic hierarchy in Nicaragua. . . . What a disgrace; what a sin! I beg you not to blame Christ for this shamelessness, nor the Church.

Father Miguel D'Escoto, 1984

In December 1982, as Church members throughout Nicaragua planned feverishly for the March 1983 arrival of Pope John Paul II, it may well have seemed to them that the papal visit would be the panacea for their many (and growing) problems. These included the rampant polarization within the Church itself, the rapidly deteriorating relationship between Church and government leaders, and the disastrous effects of the escalating contra war. Given this extremely depressing reality, the pontiff's visit was eagerly anticipated by all sides in Nicaragua. The hierarchy hoped that the pope would support its attempts to stave off the atheistic materialism of the Sandinista government and issue a message of moral support for the bishops, while the government expected him to use his moral leverage to support the incipient peace process—and possibly request a curtailment of U.S. funds to the contras.

These aspirations, however, were mutually exclusive, since there could be only one real winner. The expectations of the revolutionary government revealed its political naïveté, for the outcome of the pope's visit was never really in doubt. The Sandinistas were thus the victims of their own wishful thinking—and of their desperate desire for peace. But in all likelihood, neither side could have imagined that the papal visit, far from producing a harmonizing effect, would actually polarize the situation even further. The triumphant return of Miguel Obando y Bravo from Rome in June 1985, following his appointment as cardinal, was in many ways the logical conclusion of this entire episode—indicating the weight of official Vatican support for the traditional interpretation of the Church's mission. By extension, this implied that the tension and mistrust between the principal protagonists in the Nicaraguan saga would continue indefinitely.

Marked by continuing polarization and plummeting Church-state relations, the period 1983–85 represents the lowest point in dialogue of any kind in the Nicaraguan context—in no small part because of the unrealistic expectations raised prior to the papal visit. Throughout this period, evidence can be found to show that those on each side of the ecclesial debate believed that their vision of the Church's role was the correct one and that their Christian duty was to persist until their opponents shared their vision—or lay defeated. Dialogue, cooperation, and compromise were supplanted by an ongoing religious "dirty war," one that closely paralleled the covert war promoted by Ronald Reagan (who, like the pope, saw a moral crusade being fought between Christendom and the Infidel in Nicaragua).

The Political Background to the Religious Struggle

Anyone who visited Nicaragua in the early 1980s could not help but be struck by the impact of the contra war on the country's social fabric: funds that had been used to finance Nicaragua's spectacularly successful health, education, and agrarian reform projects were being steadily diverted to the war effort; the military presence became increasingly noticeable; and the number of funerals gradually increased as Nicaraguans on both sides of the ideological divide were killed in ever-greater numbers. Massacres of peasants by contra rebels (such as the murder of a dozen and a half residents of San Francisco del Norte in July 1982) had become commonplace. The country as a whole had entered on a war footing, and to expect the Church to remain "neutral" was unrealistic. What was surprising, though, was the passion with which both the hierarchy and the progressive Church sector adhered to their ideological positions, discounting the opinions of their ecclesial opponents with ever-mounting levels of indignation and invective: there was less room for compromise with every passing day.

A central factor in the political equation was the role of the Reagan administration, which, following its military failure in El Salvador, was determined to stamp out what it saw as the corrupting influence of Sandinismo. Accordingly the administration developed a multifaceted plan, generally referred to by the innocuous-sounding term "low-intensity conflict," to destabilize and ultimately destroy the Sandinista government in Nicaragua, even after its manifest electoral victory in November 1984. Under this plan, the CIA helped to recruit disaffected Nicaraguans into a proxy army, subsequently arming and equipping them and producing a fighting force that came to be known as the contras. From March 1981 (when $19 million was first allocated to the CIA) until the February 1990 elections, the U.S. government provided at least $300 million to this fighting force. Several contra fronts were established: the largest group was the FDN, based in Honduras; others were MISURA and MISURASATA (predominantly Miskito groups, based in the north) and Edén Pastora's ARDE (based in the south). Throughout the 1980s this fighting force (which averaged some 10,000 combatants) would engage in a policy of economic sabotage and murder, the fundamental objective of which was, in the words of Ronald Reagan, to make the Sandinista government "say uncle."

The Reagan administration also put major economic pressure on Nicaragua. It curtailed Nicaraguan imports into the United States (devastating the country's already weak economic growth under the Sandinistas); halted bilateral aid; reduced Nicaragua's sugar quota by 90 percent; excluded Nicaragua from the programs of the Export-Import Bank; blocked loans from multilateral lending agencies such as the International Monetary Fund, World Bank, and Inter-American Development Bank; pressured U.S. allies not to lend money to the Sandinista government; and imposed a trade embargo (in 1985).

In addition to this economic stranglehold, the U.S. military presence in the region was increased substantially—not only in security aid to Costa Rica on Nicaragua's southern border (a country that does not even have a standing army) and to nearby El Salvador, but also in aid to Honduras on the northern border. Between 1980 and 1984, for example, Washington's military aid to Honduras rose from $3.9 million to an astonishing $78.5 million, while the United States built several extra airports to allow for a rapid invasion of Nicaragua—at a cost of $87.85 million.[1] Moreover, a series of large-scale "joint maneuvers" were initiated with Honduras (using U.S. equipment and thousands of U.S. military personnel) in an attempt to intimidate Nicaragua.

The United States also sought to destabilize the Sandinista government by deliberately thwarting diplomatic efforts to bring peace to the region. For example, the Reagan administration claimed to support the peace initiative undertaken by the Contadora nations (Mexico, Venezuela, Panama, and Colombia) but in actual fact did all in its power to subvert the process. Reagan was obsessed with the military defeat of the Sandinistas, and nothing else would suffice. His administration engaged in wholesale doublespeak, professing to seek peace and stability while fomenting war and political instability throughout the region. Unfortunately for tiny Nicaragua, it was caught in the eye of the storm and, like Grenada before it, had to be taught a lesson in the geopolitics of U.S. hegemony.

By the mid-1980s, however, it became clear to policymakers in

Washington that the greatest pressure to be imposed on the Sandinistas would result directly from the contra war itself. Accordingly, increasingly larger funds were diverted (legally and illegally) to the contras, whose numbers rose from 4,500 in 1982 to some 15,000 by the late 1980s. It is interesting to note the influence of former members of Somoza's National Guard in the leadership of the principal component of the contras, the FDN. The commander in chief was Enrique Bermúdez, a former colonel in the National Guard, and at one point some forty-six of the forty-eight leadership positions in the FDN were held by former National Guardsmen.[2] By January 1983 more than 400 campesinos had been killed in contra raids. This seemed like a large number at the time, but it represented only a mere fraction of the many thousands who would be killed in this war. Indeed, on July 19, 1986, President Ortega announced that "the contra war had claimed 31,290 victims, 16,925 contras and 14,260 Nicaraguans who had been killed, wounded or kidnapped 'defending national sovereignty.' "[3]

In addition to the tens of thousands of lives that would be lost (out of a population of less than 3 million), the economic costs of this war were quite extraordinary. To give but one example, by the mid-1980s Nicaragua was spending just over half its national budget on defense and was faced with hundreds of millions of dollars' worth of damage inflicted by the contras. Add to this the outrageous (and, according to the World Court, illegal) actions such as the 1984 mining of Nicaragua's major ports and one could sense the moral outrage felt by many Nicaraguans. It is in this context that the observations of Archbishop Obando y Bravo and other members of the hierarchy should be considered—particularly when they deliberately refrained from criticizing the contras and even publicly doubted Washington's hand in these developments. As might be expected, rather than calming troubled waters the actions of the hierarchical Church (reflected most clearly in the positions taken by Obando y Bravo, Bishop Vega, and archdiocese spokesman Bismarck Carballo) merely added fuel to the already smoldering fire. This in turn aggravated representatives of the "Church of the poor," whose parishioners were being drafted to the front—and killed in increasing numbers. The end result was a rising spiral of distrust and frustration, polarization (religious as well as political), and mutual contempt. A decade later, the Church has still not recovered from this period of extreme bitterness and internecine feuding: while in official proclamations the bishops may refer to "reconciliation," "social harmony," and "dialogue" as desirable goals, the unfortunate truth is that they have not practiced what they preach within their own institution.

This crucial period saw many examples of this rapid increase in tensions, some stemming from old sores while others originated from new sources of conflict that developed within the rapidly polarizing national context. These will be dealt with in some detail in this chapter—in essence because it was during this period that the crisis became most acute. It was the brief visit of John Paul II in March 1983, however, that acted as a dramatic catalyst to this whole process, accentuating the clear-cut differences over ideology, the role of the Church, the nature of the Reagan administration–contra factor, and the relationship with the revolutionary process in Nicaragua. While both sides in the ecclesial debate believed that the pontiff would speak in terms that could be appropriated by them, it became increasingly clear that this was not feasible; as a result, the yawning chasm became even greater.

The Pope in Nicaragua

In the months leading up to the visit of John Paul II, the strained Church-state relationship continued to be a major political concern of truly national proportions—as revealed by a cursory glance at the headlines of either the progovernment newspaper *Barricada* or the opposition paper *La Prensa*. At the same time, however, the media increasingly focused on the pope's role as a mediator, possibly seeking a reconciliation (one of his favorite themes) between the Church hierarchy and the FSLN. Newspaper articles stressed his humble origins, belief in social justice and workers' rights (spelled out in his impressive encyclical *Laborem Exercens*), and desire for world peace. In late February 1982, the announcement by Vatican radio that the pontiff had come on a "pilgrimage of faith, peace, and fraternity"[4] heightened expectations that his visit to Nicaragua would produce something of transcendental importance. The pontiff's opening words on arriving in Managua also emphasized the pastoral nature of his visit: "I am brought to Nicaragua by a mission of an essentially religious nature; I come as a messenger of peace, to encourage, hope, and serve our faith; as a servant of the faith, to strengthen Catholics in their fidelity to Christ and the Church, and to strengthen them with love, to fill their spirits with feelings of fraternity and reconciliation."⁵ Yet by the time he left the country that evening, his public addresses—including two homilies given in León and Managua—had sent shock waves resounding throughout Nicaraguan society, the effects of which can still be felt in that country.

The arrival of John Paul II in the capital city in many ways set the tone for the rest of his twelve-hour stay in Nicaragua. As he listened to Daniel Ortega's welcome message (with an inappropriate and excessively long address on the evils of U.S. imperialism), his body language spoke volumes about his feelings toward the Sandinistas: his arms crossed, his gaze fixed firmly on the airport tarmac, and his hand supporting his down-turned head, this former actor was clearly not pleased with his hosts. A few minutes later, as Father Ernesto Cardenal

Posters welcoming John Paul II to Nicaragua.

(minister of culture) genuflected and sought to kiss his ring as a gesture of respect, the pontiff wagged his finger and lectured the priest on the need to "put his affairs in order with the Church." If reconciliation were indeed to be the keynote principle of the pope's visit, this beginning did not bode well for achieving this objective.

From Managua John Paul went to León, where he was welcomed by Bishop Julián Barni. In the cathedral the pope affirmed that he supported the people in their struggle: "Let me assure you from the outset that I understand your difficulties and accompany you with fraternal affection." He then took up the theme of fidelity to Church teachings and to Church authority, stating: "You should live united with your bishop, pray for the Church, and be true to your faith."[6]

From the cathedral he headed for the medical campus at the university, where he gave his first formal speech. The pontiff's address was delivered to a group composed mainly of campesinos, as he noted in his opening remarks. He went on, however, to state that a special message for rural workers was to be delivered later in Panama and that in León he would focus on the theme of religious education. Reiterating the views he had expressed earlier in an address to UNESCO (underscoring "the absolute right of Christian parents to refuse to see their children subjected to school programs inspired by atheism"),[7] he explained the responsibility of parents to disseminate the Catholic faith to their children. He then went to great pains to distinguish Christian education from "materialistic" instruction, claiming that man cannot be reduced to a "mere instrument of production" and so must resist these non-Catholic tendencies. He urged the faithful to proclaim the message of Christ and become "constructors of peace." Only in this way would Christians overcome "the dialectic of enmity and violence."

The climax of this rather stern lecture came in the last sentences of John Paul's sermon. Encouraging Catholics to take the sacraments regularly, he also urged them to respect—and be faithful to—their bishops, a theme touched on in his cathedral address and to which he would return later in Managua. Finally, the pontiff energetically advised his audience: "You have no need of ideologies that are alien to your Christian condition in order to love and defend mankind." With these loaded references to the necessary respect for the bishops' authority, the need for Catholic education, and the rejection of "materialistic ideology," the "pastoral" visit of John Paul II was rapidly taking on overtly political tones.

The pope's homily on Church unity given in Managua delivered a veritable bombshell to the estimated 500,000–700,000 people who attended the mass. In the words of one commentator, the pontiff "lashed out at the ideological conflicts between the government and the Catholic Church, reiterated his warning against developing a so-called popular Church alongside the institutional Church, defended Archbishop Obando y Bravo, the controversial archbishop of Managua, an antagonist of the Sandinista government, and called for obedience of this 90% Catholic country to its bishops."[8] Above all the pope emphasized the need for the unity of the Church—but on terms stipulated by the Church hierarchy. His warm support for Archbishop Obando y Bravo contrasted with his dire warnings against those who dared to question the hierarchy's authority—including, no doubt, the five priests who held government posts: "No Christian, *much less anybody who has consecrated himself to the Church,* can break that unity, acting outside or against the will of his bishops 'whom the Holy Spirit has put here to guide the Church of God' (Hebrews 20:20)" (italics added).

The pope's stated central aim was Church unity, but as the homily went on it became clear that what he was really demanding was subordination to the bishops' dictates. He called for "respect for pastoral directions given by the bishops to the clergy and the faithful"; this, he emphasized, was "a duty which was especially important for priests, religious, and other pastoral agents." One can judge the determination of the pope in issuing this message by the fact that in his homily he used the word *bishops* no less than fifteen times—revealing a man totally convinced of the need for a strong, authoritarian Church, one in which vertical communication (from the pontiff down) is the appropriate protocol.

The alternative to this ordered, united Church, the pontiff claimed, was a chaotic divisiveness that was fundamentally damaging to Catholicism. Quoting from an earlier letter issued by the Nicaraguan hierarchy, he roundly condemned the very concept of any branch or organization that challenged the institutional Church. Naturally, these remarks disturbed the Sandinista supporters and brought joy to the Church hierarchy. But for the vast majority of Nicaraguans present, it was simply a tremendous shock to see the pope deliberately ignoring the tragic reality of war and hardship in which they were living. For them Church unity was important, but far less so than their fervent desire for peace. That John Paul should ignore their plight, preferring instead to shore up Archbishop Obando y Bravo's authority, was inexplicable.

As the mass continued, the tension between ideological opponents erupted into verbal confrontation. Some Sandinista supporters briefly took control of the public-address system and made themselves heard above the proceedings. Many of the people present in the plaza broke out into chants of "We want peace," only to be told three times by a visibly angered pontiff to keep quiet. John Paul's charisma, which had been such an asset in other Latin American countries, failed him in Nicaragua as he came up against a reality that he did not properly understand or about which he had been ill-advised. For the first time in his seventeen trips abroad, the pope had not been received rapturously in all quarters; instead he had been criticized by many Nicaraguans who felt defrauded by his partisan views and, more important, by his apparent inability to understand their plight. In contrast, the supporters of the archbishop's position felt vindicated in their assessment of the dangers of a government led by atheistic materialists who had shown such disrespect for the pontiff.

The content of John Paul's two homilies failed to capture the essence of Nicaraguan reality and, as a result, caused much confusion among the populace—most of whom had been personally affected by the war against Somoza and by recent contra raids. They desperately wanted to hear a message about peace, believing that condemnation by the pope of this foreign-backed aggression would carry a moral weight around the world. Indeed, even the two most progressive bishops in Nicaragua (López Ardón of Estelí and Santi of Matagalpa) seemed to believe that the pope would call for an end to the strife. Bishop Santi, for example, noted that "the pope's visit here contains an implicit request for the war on our border to stop. As Christians and as human beings we all feel aggrieved by the shedding of our Nicaraguan brethren's blood."[9] Consequently, the pontiff's message of obedience to the bishops, the need for discipline, the value of Catholic education, and even the importance of Church unity fell flat, as John Paul resolutely continued his struggle to bring his errant flock back into the mainstream of Catholic orthodoxy. As one North American priest noted, "In Nicaragua he seemed to be a disturbed man with a mission somehow single-handedly to stave off the Marxist direction of the Sandinista revolutionary government of reconstruction and place the ideology of the Catholic Church in direct confrontation with the ideology of the Sandinista revolution."[10]

Undoubtedly the single most important reason for both the frustration of the Nicaraguan populace and the failure of the visit as a whole was the pope's lack of understanding of what had happened in Nicaragua in recent years. He seemed unable to grasp that—unlike other countries he had visited in the area—in Nicaragua the people had willingly participated in a bloody revolutionary war, the effects of which had touched virtually every Nicaraguan family. Similarly, he failed to realize that the revolution had produced tremendous social benefits for most Nicaraguans (particularly in the areas of education, health care, and agrarian reform) and that—in comparison with other Central American countries—Nicaragua did enjoy a fair degree of freedom.

The pope's inability to comprehend the historical context of this troubled nation is perhaps best illustrated by his lack of regard for the mothers of the "heroes and martyrs" (those Nicaraguans who had died in the struggle). The day before his visit to Managua, a funeral mass had been held for seventeen young militia members who had been killed by the contras. This service had taken place in the same plaza where the papal mass was held on the following day, and emotions were still running high. At the very least, one would have expected some words of consolation—even said in passing at a press conference—on this tragic event. Yet John Paul studiously avoided the topic and, in doing so, unwittingly alienated tens of thousands of Nicaraguans who desperately wanted to receive some words of condolence. Ironically, in El Salvador the pope encouraged the people to demand peace, noting in his homily: "You are, with every right, *thirsting for peace*. From your chests and throats a clamor of hope rises: we want peace."[11] Had he expressed similar sentiments in Nicaragua, the visit would have been more successful and would certainly have been more constructive in terms of easing Church-state tensions.

The pope came to Central America with two fundamental messages: obedience to Church teachings and respect for social justice. In Ríos Montt's Guatemala a "social" commentary was provided, as was the case in Honduras and Haiti (the hemisphere's two poorest countries). In the latter two countries the pope urged the Church to support the just struggles of the poor, and in Haiti he even referred to the "innate and generous religious sentiment, the vitality of the *popular nature of the*

Church."[12] In Nicaragua his message was very different. Perceiving the Church to be in mortal danger of being swallowed up by a totalitarian Marxist state, the pontiff charged forward relentlessly, using every opportunity to "save" the Nicaraguan faithful and bring them back to the Church fold under the leadership of Archbishop Obando y Bravo.

For their part, the Sandinistas can be faulted for exhibiting a certain naïveté, for they were completely unprepared for the pope's criticisms. Prior to the papal visit they had sought to ensure that the entire population would take an interest in the proceedings: a fascinating letter-writing campaign in the national media ("What would you say to the Holy Father?") was eagerly pursued, and the widespread media coverage was extremely favorable.[13] The FSLN leadership was convinced that despite its constant bickering with the archbishop (who, of course, exercised tremendous influence on the Vatican contingent), the pope would be sufficiently impressed by the reality of the Nicaraguan situation and the Sandinistas' sincere efforts to build a society that was the antithesis of the social injustice found throughout Latin America. At the very least they had expected some favorable statement on the social reforms enacted in Nicaragua (the desirability of which the pope did emphasize in other countries he visited on this trip), as well as a condemnation of the contra atrocities.

But even the pontiff's initial statement on arriving in Managua (in which he greeted the "thousands and thousands of Nicaraguans who have not been able to reach the places where we have spoken—as they would have liked") carried an affront.[14] This implication that the government had kept "thousands and thousands" from attending the celebrations was repeated in his parting remarks before returning to Costa Rica. This was ironic because the Nicaraguan government made extraordinary efforts to ensure the greatest possible access of the people to the pontiff, using an entire month's national gasoline allowance to transport Nicaraguans to the ceremonies in León and Managua. Moreover, for weeks before the pope's arrival, the media had churned out page after page of extremely favorable coverage, and the day of his visit had been declared a national holiday. Moreover the government provided free transportation for Nicaraguans to attend the ceremonies in León and Managua. In all, about one-third of the entire population from throughout the country managed to see the pope during his twelve-hour visit.

For the duration of his visit, opposition groups attempted to utilize

John Paul's presence as a means of pressuring the government, while the FSLN sought to win from the pope a call for peace and a demand for the cessation of external aggression. It was an uneven contest, for the archbishop's influence clearly held sway—as the pope said it must. Indeed, the pontiff invited the archbishop to speak at the beginning of the mass in Managua (even though this had not been agreed to in advance by negotiators representing the government and Church sectors). Moreover, the scripture texts chosen for the mass—on the construction of the Tower of Babel—were intended to embarrass the government. In addition, in the "Petitions" section of the mass, prayers were offered for political prisoners in Nicaragua, yet none were offered for the tens of thousands killed fighting in the insurrection against Somoza or for the many hundreds who had died in contra raids. In the same mass the pope ignored the traditional prayer said by the celebrant of the mass to enlighten government leaders, provoking Ernesto Cardenal to note: "In every mass the Pope has said everywhere in the world—no matter how bad the government—there has always been a prayer for those who govern. But not when the Pope came to Nicaragua. . . . It is in the text of every mass. And *here* it was suppressed."[15] Finally, it is worth noting that on his arrival in Costa Rica later that night, the pontiff came out onto the balcony of the nuncio's residence in San José and urged Costa Ricans to "pray hard for the true Christian brothers and sisters in Nicaragua."[16] These actions and statements led Vice President Sergio Ramírez (echoing the postvisit Sandinista position) to criticize the rigid ideological position of John Paul II: "He came here with a preconceived notion. He thought that here was a totalitarian regime that oppressed the Catholic people and that these Catholics would take advantage of his presence to start a rebellion. He thought this was the opportunity they were waiting for to 'liberate themselves' from religious persecution. Basically, he got off the plane as an ideological conquistador."[17]

What impact, then, did the twelve-hour stay of John Paul II have on the Church and on Church-state relations in Nicaragua? The conservative perspective is best summarized by Humberto Belli, for whom the "whole incident hurt the Sandinistas and the revolutionary Christians, alienating them even further from most ordinary Catholics in the country."[18] Phillip Berryman, whose view is that the Sandinistas expected too much ("that the Pope could cut through his own experience and ideology and the circles in CELAM and the Vatican who briefed him"), notes that the visit was "a boon to the Nicaraguan bourgeoisie and to the Reagan Administration, proof positive of Sandinista 'hostility' to religion."[19] For Rosa María Pochet and Abelino Martínez, there were two fundamental results. On the one hand, the visit sought to delegitimize "the revolution and, along with it, the mass of Christians, workers, and peasants who support the revolutionary process. In doing so it also [attacked] the attempts at renovation undertaken by the prophetic Church, and [strengthened] the arch-bishop's authority." On the other hand, the visit was an attempt to align Vatican policy with that of Washington.[20] Michael Dodson and Laura O'Shaughnessy observed that "in the short run . . . the authority of the archbishop and the Episcopal Conference was strengthened while the democratizing tendencies of Catholic doctrine were undercut," but they also noted that the main impact of the visit was to exacerbate tensions within the institutional Church and between Church and state.[21]

There was also a lesson to be learned for the Latin American Church as a whole, according to the Chilean liberation theologian Pablo Richard. Richard stated that since the papal visit to Nicaragua "the religious dimension has acquired a specific organic character within the dominant classes and imperialism. That is, Christianity is no longer being utilized simply as an ideological force, but rather there is an attempt to utilize Church structures per se, as an instrument against the Revolution."[22] Mexican theologian Canuto Barreto (who had resigned from directing the Nicaraguan National Seminary in 1982 because of disagreements with the Nicaraguan hierarchy) noted that the pope also should learn from his visit to Nicaragua: "He is a man of iron, a Pole who has become hardened in the struggle to save the old European Church along with its privileges. He will have to learn a great deal: to become the pope of the entire world, including the *Third World,* which he will also come to love with tenderness" (italics added).[23]

If the pontiff's visit had a major impact on the ecclesial nature of the religious question, it also magnified the political aspects of the same debate. The pope had sided unequivocally with the institutional Church, rejecting the "Church of the poor" and the Sandinista government. The tension in Nicaragua thus increased dramatically when the pope left to return to the Vatican, largely because that section of the Church opposed to the revolutionary process felt its position to have been significantly strengthened by the pope's conspicuous rejection of the Sandinista model. The international media coverage, which in general emphasized the unruly reception of the pontiff, reinforced the image of a Church under siege and the persona of the archbishop, while the progressive Church withdrew to analyze how it could best regroup and exercise damage control. Less than two months later, following a battle in Maracali, the discovery of contra posters produced for the FDN indicated that the controversial visit had become a propaganda tool. One poster, bearing a photograph of the pope, stated, "The Pope is with us"; another declared, "With God and patriotism we will rout communism."[24] Meanwhile, in a manual of psychological warfare and counterrevolutionary terrorism prepared by the CIA for the contra army, one of the pieces of advice was "to paint anti-Sandinista slogans." The slogan chosen as an example was none other than "Viva el Papa." In sum, whether the pope truly intended his visit to be purely of a spiritual and pastoral nature—which is highly debatable—the role he played during his twelve short hours in Nicaragua mixed spiritual and political elements until they became virtually superimposed, their lines of demarcation totally blurred.

Two Controversial Pastorals

While there were many well-publicized incidents involving infringements of human rights by the Sandinista government, scandals such as the expulsion of clergy, priests and religious involved in political activities (of both the left and right), and protests and counterprotests on a variety of ecclesio-political matters, the major tension in the wake of John Paul's visit resulted from two official documents issued by the Nicaraguan Episcopal Conference and the reaction to their publication. The first pastoral, dated August 29, 1983, commented on the issue of obligatory military service (which the conference leadership firmly opposed); the second (issued at Easter 1984) called for national reconciliation, dialogue with the contras, and an end to the war. In the context of the increasing polarization (in political as well as religious terms), these were extremely controversial positions.

The first communiqué was issued in the midst of a growing national crisis: the war against the contras had intensified throughout 1983, additional monies were being forwarded from Washington to the contra leadership, and the body count of the contras' victims had risen substantially. In sum, the contra war had become the government's major priority—yet in their August 1983 pastoral the bishops were calling on Nicaraguans to reject military service. Although the bishops claimed that their message should be interpreted in strictly moral terms ("We seek merely to shed some light on this problem from a moral and ethical perspective"),[25] this pastoral was clearly a partisan document.

The first part of the communiqué outlined the role of the armed forces in general, noting that this role could be considered legitimate only if the state itself possessed "authentic moral power" (p. 6)—which in this case did not obtain. The document went on to state that, in contrast to the "classical concept" of the armed forces' role, a new theory—the "revolutionary concept"—had arisen. In the bishops' eyes, this concept was morally unacceptable because it robbed individuals of their freedom of conscience—and should be avoided at all costs, if for no other reason than to avoid falling into the trap of totalitarianism:

> This revolutionary interpretation of sociojuridical concepts has not been legitimized in practice through popular acceptance. Instead it has been imposed, as a fact, by force of arms and other forms of state coercion.
>
> It can be easily shown that all countries with totalitarian governments have created a highly politicized army in order to defend their own ideology. This is also undertaken to force the population itself to receive political indoctrination. (p. 7)

The main point of the bishops' argument was then outlined: because the conscription law was designed to indoctrinate young men and to oblige them to assist the Sandinista political party (and not the nation) through military service in the Ejército Popular Sandinista, compliance with it served to perpetuate a totalitarian and illegitimate system. Moreover, if young Nicaraguans were not in agreement with the political program of the Sandinistas, it was fundamentally immoral to force them to serve this "army–political party" (because it deprived them of their basic human rights to freedom of thought, opinion, and political association). Then came the rub: "In light of all these arguments, when faced with this law, those who do not share the ideology of the Sandinista party can adopt a position of conscientious objection" (p. 7).

Consequently, in light of the fact that the Sandinistas could "take advantage of military discipline in order to ideologically 'manipulate' people and forcibly subject them to a determined ideology" (p. 7), the bishops were counseling the faithful to become conscientious objectors. While this advice pleased conservatives in Nicaragua (and in Washington, where the war was being fueled by President Reagan describing the contras as the "moral equivalent of the Founding Fathers" of the United States), it was poorly received by many Nicaraguans. Not only had they received little consolation from their prelates on the death of their children (indeed there had been isolated cases of priests refusing to give communion to military draftees), but now they were being explicitly counseled by their spiritual advisers to resist the draft. At a time when the contra war was negatively affecting all Nicaraguans (many of whom saw it as their duty to defend their country from the U.S.-funded forces), this action by the bishops was exceptionally controversial and ill-timed. Members of the "Church of the poor" were disturbed by this position of the Nicaraguan Episcopal Conference, so different from that taken by the U.S. Episcopal Conference, which openly criticized the Reagan policy of military aggression and supported the Contadora initiative. For many Catholics this chasm between two sister organizations—of U.S. and Nicaraguan bishops—was quite incomprehensible.

The pastoral appeared to be encouraging desertion in the face of increased military aggression from the contras; moreover, it underscored even more dramatically the role of the institutional Church—and Archbishop Obando y Bravo in particular—as the prime opposition to the revolutionary government. This attempt to delegitimize the government while damaging seriously the national defense was not, however, universally supported by all members of the hierarchy. For example, Bishop Carlos Santi (Matagalpa) claimed not to be aware of the document when it was published; his view was that it was the duty of Christians to defend their nation. Bishops Schlaefer (Bluefields) and López Ardón (Estelí) were also displeased with the communiqué. More outspoken was the Jesuit Juan Ramón Moreno, president of CONFER, who claimed the bishops were confusing "conscientious objection" with "political objection." He summarized his arguments in support of the military draft by noting: "One can be in disagreement—on a political level—with a government; yet, when external aggression is threatening, true patriots will defend their nation."[26] The controversy over military service remained a divisive issue for the duration of the contra war.

In the period following the publication of this pastoral on April 22, 1984, the situation in Nicaragua went from bad to worse. After three years of economic growth, spiraling inflation had taken a firm grip—as could be seen from a trip to Managua's "Mercado Oriental," where few could afford to buy. The lack of external funding from multilateral lending agencies only made matters worse; in 1983 Nicaragua depended on fully 35 percent of its exports merely to service the foreign debt.[27] Aid from Western Europe (which between 1979 and 1981 had amounted to 32.5 percent of total donations to Nicaragua) began to diminish noticeably—largely due to differences of opinion within Socialist International over the "radical nature" of the revolutionary government and to the election of the Kohl government in late 1982. In Washington, Congress had approved an additional $24 million for the contras in December 1983. In addition, after a power struggle between the State Department and hard-liners in the White House, the largest military exercises in Central American history (involving several thousand U.S. military personnel) took place—Big Pine II—and plans were made secretly to overturn diplomatically the Contadora peace initiative. In 1983 alone more than a thousand Nicaraguans were killed by Ronald Reagan's "freedom fighters," and there was no end in sight to the contra war. (In all some 1,700 Nicaraguans had been killed in the preceding eighteen months. To put these casualties in a perspective based on a percentage of total population, this would be the equivalent of some 136,000 U.S. citizens being killed—or almost three times the total number of Americans killed in the Vietnam War.)

Such was the general context in which the bishops released their Easter pastoral (April 22, 1984), one that proved even more controversial than the hotly debated document of the previous August. For some, this pastoral's call for reconciliation represented a commonsense approach to a military and political problem that seemed interminable, despite claims by the FSLN that the war against the contras was being won; for others, it was proof that the hierarchy was acting as Washington's "fifth column," seeking to defeat the revolutionary process from within while betraying the memory of the tens of thousands killed in the fight against Somoza and in the contra war. The Easter pastoral, then, stands as a landmark in the steadily plummeting relationship between the institutional Church and the government and in the increasingly polarized Church community.

A careful reading of the document reveals that nothing dramatically new was being said by the bishops, since many of their direct criticisms of the revolutionary process and of those Catholics supporting the "Church of the poor" had already been voiced on several occasions.

Indeed, in this document they put forward simplistic explanations for society's ills, claiming, for example, that sin persisted in the world because of the secularization of society ("Society . . . is losing its orientation toward God and is not taking the Church into consideration")[28] and religious diversionism ("Sometimes people claim to accept Christ and Church doctrine, yet at the same time they reject the Church—and thus fall into the temptation of building other 'Churches' that are simply not based on the essential teachings of the apostles and their successors, the legitimate bishops" [p. 10]). The bishops also condemned the effect of historical materialism, which deprives humans of all spiritual values.[29] They were obviously seeking to delegitimize opponents both within the government and within the Church, but their argument was more facile than insightful.

Similarly superficial were the bishops' observations on the "war situation" in Nicaragua, which they supplemented with their traditional criticisms of the Sandinistas ("Materialist and atheistic education is undermining the conscience of children and youth alike"; "Some media, using a language of hate, are favoring the spirit of violence" [p. 11]). Even their second swipe at that sector of the Church that criticized their political ideology[30] contained nothing new. Also familiar were their veiled references to "foreign powers" (the Soviet Union and Cuba, apparently) taking advantage of the Nicaraguan situation in order to "foment both economic and ideological exploitation" (p. 11). What the bishops were offering, then, was a rehashed blend of old criticisms and observations delivered in the same acerbic tone.

So why did this particular pastoral letter cause such a political explosion in Nicaragua? First, the bishops claimed that the violence in Nicaragua was largely due to internal dissatisfaction, not to U.S. funding of the contras ("It is dishonest to always justify internal aggression and violence on aggression that comes from outside" [p. 12]). Given the incontrovertible evidence of tens of millions of dollars flowing into Nicaragua (the increase in "covert" aid being paralleled by an increase in the number of deaths), and the fact that the CIA had been implicated in the mining of Nicaragua's harbors in March–April 1984, this argument was spurious at best. Moreover, the bishops' determination that an unconditional dialogue with the contras was necessary in order to resolve the crisis in Nicaragua also angered the Sandinistas, since it conferred on the contras a legitimacy (in moral and military terms) that the government—and many Nicaraguans—felt they did not deserve. (It should be remembered that in December 1983 the revolutionary government had issued a fairly generous amnesty law for all but the contra leadership and felt that this was a sufficiently magnanimous concession to the rebels.) In light of these developments, both suggestions were akin to holding the proverbial red flag before the furious bull, and reaction was not slow in coming. For Interior Minister Tomás Borge, for instance, its publication was a "criminal" act. Daniel Ortega mused that the document had probably been written at the U.S. embassy, and he referred to the bishops as "anti-Christians," "dishonest," and "immoral."[31]

The basis of the criticisms that rained down on the bishops was that, far from acting in a purely pastoral or spiritual vein, they were once again meddling in politics—and again seeking to cast aspersions on the legitimacy of the revolutionary government while distorting the reality of what was happening in the country. At the very least the document was insensitive: it made no mention of the recent mining of Nicaragua's major port but claimed that "materialist and atheistic education *is mining* the conscience of our youth" (p. 11; italics added). In addition, one could ask why the Church leadership emphasized the need for reconciliation on a political level while it spurned the same concept on an ecclesial one, consistently rejecting calls for dialogue from those supporting a more progressive interpretation of the Church's mission.

The most stinging aspect of the pastoral letter, however, was its claim that the war in Nicaragua stemmed from internal dissent, not external aggression and manipulation. The contra war was thus painted as a "war between Nicaraguans," despite abundant evidence to the contrary. This idea that the conflict was in effect a civil war implied that there were two opposing sides with legitimate value systems and military capacity— concepts that were vehemently rejected by the Sandinistas, who countered that the "mercenaries" had never held a single town in Nicaragua for a single day. Moreover, they claimed, this was an artificial war, one kept alive solely by massive infusions of military aid from Washington; if this aid were stopped, peace would rapidly return to Nicaragua.

From the government's perspective, the proposals put forward by the Church hierarchy were both politically unacceptable and morally repugnant. Any doubts the leadership might have harbored concerning the bishops' political intentions disappeared as a result of the legitimacy that the hierarchy sought to confer on the contras. Moreover, government leaders must have been aware of the similarities between the bishops' call for dialogue with the contras and that issued in December 1983 by the Coordinadora Democrática Nicaragüense (the largest internal political opposition group to the Sandinistas), which demanded such dialogue as a prerequisite for CDN's participation in the 1984 elections. (In addition, it coincided with remarkably similar requests from COSEP, the public report of the Kissinger Commission, and, of course, the Reagan administration.) In a communiqué issued almost a year later, on March 22, 1985, the bishops developed their position, offering to act as "mediator" in an "internal dialogue"—a position eagerly accepted by the contras, who viewed the bishops as their allies against the government (in somewhat the same way as the Sandinistas had sought Archbishop Obando y Bravo's intercession and mediation during prerevolutionary times, in incidents such as the hostage-taking at Chema Castillo's and the National Palace takeover).

The Easter pastoral, then, while not being particularly novel in its criticisms of the Sandinistas, nevertheless infuriated many people in Nicaragua. With its publication, religious and political tension increased quite dramatically—perhaps almost to the degree experienced in the aftermath of the pope's visit. This pastoral did not augur well for a constructive relationship between the FSLN and the Church hierarchy and made no effort to promote dialogue and reconciliation within Church circles—where both concepts were badly needed. One foreign theologian commented insightfully on the position taken by the bishops: "Without this biblical base, what the bishops are offering is not a message to unite and reconcile, but rather a firm denunciation of one particular side. . . . The final result is the use of theological language and the prestige of the bishops' position to support a particular ideological position."[32] Once again, ideological concerns held sway over religious concerns.

An issue about which a pastoral letter was expected—but never came—involved the elections of November 1984. Individual Church leaders such as Obando y Bravo and Vega (at that time president of the Episcopal Conference) did express their fundamental opposition to the electoral process at that time, indicating that the conditions for an election were inappropriate. Their observations, as well as the general guidelines provided for Catholics, were almost identical to those made in 1974 when Somoza was preparing for reelection,[33] reflecting their belief that the elections were, as in Somoza's time, not a fair and adequate reflection of the opinions of the electorate. Moreover, their skepticism regarding the electoral process closely resembled that of the Reagan administration (which was funding the domestic political opposition as well as the contras) and the same civilian opposition (the CDN), which eventually pulled out of the elections. For the revolutionary government, this close parallel could only have confirmed their worst fears about collusion between the Catholic hierarchy and the anti-Sandinista opposition both at home and abroad.

Although the bishops as a group did not publish a pastoral letter regarding the elections, Bishop Vega made his feelings on the issue known. Just ten days before the elections, he published "An Invitation to Christian Reflection." Perhaps dismayed at the lack of solidarity among his fellow bishops over the election issue, he took the opportunity to cast serious doubts on the Sandinista model: "After five years of euphoric illusions, revolutionary myths and sorrowful detours, Nicaragua is a living lesson for the whole continent. It has once again been proven that ideological dogmatism and materialist schemes do not meet basic human needs. They are mechanisms of domination, clans that ignore the fundamental rights of every person. They see human beings as nothing more than 'instruments of labor' and one more soldier for their goal of world domination."[34] Clearly, the president of the Episcopal Conference held a somewhat jaundiced view of the Sandinistas' reform program and was not in favor of their reelection.

The Role of Archbishop Obando y Bravo

Perhaps no religious figure (and certainly no political opposition figure) carried as much influence in Nicaragua during this period as Archbishop Obando y Bravo. His credibility had been established through his opposition to Somoza during the final years of the dictatorship, and since then his importance had grown with each round of the unending debate over religious-political matters. By the early 1980s he became the de facto political opposition to the revolutionary government, the perpetual thorn in the side of the Sandinistas, as he sought to impose his own beliefs (carefully veiled as "pastoral" and "spiritual" concerns) on the national agenda.

While the archbishop was undoubtedly sincere in his belief that he was protecting the spiritual interests of his flock, there can be no doubt that his role was also of exceptional political importance. Nor can there be any doubt about his innate conservatism, unbending will, and tenacious determination to oppose the Sandinista government over anything remotely tainted by what he broadly termed "materialism." While he is not a brilliant scholar nor an exceptional administrator, Obando y Bravo is a ferocious and determined fighter, extremely consistent in his conservative ideology and ruthlessly determined to have his own voice heard as that of *the* Church. Indeed, as the leading churchman in Central America—as well as the leading Church figure in Nicaragua for more than two decades—Miguel Obando y Bravo feels that it is his primary duty to speak for the Church. Writing in May 1989, the late Penny Lernoux described him well: "While Cardinal Obando was not everyone's ideal of the 'good pastor'—being autocratic, vain, and hot-tempered—there could be no doubt that the prelate had the courage of his convictions."[35] The ability to dialogue, to listen to opposing arguments, is clearly not his strong suit: rather, he believes in the necessity of authority, as well as in freedom of opinion—but only within parameters laid out by himself, as the supreme authority for the regional Church. All of this was apparent to anyone who had studied carefully the generally conservative positions taken by Obando y Bravo in the last decade of Somoza rule; either the Sandinistas were exceedingly naive in expecting him to change his weltanschauung when they came to power, or else they believed that he could be co-opted by them. In any event, as history has shown, they consistently underestimated his influence, his bent for authoritarianism, and his tenacity.

Just days after the furor over the Easter pastoral, Obando y Bravo was summoned to Rome for a lengthy meeting with the pope. Perhaps just as important, however, was a meeting he had in New York on the way back from Rome with John J. Meehan, an aide to W. R. Grace. The significance of the meeting is twofold: first, Grace is an extremely conservative—and influential—businessman whose corporation (W.R. Grace Company) was named by ex-CIA agent Phillip Agee as a front for the agency; and second, the archbishop met with Meehan to solicit funds for the archdiocese to be used in activities opposing the Sandinista government. While initially the archbishop denied that he had solicited aid from the Grace corporation, an eight-and-a-half page memorandum of the ninety-minute meeting (drawn up by John Meehan) indicates otherwise.

According to Meehan, the archbishop considered the Sandinista regime to be "far more brutal and repressive than the supporters of

Somoza," and he contended that Obando y Bravo doubted that there would be free elections in the immediate future (as noted above, these took place in November of that year).[36] The archbishop seemed convinced that there was a deliberate plan afoot by the Sandinistas to destroy the Church through the use of liberation theology, and he had devised a project to counter these efforts. Accordingly he was soliciting from the Grace corporation sufficient funding to support his Christian leadership courses, which Meehan described as "the best organized opposition in Nicaragua to the attempts of the present government to transform the country into a Marxist-Leninist society" (p. 19).

Meehan's memorandum noted that Obando y Bravo had dedicated "all his resources and skills in order to develop leaders who can oppose the Sandinistas" and, while he was not supporting any particular party or individual, he was determined to "protect the Catholic faith of his people against communism" (p. 19). The archbishop was convinced that liberation theology had to be stopped at all costs (because it challenged Catholic orthodoxy) and that the Sandinista regime was hurtling headlong on a path of godless atheism. His appeal to the Grace corporation, therefore, was for immediate funding to prevent either of these possibilities from being realized, since in the Nicaraguan context "the true Church constituted the best opportunity to stop the Sandinista advance toward Marxism-Leninism" (p. 19). Thus this extraordinary document revealed the archbishop's fears—and his determination to continue spearheading the domestic political opposition to the Sandinistas.

When viewed in this light, the archbishop's role in many of the crucially important developments outlined in this chapter becomes quite clear. His opposition to the revolutionary process was abundantly manifest and quite consistent. Thus, whether he be defending the right to conscientious objection in the face of military conscription (despite the murder of nearly two thousand Nicaraguans by contra forces), referring to the "civil war" in Nicaragua and urging dialogue with the contras, refusing to condemn U.S. military aid to the contras, or lambasting the Sandinistas for their human rights record, Archbishop Obando y Bravo was engaging in a domestic political struggle against the government. Moreover, his refusal to condemn contra raids (even when Catholic lay leaders such as the Delegates of the Word were killed) or the mining of Corinto harbor stood in stark contrast to his condemnation (in a June 1984 homily) of the assassination attempt on

ARDE leader Edén Pastora. One wonders how he reacted later when the contra leader himself reached the conclusion that, due to Pastora's refusal to work with former Somocistas in the FDN contra group, the probable author of the crime was the CIA itself, not the Sandinistas.

The key to understanding this political role of the archbishop lies in his preconciliar formation (in conservative Church settings, especially in Guatemala and El Salvador). When the sweeping reforms of Vatican II were approved in the mid-1960s, Obando y Bravo was already forty years old and not known for his openness to change. Fearing a communist takeover in Nicaragua and extremely suspicious both of Sandinista intentions in general and of some of the *comandantes* in particular, he had decided that the only way to save his country from the onslaught of atheistic Marxism was through a tacit alliance with other opponents of the revolutionary government. Hence the converging interests of the archbishop, the Vatican, the contras, the limited civilian opposition within the country, and Washington.

The development of a Church sector that opposed his authoritarian and solidly orthodox approach (as well as his extremely conservative politics) was also seen as a major threat, one that—as we have seen—had to be silenced if the institutional Church was to survive. Humberto Belli, the archbishop's friend and associate, surely echoes Obando y Bravo's view when he states that "there are many liberation theologies which are not liberating at all."[37] But in seeking to prevent such "repression," the archbishop implemented an authoritarian structure that goes directly against the flow of Vatican II and Medellín—one that discounts the concept of "horizontal" communication and that would brook no dissent. As Spanish theologian Benjamín Forcano noted in January 1983, "It is a pity and a source of sadness that here Msgr. Obando, rooted in a pre–Vatican II model of the Church, should glory in a form of absolutism which nowadays is inconceivable in Europe."[38]

It would seem, however, that this was precisely the style of prelate that John Paul II wanted for the modern Church, particularly in a society that he—like Obando y Bravo—viewed as being under the threat of Marxism-Leninism. Perhaps seeing in the embattled Nicaraguan a reflection of his earlier struggle for orthodoxy (also in the face of a perceived Marxist enemy) in his native Poland, the pope selected Obando y Bravo to become the only cardinal in Central America. The appointment, which was controversial in itself (given the existence of perhaps better qualified and more experienced prelates in the area, such as bishops Marcos McGrath in Panama and Arturo Rivera y Damas in El Salvador), became even more so in the wake of Obando y Bravo's return from the ceremony at the Vatican. Then, as has so often happened in Nicaragua, the politicization of religion (or the sacrilization of politics) took over.

Initially, the news of the archbishop's appointment to cardinal was received quite civilly. Personal congratulations were extended by Daniel Ortega on the day the appointment was announced (and Vice President Sergio Ramírez saw the archbishop off at the airport as he headed to Rome. The actual investiture (on May 25, 1985) was broadcast on Nicaraguan television, and Obando y Bravo attended a reception in his honor at the Nicaraguan embassy to the Vatican. On the way back to Managua, however, the new cardinal stopped in Miami to celebrate mass (on June 13) for the Nicaraguan community in exile. Among those present were some well-known Somocistas, as well as FDN leader Adolfo Calero and ARDE's Edén Pastora, who sat together behind the podium. So, before returning to his native Nicaragua to celebrate mass there, the cardinal took a detour to the country that was providing military aid to the counterrevolutionary forces and said mass before exiles and contra leaders. The political symbolism of this act could hardly have been lost on the Sandinistas back in Managua.

The return to the capital itself similarly went beyond a strictly religious ceremony. The contra radio station ("15 de Septiembre") urged all opponents of the Sandinistas to welcome Obando y Bravo back to Managua and to show their displeasure with the government by carrying the white and yellow Vatican flag (instead of the blue and white flag of Nicaragua or the Sandinistas' red and black banner). Tens of thousands of Nicaraguans welcomed the cardinal home the night of June 14. The following morning the cardinal said his first mass on Nicaraguan soil, which was attended by some thirty thousand faithful and concelebrated by sixty priests and five Nicaraguan bishops (four others were absent). Of significance was the fact that no bishop from Costa Rica or El Salvador and no representative of CELAM participated, nor was the apostolic nuncio present. In the mass itself, the text chosen was Apocalypse 12:7ff., which depicts the struggle of Michael against the red dragon; not surprisingly, many observers read into this the struggle of Miguel Obando y Bravo against the revolutionary government.[39]

If these events were not replete enough with political symbolism and none-too-subtle political messages, the speech of greeting to the new cardinal by Bishop Vega left no doubts about the path the Church would continue to follow. After emphasizing the need for Church unity (which, Vega took great pains to show, had to be based on the bishops' authority), he condemned "ideological discrimination" and then, in an unusual aside, concluded that things in Nicaragua had scarcely changed in nearly five centuries: "Ever since the period so long ago (and yet apparently not over yet) of the conquest, those who sought domination—and not the evangelization—of our people were opposed by the valiant missionaries and theologians who defended the social and human worth of our native people. . . . It would appear that we haven't progressed much since then."[40] The institutional Church in Nicaragua, now blessed with the approval of the Vatican, would feel invigorated as it sallied forth to do battle with the atheistic hordes.

Religious Intolerance Continues

Several other noteworthy incidents helped keep the religious question near the top of Nicaragua's national political agenda. For the most part, these were acts of harassment carried out by government supporters in a desperate response to the Church leadership's increasingly strident opposition to the revolutionary process. While this is, of course, no defense for such acts of bullying and intimidation, one can understand the degree of pent-up frustration felt by Sandinista supporters at the apparent collusion among the Church hierarchy, Washington, and the contras. By claiming that they were apolitical, concerned only with spiritual and pastoral matters, the prelates only compounded the problem.

One of the most vocal critics of the Sandinistas was Humberto Belli, who has documented in some detail the nature of the harassment exercised by Sandinista supporters against the institutional Church. For instance, on Sunday, October 30, 1983—just a month after military conscription was introduced (and two months after the bishops' communiqué on the military service law)—twenty-six churches were stormed by pro-Sandinista elements, who broke windows and doors. The auxiliary bishop of Managua, Bosco Vivas, apparently received death threats. Meanwhile bishops Pedro Vílchez and Pablo Vega denounced the abuse of human rights by elements of the armed forces, with the latter condemning local Sandinista militias of murder.[41]

While Msgr. Vega would condemn (and rightfully so) these flagrant abuses of human rights, his silence concerning the murder of the many Delegates of the Word and the thousands of Nicaraguan campesinos by the contras was quite deafening. In contrast, the Catholic Institute for International Relations in London sought to provide some badly needed perspective in its lengthy analysis of the human rights situation, noting how contra attacks had consistently targeted Catholic activists known to be supportive of the revolutionary process. Their report examines the case of the well-known Catholic lay leaders Felipe and María Barreda (killed after being tortured by the contras in early 1983) and concludes that "hundreds of lesser known Catholic activists have been killed by the contras since 1982."[42] Significantly, this is not referred to in Belli's book, nor does the name "Barreda" (despite its prominence in Catholic circles) even appear in the index. (It should be pointed out that Bishop López Ardón of Estelí *did* condemn the senseless murder of the Barredas.) Selective indignation, whatever its ideological stripe, is morally contemptible—and it is shameful that priests and religious (as well as lay observers) on both sides of the political divide were guilty of it.

One event that aggravated an already troubled situation was the arrest of Father Amado Peña in June 1984 for alleged trafficking in arms and explosives. Evidence was presented in the form of a videotape that showed Peña passing a bag containing hand grenades, explosives, and a contra flag to an accomplice; part of the same tape showed Peña talking earlier in the day with Pedro Espinoza, a contra member based in Managua, about subversive activities. Interior Minister Tomás Borge asked Archbishop Obando y Bravo to urge Peña to seek asylum at the Vatican nunciature in order to avoid arrest and thus lessen the political tension that would of necessity result. Both Peña and the archbishop maintained that the incident was an attempt to entrap the priest and discredit the Church, and so they refused to cooperate with the government. (Indeed, the archbishop noted, even before seeing the videotape, that the Church absolved Peña, who was seen as an innocent victim of government harassment.)[43] The videotape was then shown on national television, fanning the flames of discord between the revolutionary government and the Church hierarchy. Peña returned to his parish the next day but protests there by government supporters forced him to take refuge in a seminary, where he remained for almost a year.

Whether Peña (a close personal friend of the archbishop) was innocent or had in fact been involved in contra activities has never been definitively determined. Certainly his antigovernment opinions were well known to the Nicaraguan Church leadership, and the voice and image of Peña on the tape seem real. (The Church hierarchy steadfastly maintained that the whole incident was a setup and that various pieces of film had been spliced together—yet the archbishop refused the government's invitation to submit the tape to the scrutiny of experts to determine its authenticity.) Moreover, it is important to note that the government (cognizant of its own bungling of the earlier "naked priest" affair involving Bismarck Carballo) had first taken a rather low-key approach to the problem: in return for the hierarchy disapproving Peña's activities and removing him from the parish, the government would treat the episode as an isolated case and expedite the matter accordingly.

The next round in this ongoing power struggle took place on July 9, when a march—organized by Archbishop Obando y Bravo and thirty priests in solidarity with Father Peña—took place in Managua. The demonstration was clearly illegal (the state of emergency legislation banned all public demonstrations without official authorization), and Ministry of the Interior representatives officially requested the arch-bishop to cancel the march (which was billed on the Voice of America network as "the first anti-Sandinista demonstration in five years").[44] Some three hundred people participated in the mass, with Peña himself a concelebrant, which was clearly intended as a political gesture of defiance against the government.

This widely publicized march demonstrates once again the tit-for-tat policy that has characterized Church-state relations in revolutionary Nicaragua. Moreover, just as Obando y Bravo had defied the law and the Sandinistas by organizing a demonstration of solidarity with his longtime colleague Peña, so too did the revolutionary government now react against the archbishop and his followers. The government was frustrated at the archbishop's continued obstinate challenge to its authority and resorted to drastic strong-arm measures. Accordingly, ten foreign priests (only four of whom had actually participated in the march) immediately had their residence permits withdrawn by the government, in effect forcing them to leave the country.[45]

This was not the first time that the Sandinistas had used this recourse. In May 1983, for instance, the Spanish priest Timoteo Merino was expelled after being charged with supporting the ARDE contra forces in the south of Nicaragua. In October of that year, another Spanish priest (Luis Corral Prieto) and a Costa Rican (José María Pacheco)—director and subdirector, respectively, of the Salesian College in Masaya—faced a similar fate. Both had been accused of organizing opposition to the military conscription law and, despite warnings to their provincial superior, had continued in these endeavors, which led to their ultimate expulsion.

On the other end of the political spectrum was the dénouement of one of the long-standing controversies in the institutional Church, the role of the Jesuit priest (and Minister of Education) Fernando Cardenal. Earlier chapters referred to the attempts by the Church hierarchy to oblige the priests serving in the cabinet to leave their official government roles. Among those who had adamantly refused to do so, pleading conscientious objection to the request, was Cardenal. On December 10, 1984, the Jesuit headquarters in Rome announced that Cardenal (a Jesuit for thirty-two years) had been released from the order because of his refusal to leave his political post. In effect the Vatican and Archbishop Obando y Bravo had won the day, pressuring the Jesuits to expel him.

Cardenal responded with an impassioned and thoughtful "Letter to My Friends," in which he outlined the development of this saga and explained his conscientious objection to the idea of leaving his post in the Ministry of Education ("Sincerely, and before God, I believe that it would be committing a grave sin if—in the present circumstances—I were to abandon my priestly option for the poor, which revolves concretely around my work for the Sandinista revolution").[46] He noted that he had written on six occasions to the bishops, requesting an interview with them to explain his position and seek a dialogue about the matter, but none of his petitions had even been answered. For Cardenal, the issue of his expulsion from the Jesuits was nothing less than crude political pressure by the Nicaraguan bishops and by the Vatican:

> Some bishops in Nicaragua have a political agenda that both in the past and in the present is in direct opposition to the interests of the poor masses of the Nicaraguan population. . . . Here in Nicaragua there is no need for any serious religious problem between the Church and the revolution. There is no dogma of Christian faith at stake, no Catholic doctrine or hypothesis on Christian morals.

What exists here is a political confrontation. The bishops have shown themselves to be publicly united with those who attack the revolution, those who want to see the destruction of this government so that they can return to the past. (p. 16)

The Cardenal affair, then, ended in victory for the forces of reaction and orthodoxy—in much the same way that the virtual deportation of the priests following the Peña incident also represented crude political pressure against dissent. Common to both these events was an implicit insistence that opponents toe the official line and use their religious vocation as a means of legitimizing (in a blatantly political fashion) the status quo imposed from above. In this matter the respective "hierarchies" of the Church and of the FSLN were similarly dogmatic and repressive.

The harsh treatment meted out to Fernando Cardenal, together with the equally shameful expulsion of the ten foreign priests (four Spaniards, two Costa Ricans, two Italians, a Canadian, and a Panamanian) in July 1984, the furor surrounding Bishop Schlaefer's flight to Honduras in December 1983 (when it was uncertain whether he was forced by contras to accompany Miskitos being ordered to relocate to Honduras or did so willingly), official pastoral documents on highly charged political matters, and repeatedly unbalanced media coverage— all helped to fuel the fires of religious intolerance at this time. A spiral of rising retaliation—the result of frustration, insecurity, and fear, accompanied by a determination on both sides that "their" position was the only correct one—was the order of the day, no matter what the price was or who got in the way.

In the end, in a fit of anger and desperation the Sandinistas expelled priests, as did the clique of bishops who ran the Church in Nicaragua (London's Catholic Institute for International Relations estimated in 1987 that at least forty religious had been forced to leave Nicaragua because of pressure from Cardinal Obando y Bravo).[47] Elements of the revolutionary government harassed leaders of the institutional Church both for their lack of patriotism and because they adamantly rejected the model offered by the Sandinistas. For its part, the hierarchy sought at every turn to delegitimize the government (despite its significant popular support) and to return to a system that would subvert the major socioeconomic gains of the poor majority in Nicaraguan society. It was all overtly and undeniably political (despite claims to the contrary from

Church representatives in both camps), all clearly painful—and in the end, the only losers from the incessant wrangling and mutual recriminations were the majority of ordinary Nicaraguans, who for the most part were faithful (albeit confused) Catholics who supported the revolutionary process and simply wanted to be left alone.

Further Polarization

Visitors to Nicaragua at this time could not help but be struck by the invasion of the religious question into the realm of popular mythology. Billboards proclaiming "The FSLN is immortal" and "Sandino yesterday, Sandino today, Sandino forever" contrasted with bumper stickers that stated "Christ yesterday, Christ today, Christ forever." Pictures of John Paul II were posted by conservative Catholics, while those of the martyred Archbishop Oscar Romero and guerrilla-priest Gaspar García Laviana hung in the homes of revolutionary Christians (the none-too-subtle image being strengthened by slogans such as "We want bishops like Msgr. Romero"). The Vatican colors (yellow and white) vied with those of the Sandinistas (black and red). Television programs on the Sandinista network extolled the virtues of the "heroes and martyrs" and of the "revolutionary saints," while the contra forces consistently published photographs of Obando y Bravo and John Paul II in their own propaganda, often accompanied by slogans such as "The Pope is with us," "With God and patriotism we shall defeat communism," and "Christ is the liberator." Auxiliary Bishop Bosco Vivas referred critically to the religious *base communities* (which were generally extremely supportive of the Sandinistas): "They're all arms of the government—another way to mobilize the youth and women into service for the state. . . . Who knows what they do in these *comunidades*? Consecrate *tortillas* or Coca-Cola?"[48] For his part, Jesuit priest Agustín Toranzo noted that "the pope—and the Nicaraguan bishops—are committing sin by not condemning the contras."[49] Quite obviously, there was little middle ground—and very little hope of effecting any meaningful compromise.

One incident illustrates just how deeply entrenched the positions had become and how ideological considerations had basically swamped common sense and perhaps the essence of Christianity itself. In November 1984, Professor Max Azicri of Edinboro University in Pennsylvania interviewed Bishop Pablo Vega, then president of the

Nicaraguan Episcopal Conference. During the course of their meeting, Azicri raised the issue of contra attacks and referred specifically to the case of six young children from the Segovias who had been killed in a recent contra raid. Bishop Vega replied that "all forms of imperialism are evil—economic imperialism through a regime that imposes its will by force, and also ideological imperialism." He went on to note that the Soviet Union and Cuba should—like Washington—cut off their aid to Nicaragua. When pressed about the massacre of the children of Nueva Segovia, the bishop replied: "Killing the soul is worse than killing the body, according to the Lord's words, and here we have an ideology that is based on the concept that the other side is my enemy. Consequently, a bomb that is implanted in the soul is more serious."[50] Thus, while refusing to condemn those responsible for this act of terrorism, he also claimed that it was—for Catholics—a less offensive crime than Cuban aid.

The significance of Vega's response resides in the degree to which, consciously or not, the bishop had become a victim of the desensitization commonly found in war situations. Emotions had been running high for so many years without any end in sight, and the bishop's exasperation is reflected in his senseless remarks. (From the other side of the political divide, Father Miguel D'Escoto's remarks that Cardinal Obando y Bravo was "an accomplice in the assassination of our people . . . a traitor"[51] show that frustration and rhetoric were not restricted to the right wing.) These remarks illustrate well the tone of confrontation and mutual recrimination that so dominated all of Nicaragua in this period and have produced such a legacy of hatred and distrust on both sides of the ideological divide.

Historians may point to scattered and at best symbolic signs that during this period the seeds of dialogue were sown. The bishops, for instance, did not release a joint pastoral letter on the November 1984 elections—when it was a poorly kept secret that some of their number badly wanted to delegitimize the Sandinistas and the election process itself. Their collective silence before and after the election, aside from the brief and neutral guidelines they issued beforehand, was a useful contribution to a rather tense moment—particularly when the opposition coalition pulled out just a few weeks before the voting. Similarly, in December 1984, nearly two years after the pope's visit to Nicaragua, the renewal of official bilateral talks between the government and the

Church hierarchy was a welcome development. An important gesture on the part of the Church hierarchy can be seen in the presence of Bishop Vega at the January 1985 swearing-in ceremony of President Daniel Ortega, at which time the prelate gave the official invocation. Finally, one can cite the presence of Daniel Ortega at the ceremony consecrating Pablo Schmitz as auxiliary bishop of the vicariate of Bluefields in late 1984—to which Ortega had been invited by Bishop Schmitz himself.

These were all positive signs, but nevertheless they should be seen for what they were: symbolic gestures with little real meaning or impact behind them. Perhaps they can also be interpreted as subconscious acts of desperation, as both sides realized that things were getting out of hand and that some degree of pragmatism (however superficial it may be) was desperately needed. Moreover, while they may have augured well for the potential reestablishment of something vaguely resembling decent and civilized levels of dialogue, their promise was short-lived. In the Nicaraguan context at this time, for every gesture of hope there were inevitably ten of despair. The Vatican had clearly not lost sight of what had happened during the pope's brief visit in 1983 or of the continuing problems afforded by both the "Marxist" government of Nicaragua and its ally, the "Church of the poor." For John Paul II, formed in the orthodox conservative world of embattled Catholicism in communist Poland, an appropriate gesture to strengthen the Church was the appointment of Obando y Bravo as Cardinal. In doing so the pontiff initiated yet another round of tension and hostility.

Obando's first mass as cardinal for Central America before Nicaraguan exiles was clearly a political statement and perhaps may be interpreted as an act of provocation. Being photographed with contra leaders such as Adolfo Calero and Edén Pastora and making statements like "I do not object to being identified with the people who have taken up arms"[52] may well have been acceptable in the Vatican (as it certainly was in Washington), but for many back in Nicaragua these were entirely insensitive and thoughtless acts. During these years, however, when government and Church leaders were not known for their sensitivity and thoughtfulness toward their major opponents, the cardinal's first mass was a fitting epitaph to a period of polarization, recrimination, and immense frustration. So much had happened in these three short years, so many problems loomed on the horizon for the nation as a whole, that only an incurable optimist could have looked on the future of Nicaragua with anything resembling hope. The ecclesial promotion of Obando y Bravo, like the visit of John Paul II, was thus perceived as a double-edged sword. While both events represented an honor for the country, they could also be seen as an incitement for yet another round of provocation and mutual hostility. The nation thus held its collective breath and waited to see where the ecclesial chips would fall.

✝

6   IN SEARCH OF RECONCILIATION?

Church-State Relations, 1985–1990

> It is our judgment that all
> forms of aid, wherever they
> come from, that lead to
> destruction, suffering, and
> death in our families or to hate
> and division among
> Nicaraguans are to be
> condemned.
>
> Nicaraguan Episcopal
> Conference, April 1986

> We ask ourselves whether the
> Church hierarchy and the
> accompanying ecclesial
> institution, of which we are a
> part, in today's Nicaragua
> appear to be serving the poor
> majority of our fellow
> countrymen who opted for
> the revolutionary process, or
> instead are serving the
> minority who had lost their
> situation of privilege.
>
> Nicaraguan priests, religious,
> and lay people in response to
> the 1986 pastoral

THE TWO EPIGRAPHS FROM 1986—an important year in a period of low-key pursuit of what could be termed a tactical détente—hint at the potential for a truce in Church-state relations. They also, however, illustrate the wide breach that still remained between the two wings of the Church itself, as each continued to pursue a radically different agenda.

In many ways the first statement is far more remarkable than the second (which basically reiterates the traditional position of the grass-roots Church). At first glance the bishops' observation seems quite unnoteworthy, full of common sense and pragmatism. But its significance lies in the fact that in the four years since the contra war had started, this was the first time that the bishops' conference had publicly condemned military aid from *both* sides of the ideological divide. In the past, Church leaders had focused on condemning the Soviet incursions (especially in regard to "atheistic" and "materialistic" education as well as military aid) and had never been critical of the tens of millions of dollars pouring in from the United States. (Indeed, several bishops—including Cardinal Obando y Bravo himself—had lent their prestige in an overtly political fashion to the various campaigns of President Reagan to secure congressional funding for the contras.) Now, however, they were making what was for them a major shift in position by extending criticism to both superpowers. Moreover, this statement marked the beginning of a warming trend in the hierarchy's dealings with the revolutionary government, one that continued until the end of the Ortega presidency in early 1990. Thus, despite some ongoing and deeply rooted problems, during this period significant symbolic concessions were made by government and Church leaders alike, the rhetoric on both sides was toned down, and a form of pragmatic détente began to emerge in the late 1980s—a development that in 1985 would have seemed most unlikely.

Yet while a modus vivendi was gradually worked out between the Church leadership and the government during the last half of the 1980s, the same cannot be said for the opposing factions within the Church itself. The response to the pastoral letter by representatives of the "Church of the poor," for example, is illustrative on various levels. First, it shows the depth of feeling elicited by the hierarchy's call for "reconciliation" (i.e., negotiation with the contras) as well as the gaping chasm of distrust and frustration that still existed between Church factions. Moreover, as this chapter will show, the response of the grass-roots Church also rejects the idea of the contras and the duly elected government of Nicaragua as equal negotiating partners. Finally, it underscores the firmly held view that the Church hierarchy was prostituting its role as the defender of the interests of Nicaragua's masses as it rushed to support what was seen as the "preferential option for the rich." From the hierarchy's perspective—as revealed in several official communiqués and pastoral letters—the grass-roots Church remained in open rebellion, rejecting the constitutional authority of its religious superiors and threatening to destroy the essential Church unity. In short, the winds of change had failed to reach the Church itself.

The period 1985–90 is undoubtedly the most complex—and occasionally baffling—chapter of twentieth-century ecclesial history in Nicaragua. It is full of the passion and heated rhetoric that marked previous eras, but in the latter half of the 1980s there *was* some significant movement within the overall framework of Church-state relations. This does not mean that there was no substantial friction over political matters (as this chapter will show, the politicization of religion was as great as ever), but rather that a note of badly needed pragmatism was finally injected into the debate. As a result, an important breathing space was created in 1986 and 1987 that would allow Church representatives to take stock of their positions. While many problems continued (and still continue), it is nonetheless significant that the potential for discussing conflictive issues in a civilized fashion was finally discerned. The seed of dialogue (and, ultimately, of self-protection) had been sown, as participants in the religious-political debate slowly grasped the need to defuse the increasingly volatile situation. Slowly, then, and with great caution, this process has evolved—albeit with many major problems and confrontations along the bumpy road of reconciliation. But progress was indeed made, as this chapter attempts to illustrate.

The Political Background

Undoubtedly the single greatest reason for this progress was that relative success had been achieved in the smoke-filled back rooms of political power. At long last the prospect of peace in Central America loomed on the horizon, after an eternity of skillful diplomatic negotiations (culminating in the so-called Arias plan, for which Costa Rica's president was awarded the Nobel Peace Prize) and despite the continuing pressure to subvert the peace process from Washington and the mounting Nicaraguan body count. The need for political movement thus became apparent, and a small "window of opportunity" could finally be glimpsed. It is still too early to predict how the electoral victory of Violeta Chamorro will affect the balance of power in Nicaragua (much less the prospects of meaningful and lasting peace), but for the war-weary Nicaraguans the potential for peace was all that mattered. Just as peace and reconciliation were obliquely hinted at by the bishops, so too did the depressing political reality of the country finally indicate (albeit in a fleeting fashion) the potential—and the need—for change.

Many important developments within Nicaragua coalesced to produce these changing circumstances. By late 1986, for instance, it was clear that the Sandinistas had won the military war against the contras. The latter had never held a single town for a single day and had been consistently routed in clashes with the Sandinistas. (One of the largest maneuvers had been to attack Estelí with some two thousand FDN contras in the summer of 1985, but they had been repelled after several days of heavy fighting. Apart from that large-scale attack, the contras had been notably unsuccessful in their military campaign.) It was also apparent (to all but Ronald Reagan and his advisers) that, far from being the paragons of virtue Reagan proclaimed them to be, the "freedom fighters" were in fact bloodthirsty thugs and murderers—with a far worse human rights record than that of the Sandinista armed forces they hoped to overthrow. Reports of contra atrocities—found in a variety of publications put out by Americas Watch, Amnesty International, Washington Office on Latin America, Britain's Catholic Institute for International Relations, and the like—proved this beyond the shadow of a doubt. In Nicaragua the impact of this "low-intensity conflict" was widely publicized and helped steel resistance to the "mercenaries," for it was widely felt that to negotiate with them would be to betray the memory of the fifty thousand killed in the revolutionary struggle against Somoza and the many thousands killed since 1979. (Ironically, however, as the 1990 election was to show, the steady drain of resources and the ever-mounting casualties would eventually lead to a reversal of that trend, as the population voted overwhelmingly for an end to the contra war. Displeasure with the Sandinista economic record, the style of the Ortega presidential campaign, and minor corruption were also factors in the Chamorro victory, yet the nationwide desire for an end to the war was the fundamental reason for the Sandinista defeat.)

Between 1985 and 1990 the Sandinista government also instituted several major legal changes that contributed to some sort of political stability in the country. A wide-ranging amnesty law was partially successful in encouraging several thousand former contras to return to Nicaragua. Also important was the attempt (finally) to incorporate the Miskitos into the country while allowing them sufficient autonomy and control over their cultural and economic development. The repatriation scheme introduced in December 1984 had been successful, with some 10,000 Miskitos returning within the next year—thereby dealing a strong blow to the contras. Speaking in early 1986, Hazel Lau, a member of the Autonomy Commission, noted that fifteen of twenty Miskito guerrilla commanders were respecting a nine-month cease-fire and that some 13,500 Miskitos had returned to their original homes.[1] Also important were the wide-ranging consultations the government held in 1986 with mass organizations, institutions, enterprises, and unions (an estimated 80,000 people were consulted) prior to the promulgation of the new constitution.

Two major problems hung over the revolutionary government during this period and consistently threatened to destroy the Sandinista experiment: the attitude of the Reagan administration and the parlous state of the Nicaraguan economy. The economy had always been a source of widespread discontent—due to government mismanagement, the departure of skilled managerial cadres, and the ongoing cost of the war against the contras. A variety of economic reforms and "shock packages" were introduced to reverse the rapidly deteriorating conditions—but to no avail. Inflation thus soared from 343 percent in 1985 to 747 percent in 1986 and to 1,200 percent in 1987.[2] By 1988 inflation had reached an estimated 5,000 percent, with defense spending consuming a whopping 62 percent of the budget in 1987.[3]

Making this dire situation even worse was the impact of two devastating natural disasters. An extensive drought in 1987 and early 1988 destroyed an estimated $100 million in crops (approximately half the value of Nicaragua's estimated export earnings for all of 1987). The second disaster was Hurricane Joan, which ravaged the country in late

October 1988, destroying large tracts of land that produced traditional export crops—as well as leaving 116 people killed, 110 missing, and some 200,000 homeless.

As if this combination of disasters was not sufficient, one must also bear in mind the actions of the United States, whose president was obsessed with overthrowing the Sandinistas. In addition to providing funding directly to the contras, the Reagan administration went out of its way to isolate the Nicaraguan government, asking its allies not to provide aid to the Sandinistas and, in some cases (as the Iran-contra hearings showed), asking allies to provide funding for the "freedom fighters." The U.S. government also made life difficult for Daniel Ortega and members of his government when they sought to travel to address the UN and the OAS. In October 1988, to cite one example, the Nicaraguan delegation had requested sixty visas for government members and advisers to accompany Ortega on a speaking trip to the UN. But visas were granted only to Ortega and twenty junior officials; none of his ministers or media representatives—or even his wife— received this diplomatic courtesy.

Far more serious, however, was the continued military buildup in Central America. Fortified by the successful invasion of Grenada, U.S. forces increasingly participated in a variety of war games. In the fall of 1986, for instance, Costa Rica's Universidad de la Paz estimated that some thirty thousand U.S. troops were engaged in military maneuvers in the region. Spy planes frequently violated Nicaraguan airspace, Honduras continued to be fortified by U.S. military aid beyond any normal level of expectation, and Panama-based forces were increased. The shooting down in Nicaragua of a U.S. supply plane bringing arms to the contras and the capture of Eugene Hasenfus (an American aboard the plane who admitted to being on the CIA payroll) merely confirmed that Reagan was prepared to pull out all the stops in order to destroy the Nicaraguan government.

The rapidly deteriorating economic situation, the increased pressure from Washington, and the apparent lack of progress from the Contadora negotiations in the mid-1980s were all contributing factors in the Nicaraguan government's decision to amplify the decree of national state of emergency on October 15, 1985—much to the chagrin of conservative Church leaders, who reacted bitterly against the legislation.[4] Wider powers of investigation and detention, limits on freedom of speech and association (with regard to military and economic affairs), and the banning of all strikes were the main features of the new restrictions.

Some relief from this relentless and ongoing pressure came from the decision of the World Court (based in The Hague) on June 27, 1986, which found in favor of Nicaragua in its case against the U.S. policy of terrorism. The Nicaraguan government had filed suit two years earlier, alleging that the United States had violated the UN charter, that of the OAS, and an international Treaty of Friendship, Commerce, and Navigation. In the end, the United States was found guilty by the World Court on sixteen counts, including its unlawful intervention in the affairs of another state (through its support of the contras), its use of force against another state (the sabotage of ports and installations in 1983 and 1984), its overflying of Nicaraguan territory without authorization, its violation of Nicaraguan sovereignty, and its publication of a guerrilla manual for the contras ("Psychological Operations in Guerrilla Warfare") that encouraged abuses of human rights. Furthermore, the World Court found that the United States was morally bound to make reparation to Nicaragua for the economic damage resulting from U.S. actions.

While this proved a significant morale booster for the Sandinistas, it led to few tangible results: the Reagan administration responded by refusing to recognize the validity of the court's decision. (Indeed, just two days before the decision the U.S. Congress authorized an additional $100 million for the contras—in effect showing their contempt for that body's jurisdiction.) The U.S. policy of aggression continued unabated, no reparation was paid to Nicaragua, and the economy continued to grind down mercilessly. The efforts to bring peace to the region were continuing, however, and after many false starts and frustrations a faint glimmer of much-needed hope could be seen.

The key to Nicaragua's stability was the peace accord signed on August 7, 1987, by the five Central American presidents. The agreement became widely known as Esquipulas II, after the place in Guatemala where it was signed. It was Costa Rican President Oscar Arias who managed to bring to a head four years of Latin American deliberations and thus break the stalemate in which the Contadora draft treaty was mired (in no small measure because of Washington's intransigence and pressure on its regional allies). Even former Salvadorian president José Napoleón Duarte waxed eloquent at the plan, calling it a veritable "second declaration of independence for Central America."[5] Recognizing that for the first time in recent memory there was a real chance for a "made-in-Latin America" peace, the Sandinistas made a concerted effort to meet and, in some cases, surpass its treaty obligations—leaving far behind other signatory nations whose compliance with Esquipulas paled in comparison.[6]

Subsequent meetings, such as the January 1988 Esquipulas III summit in San José and the historic Sapoá agreement between government and contra leaders in March, produced a significant (if only temporary) halt in the contra war—demonstrating the possibility of realizing peace in Nicaragua. Moreover, just four days after the Guatemala accord was signed, the Sandinistas invited the Church and opposition parties to put forward a list of prospective candidates for the National Reconciliation Commission that was required by the accord—and even suggested that Cardinal Obando y Bravo should head the commission. The subsequent appointment of the cardinal as chairman and his role (along with OAS Secretary-General João Baena Soares) in ensuring that both sides complied with the Sapoá agreement exemplified once again his influence—and the role of the Church—in any major political development in the country.

The February 1990 elections, in which the bizarre United Nicaraguan Opposition (UNO) coalition headed by Violeta Chamorro emerged victorious, were in many ways the consummate expression of the nation's desperate desire for peace. The extensive analysis of the causes of the UNO victory indicates that Nicaraguans voted for the Chamorro ticket mainly because of two factors: a desire for peace and a hoped-for end to the deteriorating economic situation. Encouraged by the success of the Esquipulas II agreement: they finally dared to believe that peace could come to their war-torn land. Moreover, since doña Violeta had been the clear favorite of President George Bush (who had provided an excellent photo opportunity in a meeting with her in Washington), it was thought that she alone could bring about an end to U.S. meddling in the area. For many people, then, the February 1990 elections thus cemented the possibility of peace that Contadora, Esquipulas, and Sapoá had hinted at. Whether peace is truly at hand or remains only tantalizingly close in Nicaragua remains to be seen. But by 1990, Nicaraguans had come to see the *possibility of peace*—and that was a first.

Continuing Difficulties in Church-State Relations

It is important to note that during the period under examination, the much-needed improvement in relations between Church and government leaders came about only very gradually—and despite continued obstacles of great magnitude. Moreover, it was essentially an extremely minor change that had less to do with the desire for rapprochement than with a pragmatic decision to lessen the spiraling hostilities. What resulted, then, was a remarkably slight improvement in relations that—like the Esquipulas agreement—hinted at the possibility of reconciliation. There was no miraculous change of heart in the main protagonists nor even any significant agreement; they merely decided to tone down their rhetoric to see if any form of communication could evolve in the light of the rapidly changing political circumstances. In other words, there was no major breakthrough in the existing tension; rather, an attempt at détente in ecclesial-political matters was quietly pursued.

The first eighteen months of this period saw a direct continuation of all the problems that had so dominated the previous six years. There was, for example, continued government harassment and censorship of Church communications (the first issue of the journal *Iglesia* was seized by the government, archdiocese offices were occupied, and Radio Católica was closed down), and for several months Bishop Vega and Father Bismarck Carballo were forbidden from entering Nicaragua. Similarly, progressive priests (notably Uriel Molina) were again pressured by the hierarchy (and in particular by Obando y Bravo) to toe the official line as laid down by the cardinal. One British priest in Managua, writing in 1988, noted that "the only real religious persecution is that unleashed by the Cardinal himself, who has expelled (by 'termination of contract') over 60 priests and numerous religious sisters for their defence of the Sandinista Revolution."[7] For their part, Bishop Vega, Father Carballo, and the cardinal kept up a barrage of criticism against the Sandinistas. Vega and Carballo were particularly outspoken—especially on foreign speaking tours—and their message was eagerly seized upon by the Reagan administration in order to justify large amounts of congressional aid for the contras. While noticeably fewer pastoral letters and official communiqués were published (possibly because of disagreements among the bishops themselves), it was clear that the powerful sector of the hierarchy had not changed its official stance one iota. Meanwhile the "Iglesia de los Pobres" maintained its critical stance against a hierarchy that it saw as having sold out to class interests of the rich.

The initial period under study can best be understood by assessing the battle being enacted for the "hearts and minds" of Nicaragua's Catholics through two well-publicized campaigns headed by articulate representatives of the two wings of the Church, Cardinal Obando y Bravo and Father Miguel D'Escoto. The cardinal began his "Crusade for Peace" on June 20, 1985, shortly after returning from the Vatican following his appointment as cardinal. This four-month odyssey was a sort of public presentation to the Nicaraguan faithful, but it also carried a fundamental political message that was at times rather overtly expressed. By late October the cardinal had made seventy-two trips, largely to conservative parishes. The political nature of these "pastoral" visits was quite apparent, as a cursory glance at the main Nicaraguan newspapers will attest. In many ways it was like an opposition leader trekking across the country in an old-fashioned barnstorming campaign, especially given the constant references to the need for dialogue and reconciliation with the contras and the abolition of atheistic and totalitarian ideologies (two common themes of his crusade—and of the political opposition). Significantly the cardinal did not condemn contra atrocities, much less Washington's aid. As political theater it was superb, emphasizing the cardinal's popularity, his outspoken opposition to the Sandinistas, and, of course, the need to take the Church leadership into consideration in all political developments.

For their part, members of the grass-roots Church also produced a successful piece of political drama through the "insurrección evangélica" headed by Foreign Minister Miguel D'Escoto, which lasted from July 1985 to April 1986. There were two basic elements to this campaign: a stage of fasting headed by Father D'Escoto (July 7–August 6, 1985), then a fourteen-day "Via Crucis [Way of the Cross] for Peace and for Life," a march from the northern border town of Jalapa (in the heart of an area plagued with contra activity) to Managua (February 14–28, 1986).

The fast was planned by D'Escoto for several reasons. First, his intent was to condemn the Reagan administration's policy toward Nicaragua and to demystify the "holy war" terminology the president used to justify U.S. aggression against the revolutionary government. Second, he sought to embarrass the hierarchy, which, with few exceptions (notably Bishop López Ardón of Estelí and Auxiliary Bishop Schmitz of the Atlantic coast), continued to ignore the contra war. (D'Escoto noted that "Reagan is counting on the absolute complicity of the Nicaraguan Episcopal Conference, which, because of its silence, is also responsible for the crimes that have been committed in Nicaragua. Indeed, the conference is more responsible than Reagan himself, since the bishops' collective silence has been of enormous assistance to his arguments.")[8] Third, D'Escoto wanted to appeal to Nicaraguan Catholics of all political stripes to support the revolutionary process as it headed into a critical period. Finally, by publicizing the fast abroad, he hoped to gain international support for the peace initiative. (Fasts were held concurrently in Italy, West Germany, the United States, Mexico, Panama, France, and England.)

Within Nicaragua the fast received extensive publicity. The arrival of progressive Church leaders and Christians from around the world was covered in the local media. The participation in the fast by Bishop Pedro Casaldáliga of São Felix do Araguaia (who came, he said, with the support of twenty-three Brazilian bishops—and a warm letter of support from São Paulo's Cardinal Arns) and two hundred organizations caused sparks to fly within the Nicaraguan Church, leading the secretary of the Nicaraguan Episcopal Conference to complain about this "meddling" to the sister organization in Brazil.[9] (Sadly, Bishop Casaldáliga saw firsthand the tragic effect of the contra war, officiating at two requiem masses the day after he arrived in Nicaragua—first in León, for eight women killed in a contra ambush, and later in Estelí, for twelve soldiers killed in action.) A stinging editorial in La Prensa on August 1, 1985, did nothing but fan the flames of what was fast becoming a major incident in Nicaragua. The editorial accused D'Escoto of having arranged the fast as a means of upstaging Cardinal Obando—and because he needed to go on a diet to lose weight. It was an expression of his vain nature ("his desire to show off, to be the center of attention") as well as a tactical ploy: "he is taking advantage of the fast like a medical prescription—gaining points among those Christians who believe in his sincerity, while enjoying his role at the center of attention in all Nicaragua."[10] Once again religious events were imbued with political symbolism—from both sides of the ideological fence.

This was very much the case in the second stage of D'Escoto's campaign, the "Via Crucis" that represented a march of some 205 miles. Politics again played a role in a religious celebration, with some parishes along the way helping the participants and others closing their doors to the pilgrims. Significantly, however, Bishop López Ardón of Estelí (to whose diocese D'Escoto is assigned) personally ordered the doors of the cathedral opened and led a prayer service with D'Escoto. The culmination of this impassioned pilgrimage was a mass in Managua concelebrated by some seventy-three priests—an impressive show of support for D'Escoto's initiatives, especially when one takes into account that in the entire country there are only 310 priests (including the retired and the infirm). Some twenty thousand Nicaraguans attended the closing service in Managua's Plaza de la Revolución, possibly the largest showing of support to date of the "Church of the poor." As the marchers continued their hot and dusty trek, D'Escoto's anger at the direction of Obando y Bravo's leadership increased noticeably. In his address in Condega, for example, his frustration was open but restrained:

> With the authority of a son of God, I say to the bishops that they should reconcile themselves with their people and ask forgiveness for having remained quiet about the crimes. They have gone to Washington and Miami, and here among their people they have said nothing. Some of our bishops are a scandal. . . .
>
> At this moment, the Church in Nicaragua is, in some way, a leaderless Church, where we find ourselves abandoned by our pastors. . . . There is division, there are people who say "this is not the line of Obando." But what they must ask themselves is if perhaps it is the line of Christ, the line of the gospel. . . . We have to pray for our bishops . . . so that each bishop will speak as he must speak, independent of whether it pleases Obando and whether the Holy Father understands it or not. And we must also pray for our Cardinal of Managua, that he may come to understand the situation, that he not continue acting like an enemy of the people, that he may condemn the aggression. And would to God that when we are barely in the Archdiocese of Managua he will join this march, heading it up and celebrating the campesino mass there in Managua.[11]

Needless to say, the cardinal did not take up this invitation from Miguel D'Escoto.[12]

In addition to the religious and political tension emanating from these initiatives of the cardinal and Father D'Escoto (whose mutual antipathy is well known in Nicaragua), one of the major sources of friction resulted from the actions abroad of Church spokesmen such as Bishop Pablo Vega, Father Bismarck Carballo, and Cardinal Obando y Bravo. Their stinging criticisms of the Sandinistas were to be expected, but the form of these criticisms—and, more important, their political context (namely, when President Reagan was seeking to increase funding for the contras)—provoked a backlash of harassment by the revolutionary government.

As noted in earlier chapters, Bishop Vega had long been an outspoken critic of many features of the revolutionary government's reform programs. The tone of his rhetoric, however, rose substantially during this period, during part of which he was the president of the Nicaraguan Episcopal Conference. Speaking in September 1985 in Bonn, for instance, he justified U.S. support for the contras, noting: "A people which doesn't feel that its civil and social rights are guaranteed . . . also has the right to seek assistance wherever it can."[13]

Six months later the plot thickened when Vega was invited to Washington by the right-wing Heritage Foundation, appearing publicly with contra leaders Adolfo Calero, Arturo Cruz, and Enrique Bermúdez. He bluntly condemned the Sandinistas for their religious persecution, abuse of human rights, and cruel mismanagement of the country. Vega also expressed his gratitude for aid from the United States to promote development and freedom around the world, and he asked for U.S. support to help the Nicaraguan people escape from the pressure of the Soviet bloc. As he put it, "In Nicaragua the fundamental problem before the revolutionary triumph was underdevelopment. Now it is how to escape from the Soviet bloc."[14]

His most controversial statement, however, was in defense of his claims about the lack of human rights in Nicaragua, which he supported by noting that the Sandinistas had assassinated three priests from his diocese—a topic that was widely commented on in the U.S. media. On his return to Nicaragua, he modified his claims in a press conference given on March 12, 1986—yet in doing so he merely made matters worse. He explained that he had gone to Washington to provide his own analysis of events in Nicaragua for the legislators who were debating whether to provide $100 million to the contras. When asked whether he justified the actions of the contras, he responded: "Who is provoking these actions? That is the question to be answered."[15] He tried to brush off criticism about his claim that three priests had been killed by the Sandinistas, noting that they had in fact been Delegates of the Word, killed shortly after the overthrow of Somoza. (He did not say that the soldiers responsible for the crime had been found guilty and were serving thirty years in prison for the murders.) The bishop had been caught in a lie, one that he had fabricated in order to paint the Sandinistas as heartless (and soulless) animals—and hence increase the likelihood of additional funding for the contras. Indeed, the Reagan administration eagerly (and gratefully) latched onto his observations and utilized them to the fullest.

In early June, Bishop Vega returned to the United States at the invitation of the right-wing organization PRODEMCA (Pro-Democracy in Central America) and continued his efforts to delegitimize the Sandinistas. This was a crucial time for Nicaragua: the World Court was expected to rule any day on Managua's case against Washington, and a congressional decision on Reagan's $100 million aid package was due within a few weeks. It was in this context that Vega noted: "Each one in his own sphere. The Church has its specific function and cannot go further. But armed struggle is a human right. What remedy is left to a people that is repressed not only politically but militarily?"[16] Speaking in the New York Centro Hispánico Católico, the bishop pursued this line of argument, outlining the government persecution against the Church and stressing the need to help the contras in their struggle against "Soviet totalitarianism." Less than three weeks later President Reagan, making a final pitch for contra funding, invoked the message brought to Washington by Vega: "Reverend Father, we have listened to you, because we in the United States believe, like you, that even the most humble peasant has a right to be free."[17]

In the wake of congressional approval of the contra funding, political polarization increased dramatically in Nicaragua: government supporters felt frustrated at Washington's casual dismissal of the World Court decision and at the vast increase in contra aid, while conservative forces were understandably jubilant. One week after the congressional package was announced, Bishop Vega held a press conference in Managua that would prove to be his undoing. He infuriated the government with some of his observations—particularly his rejection of the World Court decision against Washington: "A Court can have the concrete facts within its reach or it can have only half of them. . . . It should see things from the angle of what the rights of man are and not simply the rights of governments. I believe that it would also be worthwhile to study the fact that the aggression we are suffering is thanks to the militaristic imperialism in the East as well."[18]

Vega also defended the contras' rights to take up arms[19] and refused to condemn the U.S. aid package, stating: "I cannot criticize only the $100 million, when there are other billions that are being given from the other side as well."[20] This was infuriating to the Sandinistas, who objected to clergymen like Vega throwing their weight behind campaigns to overthrow the legally constituted government of Nicaragua. What was especially galling was the bishop's attempt to justify his observations by cloaking them in terms of a "pastoral" message—when they were obviously intended to be political and manipulative. Government leaders also knew that the propaganda machine in Washington would attack them ferociously if they sought to muzzle the bishop—which added to their frustration.

The situation finally resolved itself, however, with an act of terrorism by the counterrevolutionaries: a few hours after Vega's spirited defense of the contras, some thirty-two campesinos (including twelve children) were killed in Jinotega by a U.S.-made antitank land mine. For the government, the juxtaposition of Vega's remarks and the human tragedy was the straw that broke the camel's back. As a result, Bishop Vega was escorted from his offices to the Honduran border, temporarily banished from Nicaragua because of his antipatriotic attitude. While in exile he continued his diatribe against the government, justifying on contra radio the obligation of Nicaraguans to rebel against the Sandinistas and also condemning the renewal of the dialogue between Church and government leaders in early 1987.[21]

In many ways parallel to the course pursued by Bishop Vega—though slightly less confrontational—the outspoken criticisms made by Father Bismarck Carballo on his own travels through Europe (France, Italy, and Holland) and the United States also contributed to the continuing polarization of 1985 and 1986. In April 1986 he traveled to Costa Rica to receive in the name of Cardinal Obando y Bravo an award from the conservative institution APRODEM (Pro-Democracy Association). While in Costa Rica he published an attack on the Sandinistas in the FDN contra publication *Nicaragua Hoy,* and throughout his European tour he had lambasted the "Marxist ideological aggression" destroying his homeland. In late June, as he tried to board a plane for the flight home from Miami, he was informed that he would not be allowed back into the country. Like Vega (who would face the same fate a few days later), he was temporarily banished from Nicaragua for his "unpatriotic attitude."

Several other incidents illustrate how political and religious elements continued to be inexorably intertwined and a source of friction during this period. On October 12, 1985, the first issue of the biweekly *Iglesia* (published by the archdiocese) was seized by the Ministry of the Interior—leading to charges of religious persecution by the Sandinistas. What was lost in international press coverage of the incident (which, of course, was a senseless action by the government authorities) was an understanding of events leading up to the seizure. For over a month *La Prensa* and the archdiocese's weekly bulletin had been announcing the new publication. Father Bismarck Carballo, however, had ignored repeated communications from the Ministry of the Interior stating that according to a 1981 law the journal would have to be registered officially (and that, like all publications, it would have to be submitted for approval by the censors). After first claiming that the Church was exempt from such legislation, Father Carballo agreed to comply with the law—yet he had not completed the necessary paperwork by the time the publication was ready. When Church workers began to distribute the journal in Managua and Masaya, government officials intervened, confiscated almost the entire issue, and occupied the Church offices where it was printed.

Less than three months later, another incident involving this same combination—Church-controlled media, the intervention of Bismarck Carballo (director of communications for the archdiocese), and heavy-handed government treatment—took place. On this occasion the issue was the refusal by Radio Católica (headed by Father Carballo) to broadcast the bulk of the end-of-the-year national address by President Ortega—in a gesture that piqued the Sandinistas, only the last few moments of the speech were heard on Catholic radio. The government responded by closing down the radio station—again unleashing a barrage of criticism against the government's totalitarian tactics. The official media watchdog, the Dirección de Medios de Comunicación, complicated the situation by releasing its own report and citing (with precise documentation concerning the date and time) nineteen infractions of the law by Radio Católica.

These two incidents, which revealed a somewhat immature approach on the part of both Church and government officials, are in many ways illustrative of the difficulties facing both sides. Feeling itself to be the target of government harassment, the Church again took up the role of the legal opposition to the Sandinistas. It did so, however, in a superficial manner—possibly to provoke the Sandinistas and thereby bring about international condemnation of the repression of the Church. There was nothing subtle about the actions of Bismarck Carballo, who knew that he was flagrantly ignoring the law and should have known that the revolutionary government would have no other recourse but to take the necessary legal reprisals. Nor was there anything subtle about the government's response, since officials should have seen in these actions an attempt to provoke a heavy-handed reaction—thereby generating negative international press coverage against the Sandinistas. (The radio station remained closed between January 2, 1986, and September 23, 1987. In July 1988, following its reporting of a violent opposition rally, the station was closed down for another five weeks.) As has been the case on so many occasions during the revolutionary period, the desire not to be upstaged politically by one's opponent became the order of the day—with all else being subordinated to that dictate. A tit-for-tat policy was the necessary corollary of that theory, with the end result being that religious polarization continued apace, and Nicaraguan Catholics proved to be mere pawns in this cynical manipulation that took place behind the scenes.

One final circumstance should be mentioned in evaluating the ongoing difficulties between Church and government leaders and within the Church: the continuing refusal by many bishops to condemn contra atrocities. A new element was added to this tragedy when the contras' victims were religious workers themselves. On July 3, 1987, for instance, when the Franciscan Tomás Zavaleta was killed—after driving over a land mine planted on the road just fourteen kilometers from Matiguás (in the department of Matagalpa), the hierarchy's reaction was remarkable for its refusal to apportion responsibility. Similarly, when the U.S. nun Maureen Courtney and her Nicaraguan co-worker Sister Francisca Colomer were killed (apparently in a contra ambush) and Auxiliary Bishop Pablo Schmitz and another nun were wounded in an attack outside Rosita (in the department of Zelaya), the Church hierarchy remained united in its ambiguous response to the tragedy. In both cases the evidence clearly indicated contra activity, yet representatives of the hierarchy—including Bishop Schmitz himself—refused to condemn the counterrevolutionaries.

The Zavaleta case had a major impact in Nicaragua, basically because it was the first time that a Church worker had been killed by the contras. Zavaleta was a native of El Salvador who had arrived in Nicaragua just three months earlier to work in a peasant cooperative in Matiguás. Three other people traveling with him (the parish priest, Father Ignacio Urbina, and two women members of the parish council) were gravely injured by the land mine explosion. Yet the hierarchy's reaction was noticeably unemotional. Cardinal Obando y Bravo did not attend the funeral services for Zavaleta. Nor did he or any member of the hierarchy attend the wake held that night in Managua, before Zavaleta's remains were flown back to his native El Salvador.

Similarly disturbing were the official reactions of the cardinal and, to a lesser extent, of papal nuncio Paolo Giglio when asked about the crime. When I interviewed Giglio, he stated that Zavaleta was killed "because there was war in Nicaragua." When I asked him why there was war, he replied coyly, "Because there is no peace." He carefully refrained from making any comment that could be construed as criticism of the Reagan administration's policies toward Nicaragua. When, for example, I asked who had promoted the war, he replied: "The different ideas which Nicaraguans have."

The cardinal was characteristically more blunt in his assessment of the murder of Zavaleta, although he too carefully avoided criticizing the contras or the Reagan administration. Preferring instead to point criticism at the Sandinista government, he noted in his weekly sermon at his Managua parish: "Who committed these acts? Well, that is a difficult question to answer—in a world that is so confused, and where information is so manipulated. Who is responsible for the murder? God Our Lord will know."[22] The cardinal refused to apportion any blame for the incident at all. Instead he took advantage of the murder of the Franciscan to underscore the loss of clergy who had been expelled by the government ("And we have been deprived of so many pastoral agents . . . in all they have forced seventeen priests out of Nicaragua," he noted angrily). In other words, not only did he avoid explicitly naming the contras as responsible for Zavaleta's death, but he also exploited the incident in order to criticize the revolutionary government for something that was totally unrelated to what was, in fact, a brutal murder. Moreover, he used the tragedy to criticize the government's refusal to pursue the bishops' advice on the need for reconciliation and dialogue with the "insurgents," hinting that this was the real cause of the Franciscan's death and that therefore the government was responsible.[23]

This thoughtless behavior merely aggravated an already tense situation. In the case of the deaths of the sisters and of Zavaleta, the circumstantial evidence indicated that those responsible for the crime were the contras—not only because of several confirmed reports of their activities in the vicinity those same days, but also because of the activist nature of the people killed and because the modus operandi was clearly that of the contras (not to mention the fact that the contras did not possess vehicles that the Sandinistas could blow up with land mines). Yet on both occasions—as had been the case for the thirty thousand people who lost their lives from 1979 to 1990—the Church hierarchy refused to level any criticism at the contras. The cardinal's lack of sensitivity to the Zavaleta case, his decision not to attend the funeral service, and his attempt to criticize the Sandinistas by cynically taking advantage of the tragedy were quite shocking and undeniably inflammatory. Thus, while he would claim that only God knew who was responsible for the crime, Daniel Ortega (who personally visited the survivors of the crime and paid his respects to Tomás Zavaleta) would retort: "God alone knows how much money Cardinal Obando is receiving from the CIA. . . . We don't understand the cardinal's attitude. He is supposed to be a pastor of the Nicaraguan people, but instead he's behaving like an employee of the CIA, an accomplice in their crimes."[24]

The Role of the Church Hierarchy

The key figure in the hierarchy's consistent opposition to the revolutionary government continued to be Obando y Bravo, whose demeanor was described with some insight by Connor Cruise O'Brien.[25] Mention was made earlier of his lengthy and energetic "Crusade for Peace" with which he began his tenure as cardinal. This campaign—much like that of Miguel D'Escoto—was as much (if not more) a political campaign as a religious pilgrimage. It was designed to assure the Catholic masses that peace would be attainable only if the people listened to the Church, rejecting the need to defend the revolutionary process and instead seeking dialogue and reconciliation with the contras. This, of course, was in direct opposition to the official government position, something that did not seem to intimidate the cardinal in the least. It was also a remarkably *political* stance for him to take—arguably one that went well beyond the bounds of his pastoral role.

In 1986 Cardinal Obando y Bravo made his concerns about the Sandinistas most clearly felt in the United States. As did both Bismarck Carballo and Pablo Vega, the cardinal traveled there at crucial moments when military aid for the contra forces was being discussed—and sought to tip the balance in favor of Ronald Reagan's "freedom fighters." In his trip of January 1986, for instance, he went far beyond his spiritual mission, accusing the Sandinista government of religious persecution and inviting Pérez de Cuéllar, the UN secretary-general, to intervene directly and mediate between the revolutionary government and the Church—an invitation that was declined.

While the cardinal lambasted government persecution of the Church, never did he denounce the U.S.-financed war being waged by the contras, which by this time had caused some twelve thousand casualties. On March 18, just two months later, President Reagan, in a speech defending the funding for the contras, cited the cardinal's words as proof of the need to provide aid to the "freedom fighters." In the cardinal's January 21 presentation to the Americas Society, he outlined his criticisms of the Sandinistas and explained in curious (and exaggerated) fashion why the revolutionary government had redoubled its religious persecution: "Those who flaunt power in Nicaragua took fright and decided to increase their persecution when they saw the half-million Nicaraguans who came out to greet me in June when I returned from Rome following my investiture as cardinal."[26] Obando y Bravo was deeply aware of the political role to be played by the Church—and of his own part within that process.

On May 12, 1986, the cardinal Obando wrote an op-ed piece in the *Washington Post* in which he took up many of these ideas. Coming at a time when the U.S. Congress was considering renewal of military aid to the contras, the cardinal's thoughts were an important source of information—as well as a great influence. In his editorial he referred to the exodus of tens of thousands of Nicaraguans, the censorship to which all were subjected, the general lack of freedom, the violation of human rights, and the expulsion of priests by the revolutionary government. He claimed that Church leaders found themselves caught in the horns of a dilemma, since supporting funding for the contra cause, as well as the option of condemning it or of remaining silent, were all choices fraught with difficulties. The Church, he implied, had to be apolitical, supporting the voiceless and remaining above the political fray. However, his conduct belied his actions, since in his deliberate refusal to condemn atrocities by the contras and his constant criticism of the Sandinistas (coupled with an adamant rejection of impressive social reforms realized by the revolutionary government), he was indeed taking sides—as was pointed out in a letter written by a group of Christian activists headed by the Jesuit César Jérez, the rector of the Universidad Centroamericana:

> Cardinal Miguel Obando:
> You have stated during this trip (to the United States) that you are not allied with the counterrevolutionary forces, and that your visit to these international fora is not in favor of any particular group. The facts, however, say the contrary: how can you say that you are not against the revolution when you only attack it, refusing to see anything positive in it, if you declare that it doesn't respect love, truth, justice, and the common welfare?
> How can you say, Sr. Cardinal, that you do not support the counterrevolutionaries if you have never condemned their crimes, such as the massacre of the mothers in July 1985 or the murder of the innocent children in San Gregorio? How can you say that you do not favor them, when you know full well that—now, in the United States—your words and your letters are helping the U.S. government to convince the Congress to approve more than 100 million dollars in military aid for the counterrevolution? How can you say that you are not on the side of the counterrevolution after you said mass in Miami for their leaders? You cannot deceive us, or yourself, by claiming that you are neutral.[27]

In April 1986 the Nicaraguan Episcopal Conference published an Easter pastoral letter that was in many ways a summary of the main planks of the hierarchy's position concerning the revolutionary government and the so-called Iglesia Popular. This document is a useful reference for understanding the first stage of this last period of the Church's role, as it synthesized clearly and with some vigor the hierarchy's uncompromising position—particularly toward dissent within the Church ranks. The pastoral, officially entitled "The Eucharist: Source of Unity and Reconciliation," focused on two central themes: the importance of Church unity and the need for national reconciliation. It based its arguments for the latter on the traditional Church belief in individual conversion (noting that "this needs to stem from the only source that can produce it, which is the heart of Christ"),[28] inviting all disaffected with both the magisterium of the traditional Church and the desperate national situation to look to God for advice and guidance. The pastoral emphasized, however, that this must be done in accordance with parameters drawn up by the hierarchy.

Perhaps its sharpest criticism was reserved for those sectors of the Church that were displeased with the hierarchy's role. It called for the necessary respect for its "legitimate pastors" and roundly condemned the "scandalous disobedience of certain priests and religious" who were accused of manipulating "the fundamental truths of our faith, arrogating to themselves the right of reinterpreting, and even of rewriting, the word of God—so that they can adapt it to suit their own ideology, using it as an instrument to suit their own objectives" (p. 40). This attempt by the disobedient to instrumentalize Catholics, presenting new "idols" before the faithful and foisting their own ideology on the unsuspecting masses, was—claimed the bishops—the work of a few misguided foreigners: "A belligerent group of priests, religious, and lay people of different nationalities, while insisting that they belong to the Catholic Church, in reality are working actively to undermine the unity of that Church, collaborating to destroy those very foundations on which the unity in the faith and in the body of Christ are based" (p. 40).

Church unity at all costs was the predominant message in the first part of the pastoral. The "stance of open rebellion" and of protest against the hierarchy was thus totally unacceptable for the bishops, who were determined to impose their authority on all members of the Church, whether they respected it or not. Two particular concerns were addressed by the bishops. The first had to do with what they perceived as an effort to foment class hatred by members of the "Church of the poor" who were influenced by Marxist ideology and who criticized the hierarchy for their identification with the interests of the wealthy. The second was a reaction against what the bishops saw as criticism of their alleged role as defenders of imperialist plans held by the United States. The bishops urged its critics to comply with Church teaching, in accordance with official interpretation of that magisterium, and to reject "negative or indifferent positions that adversely affect Church unity" (p. 41). The bishops were angry at being presented as the lapdogs of imperialism and were also determined to exert their authority over the rebel priests and religious. They were thus lowering the ecclesial boom on the representatives of the progressive Church sector, in essence telling them—as the pope had instructed Ernesto Cardenal three years earlier—to "put their affairs in order." In both cases, however, it was a matter of the progressives regularizing their situation according to guidelines laid out by the bishops: thus "ecclesial reconciliation" meant that critics of the hierarchy had to accept unquestioningly the latter's dictates on religious matters.

The second main thrust of this pastoral was to emphasize the need for reconciliation on the national level. This was extremely difficult, the bishops noted, since the revolutionary government was doing all in its power to limit and indeed manipulate the Church's role:

> There is an attempt to silence and bind the Church, to subjugate it, while half-truths and institutionalized lies continue to bring applause from naive bystanders.
>
> The Church is accused of keeping silent on national developments—yet its only radio station has been stripped from it, and every news item about both injuries committed against it and its defense against critics is censored in the official media.
>
> The Church is requested to raise its voice in favor of peace—yet when it does so through the path of reconciliation and dialogue, it is slandered and attacked. It is not a set of moral guidelines that is wanted—instead the government wants a declaration that it can manipulate. (p. 41)

Faced with these circumstances, the hierarchy vowed to continue fighting for peace and reconciliation. Unlike the path of confrontation laid out by the government, however, they proposed the traditional approach of individual conversion, since "in the last instance the root of all evil is to be found in man's heart; this evil produces in both the minds and hearts of people irreparable damage" (p. 41). Appeals to Christ's love were thus the necessary antidote for the desire for revenge and the widespread hatred that was tearing Nicaraguan society apart. By Christ's love and through mutual repentance and pardon, Nicaragua could finally emerge from the increasing spiral of death and destruction. It was necessary, then, to reject all "foreign meddling and ideologies," the bishops noted, since only then would Nicaragua be able to discover its own solutions.

This pastoral letter was important, not only because it explicitly expressed the bishops' position on the need for Church authority, but also (and more important) because *for the first time* it indicated the need for an indigenous solution to Nicaragua's woes. In the past the bishops had criticized "Marxist influence" and Soviet imperialism but had studiously avoided leveling any criticism at the ideology of capitalism and the policies of the United States. While they did not name Washington specifically, nevertheless they did state that Nicaragua should be left to resolve its own difficulties: "It is our judgment that *all forms of aid, wherever they come from,* that lead to destruction, suffering, and death in our families or to hate and division among Nicaraguans are to be condemned. To opt for the annihilation of the enemy as the only way to achieving peace is to opt inevitably for war" (p. 41; emphasis added).

While the bishops should be commended for finally condemning (no matter how hesitantly) military aid from the United States—after years of attacking Soviet aid to the Sandinista government—above all else they advocated reconciliation *on terms laid out by them*. Thus, reconciliation within the Church meant, in practice, that members of the "Church of the poor" should reject their profoundly felt beliefs regarding the need to exercise the "preferential option for the poor" and instead subordinate themselves and their beliefs to a form of ecclesial conduct that they considered to be outdated and ineffective. Moreover, reconciliation within the political context of revolutionary Nicaragua meant of necessity that the Sandinistas should enter into agreement with the contras as equal negotiating partners (despite the fact that the latter had little political or military credibility and were guilty of widespread atrocities). No differentiation was made between the aggressors and their victims—nor did the bishops ask the contras to lay down their weapons and cease their wanton destruction as a necessary first step toward meaningful reconciliation. In reality, then, the form of reconciliation suggested by the hierarchy meant "not to opt now in favor of the poor, but rather to opt for poor and rich alike, for all. In other words not to opt, but rather to abstain from doing so. The people putting forward this proposal feel that they are truly reconciling two different perspectives, yet in reality all that they are doing is attempting to avoid the conflict . . . while asking the sheep to accept living peacefully with the wolf."[29] Such a proposal was profoundly distasteful both to the revolutionary government and to the progressive Church sector.

One could also argue that the idea of "individual conversion," which the bishops presented as the key to resolving this bloody conflict, had not proved particularly successful in Nicaragua thus far—as the daily body count clearly showed. Thus, the bishops were again adopting a political approach that would favor their (essentially conservative) view of the status quo, in essence urging that Nicaraguans shun a battle against the forces of violence and instead seek reconciliation with those who desired to turn back the hands of time. For the hierarchy, this was the only humane manner in which to proceed; conversely, many revolutionary Christians sought to show that God was not impartial in this struggle but did take sides against the oppressor: "Throughout the entire Bible God appears as the liberator of the oppressed. He does not maintain a position of neutrality. He does not attempt to reconcile Moses and the Pharaoh, the slaves and their Egyptian oppressors, or the Jewish people and their other oppressors. Oppression is a sin to which one can not yield concessions. Quite simply, oppression has to be eradicated."[30]

Two years later the bishops published another key pastoral letter to celebrate the feast day of Saints Peter and Paul. While some of the same themes are addressed (the need for reconciliation and for a change of heart from "the so-called Iglesia Popular, which aggressively strives for an alliance between the Christian faith and a materialist ideology possessing moral practices that are unacceptable for Catholics"),[31] the tone of the document is noticeably less belligerent. The bishops are still in disagreement with the revolutionary process, noting the "disillusionment of those who placed their hopes in, and were prepared to give their lives for, a particular political project—and now feel defrauded by their leaders" (p. 14), but now they focus more directly on specific social problems, and their criticism is far less emotional than before.

One can detect in the pastoral the bishops' continued opposition to the revolutionary government (they direct part of their exhortation, for example, not to the "counterrevolutionary forces" but to the "Nicaraguan resistance"). Moreover, they continue to emphasize the need for pardon, for individual conversion, and for the destruction of resentment—as they had done in their earlier letters of 1984 and 1986. One can discern, however, almost a grudging respect for government efforts to realize a meaningful dialogue with the contras, and even though there has been limited progress ("Political dialogue, amnesty, democratization, and the cease-fire have all stalled" [p. 14]), the bishops are aware that significant concessions had been made by the Sandinistas. In sum, while still expressing heartfelt opposition to the revolutionary model, the Church hierarchy had toned down its criticism somewhat—almost certainly because of a combination of pressures from the Vatican, major concessions by the revolutionary government, and significant progress in negotiations to bring about peace. (In January of that year the Central American presidents had signed the Esquipulas II treaty, followed in March by the first face-to-face negotiations between Sandinista and contra leaders at Sapoá.) At long last, some members of the Nicaraguan Episcopal Conference seemed to understand the Sandinista position a little better.

Positive Developments in the Church-State Relationship

The central thesis of this chapter is that despite formidable obstacles (not the least of which was a set of deeply rooted prejudices held by members of the Catholic hierarchy) between 1985 and 1990 significant progress was gradually made in defusing some of the tension that existed between the leadership of the Church and the revolutionary government. Unfortunately, the same cannot be said about the tension within the Church itself, where radically different interpretations of the Church's mission are still passionately held and where the Church's emphasis on reconciliation seems not to be practiced.

If one accepts that there was some sort of informal (if unspectacular) détente between the revolutionary leadership and the Church hierarchy in the late 1980s, then it is logical to ask, why did this happen and how did this change come about? As we have seen, this extremely gradual process—in no small measure a deliberate tactical maneuver by both sides—was the result of steadily converging interests, especially as the possibilities for a peace accord became apparent. The first part of the question, then, can be answered simply by stating that it was in the best interests of both sides to tone down their strident condemnations, replacing their mutual recriminations (and at times undisguised hostility) with a significant dose of realpolitik. The peace process was a major influence in the defusing of this tension—particularly after Cardinal Obando y Bravo became involved both as a mediator and as head of the Reconciliation Commission. In this context the position of the Vatican modified significantly, which led to gestures and indications of willingness to dialogue by the hierarchy. For its part, the revolutionary government had already shown a willingness to negotiate—largely because of the recognition that the continued opposition of Cardinal Obando y Bravo was a hindrance to national peace and stability. The picture was completed by the rhythm of the peace process, skillfully directed by Costa Rica's Oscar Arias, with which the revolutionary government showed itself more than ready to comply. Indeed, no other country in Central America did as much as Nicaragua to fulfill the requirements of the Contadora and Esquipulas accords.

The evidence to show *how* this came about is far more difficult to piece together in a concise and logical fashion since it is in general fragmentary, occasionally confusing, and almost always of a circumstantial nature. There is, then, no clear-cut explanation of how the need for a new approach came to modify the behavior of both Church and government leaders. Nonetheless, the sheer weight of this evidence is quite compelling—all the more so if one reexamines the position taken by Church leaders just three or four years earlier.

One can cite, for example, the gradually changing position of the Vatican toward the revolutionary process. In December 1985, the pope—perhaps still remembering his own difficult experience in Nicaragua—criticized in no uncertain terms the conduct of the Sandinistas. At that time the pope emphasized the need for dialogue with the contras as the only viable route to effective reconciliation in Nicaragua, and he reiterated traditional Catholic doctrine concerning the need for an individual conversion or "change of heart." He ventured directly into the political realm, after alluding to the expulsion of ten priests in the wake of the Peña case: "I know too how you all suffer because of different kinds of obstacles placed before the Church, and about various kinds of intimidation and humiliation to which priests and faithful Catholics are subjected."[32] In his references to "intimidation and humiliation" and in his emphasis on the need for reconciliation, he was supporting the Nicaraguan hierarchy totally—and was warning the revolutionary government of that fact.

By the following year, however, there had been significant change in the Vatican's position, largely because of the influence of a new papal nuncio, Msgr. Paolo Giglio, appointed in July 1986. His predecessor, Msgr. Cordero Di Montezemelo, was rumored to have had serious differences of opinion with the cardinal, supporting a conciliatory policy toward the Sandinista government, and was subsequently transferred to the nunciature in Uruguay. The new nuncio, a conservative and pragmatic man,[33] raised expectations from the moment he arrived in Managua, declaring himself in favor of a dialogue between the United States and Nicaragua and even offering to mediate such negotiations if both sides deemed it advisable. In November 1986, he noted that thus far, while the Sandinistas had offered to negotiate with Washington on several occasions, it was the United States that refused to participate in such negotiations.

While Giglio is certainly no liberal (and, of course, as a consummate diplomat has to reflect the conservative and orthodox policies of the pontiff), he has shown himself to be a highly capable politician. (Moreover, unlike his predecessor, who had to divide his time between Nicaragua and Honduras, Giglio is assigned specifically to deal with the thorny situation in Nicaragua.) His seven years' experience in China— where he dealt extensively with the nationalist Catholic Church and was extremely successful in negotiating a gradual defusing of tension between nationalists and "Vatican-leaning" Church members—will stand him in good stead in Nicaragua.

The new nuncio arrived just as the Church-state relationship was deteriorating dramatically: Cardinal Obando y Bravo, Father Bismarck Carballo, and Bishop Vega were in the midst of their international speaking tours in which they consistently denounced the Sandinistas (knowing that their declarations would help the Reagan administration's bid for contra aid); the revolutionary government then retaliated by expelling Vega and refusing entry to Carballo; in April 1986 the revolutionary government had censored the hierarchy's Easter pastoral letter; Radio Católica remained closed; and the war situation had escalated. Despite these inauspicious beginnings, by the end of September the nuncio had revived the almost moribund dialogue between representatives of the hierarchy and the government, offered to negotiate between Washington and Managua, and had made it clear that a new, more flexible Vatican policy toward the Nicaraguan situation was required.

In addition to the nuncio's pronouncements, several other factors contributed to the change in the Vatican's position. On June 19, 1986, Vice President Sergio Ramírez was received by the pope in a private audience; later he met with Vatican Secretary of State Casaroli. Bishop Vega, who spent a month in Rome after his expulsion from Nicaragua, was treated coolly at the Vatican: the official Church press largely ignored him, while Vatican radio did not air an interview taped with him on July 29. The Vatican may have decided that the revolutionary government was not in danger of imminent collapse (and, conversely, that the contras were incapable of a military victory), that the revolutionary government had sought to comply with recommendations on peace for the region, and that it was an appropriate time—particularly with the appointment of the new nuncio—to tone down its critical rhetoric.

The Vatican also appears to have been a little embarrassed by the vehemence of the denunciations of the revolutionary government made by members of the Nicaraguan hierarchy—particularly when important members of bishops' conferences in Latin America and the United States were decrying their defense of the Reagan policy in the region. Finally, given the degree of popular support still shown the revolutionary government (despite a disastrous economic situation, the military draft, and what the Vatican had always seen as religious oppression), the Vatican apparently decided on a different course of action that could be interpreted as an "ecclesial cease-fire," or at least a tactical accommodation in its dealings with the revolutionary government. The end result was the September 1986 meeting of Daniel Ortega, Cardinal Obando y Bravo, and the papal nuncio and a revival of bilateral negotiations between leaders of the Church and government, the objective of which was to seek the normalization of relations between the two.

Two months later the Congreso Eucarístico Nacional took place in Managua. A variety of religious leaders attended, including three cardinals, bishops from sixteen countries, and Mother Teresa. The congress deliberately ignored the political reality of Nicaragua (despite the ongoing trial of Eugene Hasenfus, whose plane had recently been shot down while on a CIA operation to transport arms to the contras, an incident that received worldwide media attention). Yet while Sandinista leaders may have decried the lack of attention given this incident at the congress, they must have been struck by the fact that the Church leadership sought to keep the proceedings as apolitical as possible—and refrained from the denunciations that just a few months earlier they might well have issued. For his part, President Ortega met with several Church leaders attending the conference, including Cardinal Bernard Law of Boston, Msgr. Antonio Quarracino (president of CELAM), Cardinal Opilio Rossi (a special papal delegate), and Mother Teresa. (Significantly, after earlier refusing permission for the Missionaries of Charity to work in Nicaragua, Daniel Ortega—when asked by Mother

Teresa if she could bring four sisters to Nicaragua—informed her that she could indeed found a religious community in Nicaragua and could bring as many as four hundred workers into the country.)

The signing of the Esquipulas II accord in August 1987 was an important catalyst for the development of this policy of détente. Subsequently the government permitted the reopening of Radio Católica and the return to Nicaragua of clergy who had been refused entry (Bishop Vega and priests Bismarck Carballo and Benito Pitito). The establishment of the National Reconciliation Commission (composed of Cardinal Obando y Bravo and Msgr. Bosco Vivas as his supplementary member, Vice President Sergio Ramírez, Mauricio Díaz of the PPSC and Erick Ramírez of the PSC as his supplementary member, Gustavo Parajón of the Protestant CEPAD and Gonzalo Ramírez of the Red Cross as his supplementary member) was a major step in developing credibility about a viable peace accord through this grouping of highly regarded Nicaraguans representing many diverse interests. The naming of Cardinal Obando y Bravo as head of the National Reconciliation Commission (a position supported by the government), and then as mediator in the dialogue between the government and the contras, fortified this credibility. Indeed, at the inaugural session of the commission, President Ortega and the cardinal were seen praying together—an important symbolic gesture. As a result, despite the occasional discordant note,[34] the new climate of rapprochement began steadily—if slowly—taking hold.

Several other factors contributed to this process of détente. Among these was the visit of President Daniel Ortega to the Vatican on January 29, 1988. There he met privately with John Paul II and with Cardinal Casaroli, the Vatican secretary of state. The continued meetings and dialogue between representatives of the hierarchy and the government also contributed to the new climate of rapprochement. Moreover, on New Year's Day, 1990, Obando y Bravo condemned the murders of Sister Maureen Courtney and Sister Francisca Colomer. Although he refrained from placing blame on the contras, his condemnation of the event contrasted sharply with his response to the murder of Tomás Zavaleta.

The pastoral letters produced by the hierarchy in the late 1980s, although still critical, are generally far less provocative than those issued earlier in the decade. Consider, for instance, the May 30, 1989, "Pastoral Letter on Family Catechesis." Although it takes issue with "a materialist form of education that encourages atheism, imposing upon Nicaraguan children and young people the ideology of a minority—something which goes against the desires, beliefs, faith, culture, and moral principles of their parents (and in doing so violates their legitimate rights),"[35] this pastoral nevertheless limits itself to the realm of education and the family role. Gone are references to the abuses of human rights, the division caused by the "Church of the poor," and the need for reconciliation with the "insurgents." The focus instead is on a critique of the educational system and the crisis of the family in Nicaragua ("Such an image can always be seen when attempts are made to bring up a family outside the faith," the bishops note in self-congratulatory fashion [p. 23]).

The final piece of evidence to show the evolution of the Church's role during this period is the hierarchy's reaction to the elections that took place in February 1990. In the 1984 elections the official Church response had been cool in the extreme—to no small degree because their outcome helped legitimize the Sandinistas at a time when the Church leadership was bound on a path of confrontation with the revolutionary government. In 1990, while the Episcopal Conference understandably preferred the UNO coalition over the FSLN, it tried to be honest and open in its "orientations" to Nicaragua's Catholics. The bishops advised the faithful that it was their "duty" to vote in the elections and seemed to encourage them to consider selecting the UNO option: "Christians should not support ideologies that are based on hatred and that give rise to divisions in both society and our families, while encouraging attitudes of hedonism and violence that are in opposition to Christian morals."[36] Yet the rest of the letter is balanced, telling Nicaraguans to vote with their conscience and without fear of expressing their political preferences, since this would undoubtedly assist the efforts to bring peace to Nicaragua.

In 1984 the hierarchy had avoided any action or statement that could have been taken as justifying or legitimizing the election, but in 1990, on the day of the election itself, it was a very different matter. The front page of the election-day issue of *Barricada*, for instance, was devoted to a study of Daniel Ortega and Miguel Obando y Bravo. A large photograph of the two of them together and the emotional and melodramatic lead article, "Daniel and Miguel: Let's Vote for Peace," tried hard to show the similarities in the position of the two leaders:

The mother of former Nicaraguan president Daniel Ortega attends mass at
Santa María de los Angeles, a church where Father Uriel Molina developed an
important Christian base community.

They are two men born amidst the bustle of the mining area,
where gold flourished—but which neither of their families ever
received. . . . Both men gave their lives, in a total and
uncompromising fashion, to the mission of serving others. If it
was true that a religious vocation was shared by both, it is also true
that both decided to undertake a mission in their lives with
religious fervor. They faced no other alternative but to give of
themselves, above their humble backgrounds; without passing
through the sins of this world; with devotion and faith that was
both religious and political. Whereas Daniel spent seven years in
Somoza's prison, Obando spent seven long years meditating on a

faith and religious vocation (that were never in doubt) in Salvadorian seminaries.[37]

This panegyric to the "two natives of Chontales" is all the more extraordinary when one considers that it appeared in the "official organ of the Frente Sandinista de Liberación Nacional." It symbolizes the manner in which the revolutionary government and the Church hierarchy had reached some sort of an understanding—somewhat superficial and based on tactical considerations, of course, yet nevertheless an important step in search of détente. The other pro-Sandinista newspaper, *El Nuevo Diario,* also carried a major article on Obando y Bravo, who was apparently exercising his right to vote for the first time. Calling upon all sides—including the Bush administration—to respect the popular decision, the cardinal noted: "If the Frente Sandinista wins, we must accept it; and if the other side wins, then the same thing applies."[38] For its part, in the wake of the electoral victory by UNO, the hierarchy issued an important document on March 1, 1990, "Guidelines of the Nicaraguan Episcopal Conference on the Postelection Period," in which—in extremely measured and careful tones—the bishops called for an end to the war, praised the fairness of the electoral process, condemned the acts of violence committed by those displeased with the election results (although they still refrained from condemning continuing contra attacks), and congratulated the government on their acceptance of the democratic results.[39] Clearly, tension between the Sandinistas and Cardinal Obando y Bravo had subsided noticeably. And whereas the cardinal was undoubtedly delighted (and probably surprised) with Violeta Chamorro's electoral victory, it seems fair to assume that—had the Sandinistas won—the pursuit of what could be termed ecclesial détente would have continued nonetheless.

Dialogue or Negotiation?

This chapter has focused on what is undoubtedly the most complex and emotional period of Church-state relations in recent Nicaraguan history. Major problems and significant confrontations, which had been commonplace in the previous period, continued to characterize this troubled relationship. Moreover, within the two wings of the Church, vitriolic attacks continued—as Church leaders and representatives of the "Church of the poor" hurled insults at each other and refused to seek a modus vivendi. Some uncompromising members of the hierarchy, such as Obando y Bravo and Vega, showed extremely little flexibility, refusing to dialogue with their ecclesial opponents while insisting that they accept unquestioningly the dictates of the Church leadership. In this ongoing intraecclesial power struggle, the predominant role of the archdiocese of Managua—and of the archbishop's personal tenacity—should not be underestimated.

At the same time, however, this was a period of significant change, as both the revolutionary government and the Church hierarchy decided to tone down their inflammatory rhetoric against their respective foes. The sight of Daniel Ortega and Miguel Obando y Bravo praying together and the lavish praise bestowed on the cardinal in *Barricada* are developments that would have been inconceivable just a short time earlier. In short, there was substantial movement on each side to seek accommodation with the other. Unfortunately, this political détente has not been accompanied by religious reconciliation within the Church itself. For a variety of reasons—not the least of which is the hierarchy's determination not to allow the grass-roots Church to take root and thereby challenge its authority—such reconciliation appears to be extremely unlikely in the near future.

A question that surrounds the modus vivendi that developed between the Sandinistas and the Church hierarchy is whether it sprang from a genuine desire for dialogue or was based on the need for a pragmatic solution to problems that were threatening to career out of control. The answer appears to be that although Church and government leaders in earlier periods had paid lip service to the importance of meaningful dialogue, they had never pursued it with any determination or serious intent. This was especially true in the case of the cardinal, who for many years regarded the Sandinistas as anathema and their reform programs as virtually diabolical. Subsequently, however, both Church and government leaders saw that it behooved them to pursue a path of gradual détente: such a course served each side's self-interest, enhancing their credibility and influence both at home and abroad. Both Church and state, then, sought to improve relations because it was tactically advantageous to do so. It is a tragedy for the Nicaraguan Church as a whole that the same tactical benefits could not be discerned within the Church itself, since the sometimes vicious infighting within ecclesial circles has left many profound scars. Religious orthodoxy has thus triumphed—but at a cost that has yet to be fully appreciated by the main protagonists.

✝

PROPHETIC STANCE OR

POLITICAL ACCOMMODATION?

The situation of our country is
very difficult. I invite all our
brothers to try to solve our
problems through
conversation, to avoid
bloodshed, acts of violence.

Cardinal Miguel Obando y
Bravo, May 16, 1990

SPEAKING TO REPORTERS IN Managua on his way to meet
with former president Daniel Ortega, Cardinal Obando y Bravo once
again threw himself into the political fray. This time it was to resolve a
massive labor dispute that had crippled Nicaragua's civil service,
telecommunications, hospitals, transportation, banks, and schools as
workers demanded significant pay increases from the new UNO
government. For more than a decade they had tightened their belts and
put up with spiraling inflation and increasing deprivation. Now,
however, given the Bush administration's support of Violeta Chamorro,
the moment seemed right to push for a significant increase in their
salaries. It was an extremely tense time for Nicaragua: the contras still
had not demobilized, Sandinista youth cadres were calling on the
government not to cede power to the Chamorro coalition (which had
already started to come apart at the seams), and virtually the entire civil
service was threatening to close down the country's schools, hospitals,
communications services, and all the ministries. There were serious
questions too about the country's armed forces (still headed by
Humberto Ortega, brother of the former president) and a widespread

fear that the situation could easily get out of hand. This was the context in which Obando y Bravo stepped into the fray in an effort to reconcile such diverse potential crises.

It is fitting that a quotation from the cardinal head this final section, for he has been the most influential Church representative in Nicaragua for the last two decades, a man who has often dominated the national religious—and often political—stage. In the days following the February 25, 1990, election he had already mediated in several minor disputes between UNO and the FSLN, and he played a prominent role in the actual swearing-in ceremony of Violeta Chamorro, at which he addressed the crowd for a full thirty minutes—an unmistakable sign of the authority he possessed.

Yet while the cardinal has played a seminal role in Nicaraguan political life for some twenty years (and will undoubtedly continue to do so in the future), his contribution has not been totally positive. Indeed, his single-minded determination in his personal crusade to bring the "errant wing" of the Church back into the ecclesial fold has in many ways been counterproductive—particularly if one accepts the central thrust of the policy of aggiornamento so carefully emphasized by Vatican II and Medellín. The legacy of frustration and despair that remains among liberal clergy will take many years to dissipate. Thus, while orthodoxy has indeed won the day, and while the progressive Church sector and its "preferential option for the poor" have beaten a strategic retreat, the scars of a long and extremely bloody struggle remain. It behooves the cardinal to apply some soothing balm over these festering wounds—yet this is a policy he will probably choose to ignore since it goes directly against the very grain of his own vision of the Church's role, compromising the structure and authority needed to ensure its prominence.

The political role of the cardinal is well illustrated in a cartoon published in the October 26, 1988, issue of the *Guardian,* which shows the cardinal driving into the U.S. embassy and then visiting *La Prensa,* the offices of the democratic opposition, and the business council COSEP. He stops his car to chide a priest who is giving bread to a poor campesino, telling him, "How many times must I tell you the Church shouldn't get involved in politics?" This emphasizes what has been a constant of the hierarchy's position for several centuries—namely, the inconsistent, even hypocritical, attitude regarding the role of the Church in politics. The official line is that the Church should interest itself only in purely spiritual matters, in pastoral concerns. The problem with such a blanket statement is that it has never reflected reality and probably never will.

Yet the Nicaraguan hierarchy, under Cardinal Obando y Bravo, continues to maintain this argument even while it breaks its own guidelines by participating overtly in political matters. The key to this inconsistency is that the hierarchy elects to determine the very parameters of political activity, and in doing so it defines those facets that it regards as unwholesome. By the same token, the hierarchy *does* allow (and even actively encourages) that political activity which strengthens its own political, moral, and social stance. In other words, there is an obvious double standard concerning what is permissible in the political realm—with the key to proper political participation held firmly in the hands of the hierarchy.

The current period in Nicaragua is marked by the dramatic extent to which the Church has been caught up in the maelstrom of political tension—and there has certainly been more than enough grist for the ecclesial mill. Yet as the history of the Nicaraguan Church reveals, this is but the latest (if most extensive) period in which the Church has pursued political options. Indeed, the idea of an apolitical Church, devoted solely to spiritual matters, is absurd and ahistorical. From biblical times hence, the role of religion has revolved around making choices—many of which are of a strictly political nature. The courageous position taken by Bishop Valdivieso in the sixteenth century as he sought to protect the native population was thus as political an action as Archbishop González y Robleto's spirited defense of the Somoza dynasty. That is to say, both prelates pursued a clear-cut political option.

If the Church in Nicaragua (and indeed throughout the world) has never been apolitical, a corollary to that observation is that in most cases its leadership has tended to support the status quo. This is not surprising, since it is the middle-class and wealthy sectors of society who send their children to the exclusive (and often highly regarded) private schools run by the Church, who provide funding for charitable works and a variety of Church projects, and whose social interests most closely resemble those of the hierarchy. While exceptions like Valdivieso may be found, a dispassionate study of Church history reveals that more conservative Church representatives are the norm. In the case of contemporary Nicaragua, this has been particularly obvious, with the Church hierarchy strongly supporting positions shared by COSEP and the democratic opposition, while consistently shunning the "radical" reforms of the Sandinistas. A message of visceral anticommunism (which has been used extremely loosely to encompass anything to the political left of the Christian Democrats), accompanied by diatribes against any form of structural reform (be it in educational or agrarian matters), was thus to be expected. In Obando y Bravo's case, when such a stance was allied with a policy of deliberately ignoring the wanton abuses of the contras, which brought pain to tens of thousands of Nicaraguan (Catholic) families, the cardinal had arguably lost contact with his essential mandate as pastor of the entire Nicaraguan population.

What aided, and indeed emphasized, this identification with conservative interests was the impact of the Cold War. For Catholics and members of the "free world" born during this era, a staunchly anticommunist philosophy was inbred over a period of many years. Members of the Church hierarchy were also socialized along these lines. This philosophy led them to secure a niche for themselves in Somoza's Nicaragua and to view the dictator as an imposing bulwark against the encroachments of international communism. After the revolutionary victory of Fidel Castro in nearby Cuba and, even more dramatically, the entry of Havana into the Soviet sphere of influence, the Church leadership decided that the threat of communism posed the greatest potential danger for Latin America.

The July 1979 victory of the Frente Sandinista de Liberación Nacional, while promising to usher in a new era of social justice and much-needed reforms, also represented for many Church representatives an updated version of that danger. For while the Christian sector as a whole—indeed, virtually the entire population—had participated in the overthrow of the dictator, it was clear that there were "hard-liners" in the Sandinista camp who were avowed Marxists. Indeed, the eve of the revolutionary victory saw Obando y Bravo in Caracas seeking to patch together a coalition that would take political control of Nicaragua—precisely so that the relatively inexperienced Sandinistas would be marginalized. To a large degree, then, it was an inbred, almost instinctive fear of anything that smacked of Marxism that profoundly concerned the hierarchy. Reading through scores of Church documents, sermons, communiqués, pastoral letters, and the like, one is tempted to conclude that the hierarchy in Nicaragua would accept virtually any form of government *provided that it was not Marxist*.

This Cold War atmosphere that permeated the Nicaraguan hierarchy's weltanschauung (and therefore colored its views of the Sandinistas, even though the dreaded "hard core" was remarkably limited and the despised reforms were quite mild in comparison with anything found in Cuba) also made itself felt in the Vatican and in Washington. In the United States, the election of Ronald Reagan augured ill for the future of revolutionary Nicaragua—especially in light of his poor grasp of international affairs, simplistic understanding of Latin America, and knee-jerk reaction to any form of nonconservative political philosophy. The destruction of the Nicaraguan revolution soon became a deeply embedded personal obsession, and Cardinal Obando y Bravo became for Reagan a symbol of the "heroic resistance" against the inhuman "totalitarianism" of the Sandinista government.

While Reagan would provide the material aid to depose the revolutionary government and would stop at nothing in order to do so, it was the Vatican that legitimized Obando y Bravo's outspoken attacks on the Nicaraguan government, and it sought to use all its powers of spiritual authority to sway the population against the Sandinistas. John Paul II, himself a refugee from an authoritarian Marxist government (and originating from an extremely conservative Church), saw in the Nicaraguan context a similar situation to what he had personally experienced in his native Poland. An uncompromising, tenacious, and authoritarian Church leader, he saw in Obando y Bravo a person whose situation closely resembled his own bitter experiences, and he therefore decided to support Obando y Bravo in opposing the Latin American version of this totalitarian and atheistic oppression. Once again, the political realm of the Church should be underscored—this time manifested through the personal intervention of the pontiff himself, who did all in his power to aid the embattled bishop (including promoting him to cardinal).

One final characteristic of Catholicism in Nicaragua should be noted. In this study, I have attempted to show that politics has been an omnipresent concern of the Church since the cross and the sword arrived in Nicaragua some five centuries ago. Moreover, in an effort to stabilize its influence and to protect its own social identity (thereby strengthening its capacity to evangelize), the Church leadership has tended to side with those exercising power and influence. The end result is that in general the Church has been co-opted, choosing to look after its own interests (temporal as well as spiritual) as its primary objective. Thus charity was often preferred to social justice, since the latter could

Children waiting for food at a local store, Managua.

well lead to an examination of the Church's political allegiances—potentially reducing the institution's own well-being and influence.

The emphasis on charity as opposed to justice is a theme commonly expressed by Cardinal Obando y Bravo. In early 1991, for example, after it had been shown that Nicaragua's inflation rate for 1990 was the worst in Latin America (13,500%),[1] the Chamorro government devalued the currency to one-twentieth of its previous worth. This move made life very difficult for most ordinary Nicaraguans, yet the cardinal supported President Chamorro—although he did hope that "those with resources will not seek to take greater advantage of the poor, since we all have to practice charity."[2]

Yet there has always been a courageous minority of priests and religious who preferred to practice what they preached and who were shocked and dismayed at the manner in which their religious superiors had been co-opted. At crucial times in Nicaraguan history these

Churchmen and -women took a stand to support the interests of the marginalized and fought against what they perceived as injustice, as can be seen in their defense of the indigenous peoples at the time of the struggle for independence, in the era of William Walker's piracy, and during Sandino's opposition to the U.S. marines. Their presence is also seen among those people who dared to stand up to the Somoza dictatorship during its four decades of brutality and corruption.

Always these priests and religious (and occasionally a bishop) were a distinct minority, often the butt of criticism and censorship by the Catholic hierarchy—in essence because they were making life difficult for the bishops. Moreover, they were often criticized by their fellow priests and religious who regarded them as being too "political" (without admitting that there is no such thing as being apolitical and that in criticizing their colleagues they too were pursuing a political option). The end result has been a form of religious polarization, a divided Church that is as old as the very presence of Christianity in Nicaragua. The only difference is that since the mid-1960s (until recently) there has been a legitimizing wind of change emanating from Church magisterium, one that has inspired Church representatives to become the "voice of the voiceless."

In recent years, under an extremely conservative pontiff, a form of authoritarian orthodoxy has steadily replaced the upsurge of ecclesial liberalism that flourished in the late 1960s and early 1970s. Some theologians have been obliged to remain silent on ecclesial matters for extensive periods, retiring liberal bishops have been replaced by staunch conservatives, and priests with controversial positions on Church doctrine have been admonished and told to remain silent. This has been particularly noticeable in Latin America, where liberation theology had developed quite swiftly during the last thirty years. In the Nicaraguan context, this process of polarization has led to two distinct camps, one supporting the modernizing trend unleashed by the radical reforms of Vatican II (1962–65) and Medellín (1968) and the other seeking to turn back the hands of time and stifle this outburst of liberalism. Yet this division can be found to various degrees throughout Latin America, in Brazil and Peru, Chile and Argentina. Perhaps more germane to our argument, it has been a commonplace feature of Church history for several centuries—except that it did not have the (temporary) legitimation of the above-mentioned reforms. Valdivieso was thus a member of the dreaded "Church of the poor" several centuries ago, and if he were alive today he would undoubtedly be regarded with some suspicion both by the cardinal and by the Vatican.

This acceptance of the Church as a political body, exercising substantial influence throughout the world, is at times difficult to accept, trained as we are to see Church leaders as being "above politics." The Vatican, however, has serious vested interests in the Nicaraguan case, not only because an inability to rein in this errant wing would send all the wrong signals to the many supporters of liberation theology around the world, but also because within the next decade the majority of the world's Catholics will live in Latin America—hence the need for general orthodoxy in Church magisterium if the universal Catholic Church is to be a credible, unified Church. Thus, at the moment Nicaragua just happens to be in the eye of the ecclesial storm, a storm that—from the Vatican's perspective—simply has to be subdued.

What next for the Church in Nicaragua? With the new government in power for so short a time it is foolhardy to speculate excessively. Nevertheless, certain observations can be made. The Catholic hierarchy is in general delighted that doña Violeta—in every sense a traditional, respectful Catholic—is in power, for she and her political backers represent the class of managers and politicians with which the hierarchy feels most comfortable, the class whose interests most closely resemble the hierarchy's own. The Church leadership will continue to present itself as being "neutral," although it will have a much more supportive relationship with Chamorro than with the Sandinistas. Thus, no fulminating pastorals condemning atheistic and materialistic education will be produced, no Virgins will be discovered miraculously crying over Nicaragua's march toward totalitarianism.

Meanwhile, the progressive Church in Nicaragua will continue to face great difficulties. No longer does it have the moral and political support of the government, and its international credibility has undoubtedly suffered as a result of the Sandinistas' electoral loss. Moreover, Cardinal Obando y Bravo gives every indication that he does not support for the Church the reconciliation he urged in order to achieve a national political settlement. Finally, the Vatican leaders, who in the mid-1980s sought to rein in liberation theology by imposing silencing orders on leading theologians and replacing retiring bishops with solid conservatives throughout Latin America, will maintain their ecclesial pressure in order to ensure that official orthodoxy—as outlined by them—will prevail.

It remains to be seen whether the grass-roots Church can reciprocate Daniel Ortega's claim that the Sandinistas will return to basics, building up their membership and "ruling from below." Certainly, the ecclesial odds stacked against the progressives would indicate that this is no easy task. But despite the awesome obstacles to be overcome within the Church, the solid bedrock (if minority) support enjoyed by the "Church of the poor" is also quite substantial. It also remains to be seen how, after something akin to normalcy returns to Nicaragua, the progressive wing of the Church will react to the cardinal's guidance. It is not beyond the realm of possibility that some of his fellow bishops might speak out in favor of a softening of his approach. The hierarchy has never been totally united behind Cardinal Obando y Bravo's often single-track approach, and although this minority opinion has never been particularly vocal, it nevertheless exists. Much will also rest on the shoulders of the progressive Church leaders, and on how they react to the new circumstances. In sum, it is time for the progressive sector of the Church to come fully to terms with the reality of a Chamorro government (and all that implies) and then determine how they can participate effectively in this context. Certainly the challenges facing the progressives are great indeed—but the grass-roots Church was able to rise above even greater adversities in the last decade of Somocismo.

The future thus looks confused for Nicaragua as a whole, with so much hinging on whether Violeta Chamorro and her loose multiparty coalition (aided by a desired infusion of U.S. aid) can improve Nicaragua's economic fortunes, bring peace and stability to the region, and improve living conditions for Nicaragua's population. But whatever the future brings to this embattled country, the Church—in both its wings—will be intimately involved, in politics as in every other sphere. It was ever thus, despite popular beliefs to the contrary, and to expect anything else would be both erroneous and naive.

✝

NOTES

Chapter 1

1. See Franzella Wilson N., Jilma Soza A., and Matilde Gutiérrez D., "Investigaciones para la historia de la Iglesia en Nicaragua" (master's thesis, Universidad Centroamericana, Managua, 1975), vol. 1, 7.

2. In his authoritative history, Jorge Eduardo Arellano refers to the mass baptisms occurring in the wake of the arrival of one of the first Spanish conquistadores, Gil González Dávila: "In this manner some 9,018 people living in the territory of the Indian leader Nicaragua . . . and some 12,067 of Nochari 'province' were baptized. In addition some 10,000 in what is now Costa Rica were also christened, giving a total of 32,264 baptized Indians in one campaign." See Jorge Eduardo Arellano, *Breve historia de la Iglesia en Nicaragua (1523–1979)* (Managua: n.p. 1980?), 9.

3. Ibid., 11.

4. Ibid., 13.

5. Quoted in Oscar González Gary, *Iglesia Católica y revolución en Nicaragua* (Mexico City: Claves Latinoamericanas, 1986), 1:49–50.

6. Ibid., 60.

7. See ibid., 67, and Edgar Zúñiga, *Historia eclesiástica de Nicaragua: La Cristiandad colonial (1524–1821)* (Managua: Editorial Unión, 1981), 31.

8. In their decree of May 2, 1527, for example, the Reyes Católicos spoke of the exploitation to which the natives were subjected and explained Alvarez Osorio's mission in Nicaragua: "Since there are so many Indians in Nicaragua, and it is such a rich area, we have agreed to send a conscientious representative to be the protector and defender of these people, looking out for their proper treatment, protection and conversion. He will be charged to ensure that they not be maltreated without good cause, and will also make certain that the regulations designed to protect their fair treatment be respected." Quoted in Wilson, Soza, and Gutiérrez, "Investigaciones," vol. 1, 25.

9. Cited in Zúñiga, *Historia eclesiástica*, 89.

10. Cited in González Gary, *Iglesia Católica*, 77.

11. Ibid., 82.

12. Writing to the king of Spain in 1676, Bishop Navas y Quevedo indicated that—more than 150 years later—the situation of the Indians had not improved: "In two entire years the effect of two major plagues would not have brought about as much damage as has been inflicted on these poor Indians by the Governor of Nueva Segovia. The Indians have been stripped of their mules, honeycombs, cattle, and horses, and they are virtually never left alone." Cited in Tayacán, *Historia de la Iglesia de los Pobres en Nicaragua* (Managua: CEHILA, 1983), 21.

13. It is interesting to note, however, that the lower clergy were often displeased with the political stance of their religious leaders, and indeed at times they were involved in attempts to bring about independence from Spain. Among the best-documented cases are the uprisings of 1725 and 1727 in León, in which several priests participated. For further information, see González Gary, *Iglesia Católica*, 92–93.

14. Ibid., 22, 26.

15. Cited in Arellano, *Breve historia,* 51.

16. Among the reforms brought in by García Jérez were prohibitions against blaspheming, "providing shelter to unknown persons, possessing any type of armament, intoxication. Fines were imposed on those who illegally processed alcohol and on those who did not stop when ordered to do so by the security forces. People were also prevented from engaging in gambling, and young and lazy citizens were prohibited from entering billiard halls. The heads of families were obliged to keep their children at home. . . . In addition anybody who sought to lead a public disturbance would be shot to death, and anybody who participated in such a mob or insulted the authorities would be sent to serve in the Spanish army." Cited in Zúñiga, *Historia eclesiástica,* 304–5.

17. Tomás Ruiz deserves more ample study, since he was clearly the most radical priest seeking reform. The brief biographical details that we do have indicate that he was a fascinating figure: not only was he the first Nicaraguan Indian to become a priest (and the first to obtain a doctorate in law), but he was also a leading political activist. Indeed, since 1805, when—together with the Franciscan José Antonio Monino—he had led the first public demonstration in Nicaragua (at El Viejo) against Spanish domination, Ruiz had been a major influence on those members of the clergy seeking radical reform. For further information, see González Gary, *Iglesia Católica*, 98–99.

18. John A. Booth, *The End and the Beginning: The Nicaraguan Revolution* (Boulder, Colo.: Westview, 1982), 12.

19. Cited in Donald C. Hodges, *Intellectual Foundations of the Nicaraguan Revolution* (Austin: University of Texas Press, 1986), 111.

20. Cited in Manzar Foroohar, "The Catholic Church and Socio-political

Conflict in Nicaragua, 1968–1979" (Ph.D. diss., University of California, Los Angeles, 1984), 102.

21. Ibid.

22. Bishop Ulloa y Larios, for example, in a pastoral letter issued in León on May 24, 1887, outlined the necessary tariffs to be given to the Church by the faithful. Among these *aranceles* to be paid parish priests were one of every seven "calves, colts, young mules, donkeys, goats, and pigs," as well as a similar portion of chickens, ducks, coffee, cheese, cotton, corn, etc. This was justified "since the payment to Ministers of the Altar of the year's first fruits (*las primicias*) has always been a worthy custom of religion, a tribute offered to God Our Lord to thank Him for the immense benefits we have received from His paternal interest in His creatures." Those who chose not to make such contributions were warned of the penalty facing them: "the Sacred Councils and Sovereign Pontiffs have ordered excommunion against those who in any way disobey this order and retain in their power these Sacred products," and they were warned that absolution for their sins would not be given. See *Cuaderno que contiene dos pastorales del Ilmo. Sr. Obispo de Nicaragua Dr. D. Francisco Ulloa y Larios* (León, Nicaragua: Tipografía del Istmo, 1893), 2, 4–5.

23. In a note to the U.S. embassy, Díaz revealed his slavish dependence on U.S. military support: "The serious dangers which beset us can only be destroyed by skillful and efficient aid from the United States, like that which produced such good results in Cuba. For this reason it is my intention, through a treaty with the American Government, to modify or enlarge the Constitution . . . permitting the United States to intervene in our internal affairs in order to maintain peace." Cited in George Black, *Triumph of the People: The Sandinista Revolution in Nicaragua* (London: Zed Press, 1981), 8.

24. "As well as having its European debts cancelled by new loans, the Díaz government received working capital and stood by while the Americans appointed a controller of customs revenues and assumed effective control of Nicaraguan finances, handing over U.S.-stipulated sums to the Nicaraguan Government on a monthly basis. Customs revenues, the railways, and the national steamship company were offered as security against loans contracted at punitive rates from the U.S. banking houses of Brown Brothers and Seligman, and American administrators were duly appointed to each of these utilities. 51% of shares in the Banco Nacional were handed over to U.S. bankers, and the tax laws and currency overhauled according to Washington's wishes. By the time of the presidency of General Emiliano Chamorro, who came to power in 1916, financial control had been neatly formalised in a three-man committee composed of the Nicaraguan Minister of Finance and two North Americans. . . . Even this paled, however, by comparison with the latest canal treaty . . . which gave the United States exclusive rights in perpetuity to construct a canal

on Nicaraguan territory. . . . In exchange the Nicaraguan Conservatives received $3 million, which went straight to New York to pay off interest on loans. The handover of Nicaragua was complete." Ibid., 9–10.

25. See Arellano, *Breve historia,* 83.

26. Cited in Foroohar, "Socio-political Conflict," 108.

27. Cited in Arellano, *Breve historia,* 81. In this dramatic appeal, the Nicaraguan bishop then explained to his North American colleague the extent of the military occupation, particularly as it affected his own churches: "Intervention! Most eminent Cardinal, you cannot imagine how harsh that word is. . . . You have never experienced the double sorrow—as a bishop and as a citizen—of hearing the echo of heavy military boots resound beneath the nave of our churches. You have never cried with pain upon seeing the crucifix taken down from our cathedral—to be replaced with the flag of the conqueror now flying on the cathedral towers. . . . You have not seen the sanctuary changed into a military barracks, and the altar where communion is sanctified turned into a serving table for the soldiers' meals" (pp. 80–81).

28. Cited in González Gary, *Iglesia Católica,* 148–49.

29. Ibid., 145.

30. Cited in Arellano, *Breve historia,* 86.

31. This event caused Church historian Arellano to comment as follows: "When José María Moncada accepted the commemorative medal of the First Eucharistic Congress from the hands of Msgr. José Antonio Lezcano, the Church was in essence abandoning itself to the dictator of the day in order to protect its interests and retain its traditional hegemony. Indeed, it was also maintaining its complicity—established many years earlier—with North American imperialism." See Arellano, *Breve historia,* 84.

32. Pedro Buissink, *Primer anuario eclesiástico de la Iglesia Católica en Centro América* (Escuintla, Guatemala: Talleres Sánchez y de Guise, 1924), 43–44.

33. Cited in Arellano, *Breve historia,* 87–88.

Chapter 2

1. For an insightful study of Anastasio Somoza García's rise to social and military prominence, read Bernard Diederich's eminently readable study *Somoza and the Legacy of U.S. Involvement in Central America* (New York: E. P. Dutton, 1981), especially 1–50.

2. See Booth, *End and Beginning,* 68–69. Booth estimates that by 1945 Somoza's personal wealth was between $10 and $60 million: "This was just the beginning, however. . . . [He] converted his virtually absolute political dominion into immense economic power. The public purse became his own, government enterprises became lackeys to his personal interests, and regulatory powers stifled his competition. Unchallenged conflict of interests, theft,

embezzlement, and graft generated wealth that financed his somewhat more legitimate investments" (page 68).

3. Philip J. Williams, "The Catholic Hierarchy in the Nicaraguan Revolution," *Journal of Latin American Studies* 17 (November 1985): 347–48, n. 23.

4. See "Two Intercepts Dated April 5, 1945," *Confidential U.S. Diplomatic Post Records. Central America: Nicaragua 1930–1945*, reel 37, frames 169–71.

5. Cited in José Antonio Lezcano y Ortega, *Predicación pastoral en las Dominicas de un año litúrgico* (Managua: Carlos Heuberger, 1939), 5.

6. Ibid., 88–89.

7. Lezcano continues developing this argument, warning his readers not to despair at apparent discrepancies between bad Christians who may receive material rewards and good, humble Christians who do not: "This is because God follows the same approach as do doctors with their patients. Therefore, the patient who can be cured is subjected to all kinds of painful treatment and discomfort, whereas the one who has an incurable disease is allowed to do as he will, since his death is certain." Ibid., 139.

8. Ibid., 195.

9. Ibid., 127.

10. Ibid., 130.

11. Cited in Williams, "Catholic Hierarchy," 19.

12. See *Recuerdos del primer congreso catequístico nacional de Nicaragua (Celebrado en la ciudad de León del 28 de diciembre de 1938 al 1o. de enero de 1939* (León, Nicaragua: n.p., 1939?), 47.

13. "I am pleased to learn, through the respected voice of Your Excellency, that the preliminary stages have been successfully completed. The enthusiasm for the congress is indeed extraordinary, and indeed it bears eloquent witness to the strong sentiments of spirituality held by the Nicaraguan people, who exercise their religious devotion within the broadest freedom guaranteed by my government." See the *Album del magno congreso nacional del Apostolado de la Oración y de las Juventudes Marianas de la república de Nicaragua* (Managua: Secretariado Nacional del Apostolado de la Oración de las Congregaciones Marianas, 1942), 70.

14. See Finley to Sec. of State; Dis. 2799, January 8, 1945, Managua; "President Somoza Attended a Eucharistic Congress at Leon December 31–January 3 Whose Significance Was Political Rather than Religious," *Confidential U.S. Diplomatic Post Records. Central America: Nicaragua 1930–1945*, reel 36, frame 676.

15. Congreso Eucarístico de Cultura Católica, *Album conmemorativo del congreso inter-Parroquial de cultura católica y primer eucarístico del Departamento de Masaya (3 al 8 de enero de 1950)* (Managua: Católica, 1950), 48.

16. Ibid., 53.

17. See Lacayo Swan's comments in the *Memoria del pequeño congreso de*

hombres católicos, Celebrado en el Instituto Pedagógico (Managua: San José, 1953), 16–17.

18. Statistics cited in Black, *Triumph of the People,* 37.

19. See Williams, "Catholic Hierarchy," 346–47.

20. Cited in Arellano, *Breve historia,* 91.

21. "Carta Pastoral Eclesiástica del Excelentísimo y Reverendísimo Monseñor Doctor Don Vicente Alejandro González y Robleto, Arzobispo de Managua. 3 de Agosto de 1959," 5–6. Page references to subsequent quotations are given in the text.

22. "All the authors coincide in denying this course of action. If it were to be employed, it would give full rein to anarchy. The people would then hold sovereign power, higher even than that held by their ruler. They would then not only be the judge of their own case, but also the master of the nation's sovereignty. We would then fall into the agitated river of the most troubled demagogic theories." Ibid., 12.

23. By way of contrast, Philip Williams notes the exceptional position taken by Bishop Calderón y Padilla, who published his own pastoral letter two weeks later "in which he qualified the principle of divine origin of authority by saying, 'The authority is null when there is no justice.' He went on to add that when the civil authority is in open opposition to 'divine laws,' man is free to oppose the civil authority. In such cases, resistance is a duty and obedience a crime." See Philip J. Williams, *The Catholic Church and Politics in Nicaragua and Costa Rica* (London: Macmillan, 1989), 22.

24. In particular, a presentation by Dr. Ernesto Castillo, of Managua's Universidad Centroamericana, included a detailed description of Nicaragua's "human reality." Among the "lowlights" of Castillo's lengthy talk some figures stand out: there were only 4,410 hospital beds for 1.8 million inhabitants, and for every 10,000 inhabitants there were only 4.8 doctors, 22 nurses, and 0.4 dentists. He put this in perspective by noting how "in order to defend just one family [i.e., the Somozas] with the national military more than 36 billion córdobas had been spent in the 1967 budget. On the other hand, in order to defend the health of 1.8 million Nicaraguans, only 19,282,000 córdobas had been planned" (p. 148). In the field of education there was a similar disproportionate treatment of the poor: only 16 percent of children between the ages of fourteen and eighteen were in school, while for the cost of the recently completed National Theater, some 1,536 new schools could have been built. Land tenure patterns also showed a lack of balance: 1.6 percent of large landowners controlled 42 percent of the country's arable land, while some 35 percent of the population owned only 2.5 percent. See Castillo, "Realidad Humana de Nicaragua," in the *Encuentro pastoral. De cara al futuro de la Iglesia en Nicaragua (1o. Encuentro pastoral, Managua, 20–25 enero, 25–1 febrero 1969)*

(Managua: Fichero Pastoral Centroamericano, 1969), 141–59. Page references to subsequent quotations are given in the text.

25. Ibid., 38.

Chapter 3

1. Bernard Diederich, for instance, estimates that by the end of 1967 there were only about fifty wholly committed FSLN members. See Diederich, *Somoza*, 85.

2. "In the first six months after the quake the national emergency committee received $24,853,000 in cash. The United States had sent $32 million in government funds, plus an additional $112,181 from private sources. But the Nicaraguan treasury listed the United States as providing only $16.22 million. No one seemed concerned to explain the discrepancy." See Diederich, *Somoza*, 100.

3. See Phillip Berryman, *The Religious Roots of Rebellion: Christians in Central American Revolutions*, 65.

4. Edward L. Cleary, *Crisis and Change: The Church in Latin America Today* (Maryknoll, N.Y.: Orbis Books, 1985), 18.

5. For further information, see Michael Dodson and Laura Nuzzi O'Shaughnessy, *Nicaragua's Other Revolution: Religious Faith and Political Struggle* (Chapel Hill: University of North Carolina Press, 1990), 87–90.

6. Ibid., 91.

7. See Ernesto Cardenal, *The Gospel in Solentiname*, Trans. Donald Walsh, 4 vols. (Maryknoll, N.Y.: Orbis Books, 1976–82).

8. See "Cómo se formó una comunidad cristiana," *Testimonio*, no. 10 (September 1969): 12.

9. See Félix Jiménez S., "Historia de la parroquia San Pablo Apóstol a XX años de fundación con Cristo y la revolución, 1966–1986" (Managua; 1986?, mimeo.), 6.

10. "If we summarize this first stage, it is fair to say that the parish model resulting from San Pablo is totally different from any traditional structure then existing in Nicaragua. The San Pablo model brought a number of innovations: revolutionary pastoral and theological elements for the Nicaraguan Church; extensive lay participation in both the life of the Church and the community; a strengthening of family and marital relationships; the discovery of the importance of the Bible; and the celebration of the Eucharist in which all shared and participated. All are examples of the San Pablo community model which made an important contribution to the renovation of the Church in Nicaragua. These ideas, together with the personal charisma of the parish's founder, Father José de la Jara, make this stage one of the happiest moments in parish history.

"On a personal level, the major contribution of this stage is that it gave back to people the *dignity and self-respect* which the system of exploitation and so many years of dictatorship had taken away from them. Consequently, as people entered the Christian community, they began to feel that they possessed a personal value, and had to be taken into account." Ibid., 14.

11. See González Gary, *Iglesia Católica,* 242.

12. One of the parishioners, Antonia Cortéz, described the nature of religious life when Uriel Molina arrived: "Before Father Uriel arrived, religion was practiced in a very ritualistic way. This was the case throughout Nicaragua: processions, rosaries, spiritual retreats. . . . But at the same time injustices were growing. Only a few priests felt the people's suffering, and perhaps that's why they began to work here, raising the consciousness of the people, opening our eyes to the fact that it was not just a matter of praying but also of knowing our rights." Interviewed in Margaret Randall, *Christians in the Nicaraguan Revolution* (Vancouver: New Star Books, 1983), 131.

13. Ibid., 137.

14. Randall, *Christians,* 129–30.

15. Humberto Belli, *Breaking Faith: The Sandinista Revolution and Its Impact on Freedom and Christian Faith in Nicaragua* (Garden City, Mich.: Puebla Institute, 1985), 26.

16. One of these members, Mónica Baltodano, explained the origins of her involvement with the group: "I became a member of the Frente in 1973. Earlier, in 1970, a group of *compañeros* had been affiliated with the Christian group. There we underwent our revolutionary apprenticeship, as we started to see reality. . . . Fernando Cardenal and several progressive priests participated. In these meetings we gradually became aware of the need for a change in our country—one which did not have to be only one of personal change, but rather of existing structures." Cited in González Gary, *Iglesia Católica,* 277.

17. See Randall, *Christians,* 194–95.

18. Foroohar, "Socio-political Conflict," 310.

19. See "Resonancias de Medellín en la Iglesia de Nicaragua," *SID,* no. 25 (March–April 1976): 13.

20. Roberto Sánchez, "Uso o no uso de la sotana: gran problema," *Testimonio,* no. 5 (May 1, 1969): 5.

21. See "Obispo de Granada Renunciará al Obispado dentro de 5 años," *Testimonio,* no. 5 (May 1, 1969): 12.

22. Msgr. Noel Buitrago, for instance, was quoted as saying—as he blessed a new building—that he was there "to implore the blessing of God Our Lord, and to bless these works of progress, which have resulted from the skillful hands of our great president, General Anastasio Somoza Debayle.

"May God Our Lord send from heaven His blessing to our beloved president and protect him for many years so that he can continue to assist all Nicaraguans.

"Carry on, General, along your very long path, sowing in all four cardinal points progress and work." See *Testimonio,* no. 9 (August 1969): 16.

23. From an article in *Novedades,* "Somoza es símbolo de la unidad nacional, dice el Padre Roche," reprinted in *Testimonio,* no. 11 (October 1969): 3.

24. "El Encuentro pastoral después de un año," *Testimonio,* no. 12 (February–March 1970): 4.

25. In one issue the editors sought to explain, as a form of self-defense, the fundamental nature of their concern for the much-needed social changes in Nicaragua: "It is more urgent to improve the foul promiscuous slums found in our cities than to create parks for the tourists to see.

"It is more urgent to build many modest but decent chapels throughout the suburbs than to invest thousands of córdobas in marble altars and sumptuous decorations in the city center.

"It is more urgent to sow elementary schools throughout our country than to spend vast amounts remodeling schools, universities, and official buildings.

"*Testimonio* has nothing against parks, the construction of churches, or the modernization of other buildings. *Testimonio* merely states that in a well-organized family with a limited budget one has to begin with the most urgent needs." See "*Testimonio* no está contra nadie," *Testimonio,* no. 6 (May 1969): 10.

26. See the editorial in *Testimonio,* no. 16 (April–May 1970): 2.

27. From an article in *Novedades,* reprinted in *Testimonio,* no. 11 (1969): 3.

28. "Carta pastoral de los Obispos de Nicaragua, Sobre los principios que rigen la actividad política de toda la Iglesia como tal," Managua, March 19, 1972, p.8. Further page references are cited in the text.

29. "Declaración de la Conferencia Episcopal de Nicaragua reunida en sesión extraordinaria" (May 27, 1974), *Encuentro,* no. 14 (July–December 1978): 87.

30. In an incisive analysis, Andrew Bradstock summarizes some of the innovations shown by the hierarchy in the period under study: "Obando's first letter as archbishop spoke of the Church's commitment to denounce injustice and work towards a peaceful transformation of society, and in June 1971 the bishops voiced popular concerns about the distribution of wealth and 'organizational structures' in the country. In 1972 they criticized the new constitutional arrangements and echoed calls for a 'whole new order.' In February 1973, in the wake of the earthquake in Managua, the bishops suggested that the need for material reconstruction after the disaster symbolized the need for the construction also of a new and more just society. A few months later they issued a denunciation of the violence and abuse of human rights perpetrated by the government. At the end of 1973 Archbishop Obando used the mass organized to remember the Managua earthquake as an opportunity to criticize the dictatorship, offending the president to the extent that he walked out during the Archbishop's speech and had the National Guard unplug the

amplification equipment." See Andrew Bradstock, *Saints and Sandinistas: The Catholic Church in Nicaragua and Its Response to the Revolution* (London: Epworth Press, 1987), 24.

31. Miguel Obando y Bravo, "La familia en Nicaragua," *Boletín de la Arquidiócesis de Managua,* no. 15 (August 1973): 4.

32. Miguel Obando y Bravo, "Mensaje de Navidad y Año Nuevo del Excmo. e Ilmo. Mons. Miguel Obando y Bravo, Arzobispo de Managua," *Boletín de la Arquidiócesis de Managua,* no. 18 (November 1973): 5.

33. "It is especially noteworthy that ethical norms in the field of sexuality have begun to experience great difficulty. . . . The high rate of traffic accidents: this is one of the problems which, even though on the surface it may not appear so, affects aspects of moral life such as sexuality and delinquency." See Miguel Obando y Bravo, "Mensaje de Navidad y Año Nuevo," *Boletín de la Arquidiócesis de Managua,* no. 31 (January 1975): 6–7.

34. Miguel Obando y Bravo, *Boletín de la Arquidiócesis de Managua,* no. 35 (May 1975): 6.

35. Miguel Obando y Bravo, "A los hombres que trabajan en la información," *Boletín de la Arquidiócesis de Managua,* no. 46 (April 1976): 5.

36. Miguel Obando y Bravo, "Discurso de Mons. Obando al inaugurar el período legislativo de 1976," *Boletín de la Arquidiócesis de Managua,* no. 48 (June 1976): 4.

37. Miguel Obando y Bravo, "Etica empresarial: Conferencia dictada por el Excelentísimo y Reverendísimo Mons. Miguel Obando y Bravo, Arzobispo de Managua, a la Cámara de Comercio América," *Boletín de la Arquidiócesis de Managua,* no. 49 (July 1976): 6.

38. Miguel Obando y Bravo, "Problema ético de la publicidad," *Boletín de la Arquidiócesis de Managua,* no. 50 (August 1976): 5.

39. Miguel Obando y Bravo, "Mensaje . . . a los sacerdotes y Delegados de la Palabra en la zona rural de Managua," *Boletín de la Arquidiócesis de Managua,* no. 54 (December 1976): 5.

40. "Carta de Monseñor Salvador Schlaefer" (May 20, 1975), *Encuentro,* no. 14 (July–December 1978): 91.

41. "Mensaje de la Conferencia Episcopal de Nicaragua, renovando la esperanza cristiana al iniciarse el año 1977," *Encuentro,* no. 14 (July–December 1978): 96.

42. Conferencia Episcopal de Nicaragua, "Mensaje al pueblo de Dios al iniciarse el año 1978," *Encuentro,* no. 14 (July–December 1978): 100.

43. "We finally wish to remind you: the ultimate motivation for the Christian to intervene actively in the construction of peace, here on the earth, is love. A just society, at peace, is a part of the Lord's plan. Love should be present in all situations, at the time when we choose strategies to attain peace." See "En

la hora presente: Mensaje de los obispos Católicos de Nicaragua ante la grave crisis de la Nación," *Encuentro,* no. 14 (July–December 1978): 103.

44. "Conferencia Episcopal de Nicaragua a los hombres de buena voluntad" (August 2, 1978), *Encuentro,* no. 14 (July–December 1978): 108.

45. "Mensaje del Señor Arzobispo y su Consejo Presbiteral en las actuales circunstancias que vive el país" (August 3, 1978), *Encuentro,* no. 14 (July–December 1978): 114.

46. See "Carta de la Iglesia al Presidente de los Estados Unidos," *Encuentro,* no. 14 (July–December 1978): 119.

47. See "Sacerdotes protestan represión," *La Prensa,* September 8, 1978.

48. "Arzobispo estuvo en serio peligro," *La Prensa,* September 11, 1978.

49. "Atropello a Padre Baltodano," *La Prensa,* September 30, 1978.

50. Cited in Williams, *The Catholic Church,* 37.

Chapter 4

1. "Mensaje de la Conferencia Episcopal Nicaragüense," in Centro de Estudios y Publicaciones (hereafter CEP), *Nicaragua: La hora de los desafíos* (Lima: CEP, 1981), 69.

2. Conferencia Episcopal Nicaragüense, "Compromiso Cristiano para una Nicaragua nueva," in CEP, *Nicaragua: La hora,* 74–75.

3. "It is sufficient to read all our publications to see that our crusade was totally Nicaraguan and original. I can state that the Cuban advisers who participated in the crusade were not in a position to impose anything . . . and can say in all honesty that after working for thirteen months in the crusade (including five days that I spent in Havana), nobody told me what I had to do, nor did they seek to impose anything." See "Entrevista a Fernando Cardenal," in CEP, *Nicaragua: La hora,* 45–46.

4. Cited in Belli, *Breaking Faith,* 207.

5. See the "Decreto de la Junta de Gobierno de Reconstrucción Nacional sobre Navidad," in CEP, *Nicaragua: La hora,* 101.

Belli quotes a Sandinista functionary, Julio López, who, in December 1979, had planned to exploit the Christmas celebrations to the FSLN's advantage: "After the triumph of the People's Sandinista Revolution we are working to reorient the celebration of Christmas. We want to make it a special day for the children, one with a different content, fundamentally political. In essence, we want to rescue for the revolution a tradition that, although religious, is established among our people. It is thanks to our Sandinista revolution that now our children can celebrate their Christmas in freedom and grow up in a homeland that assures them their future and their happiness. This is the central thought of the celebration." See Belli, *Breaking Faith,* 141.

6. "Carta abierta sobre las prohibiciones religiosas en Nicaragua," in CEP, *Nicaragua: La Hora,* 136.

7. Laura Nuzzi O'Shaughnessy and Luis H. Serra, *The Church and Revolution in Nicaragua* (Athens, Ohio: Ohio University Center for International Studies, 1986), 78.

8. See Williams, *Catholic Church and Politics,* 60.

9. In their "Carta abierta de comunidades eclesiales de base al CELAM," they criticized the approach of the organization: "In order to understand the situation you have delegated a cardinal who then interviewed the Nicaraguan bishops and one or two other people. Once again, however, you have excluded the masses of the people of God, where there are many priests, religious, and lay people who have lived through the Nicaraguan drama, day and night, next to the people. You are content with a report that will be sent to Rome, where the understanding of events in Nicaragua is even less." See their document in CEP, *Nicaragua: La hora,* 100.

10. See Williams, *Catholic Church and Politics,* 89.

11. Cited in Belli, *Breaking Faith,* 111.

12. Cited in O'Shaughnessy and Serra, *Church and Revolution,* 22.

13. See Michael Dodson and Laura Nuzzi O'Shaughnessy, "Religion and Politics," in *Nicaragua: The First Five Years,* ed. Thomas Walker (New York: Praeger, 1985), 134–35.

14. Williams, *Catholic Church and Politics,* 58–59.

15. See "Nicaragua," *Latinamerica Press* (Lima), October 27, 1988, 2.

16. The report in *La Prensa* shows the degree to which religious news was manipulated: "At the very moment when crowds of people, possessed by the devil, attacked Auxiliary Bishop Msgr. Vivas with blows, impious hands tore off his sacred chain and threw it like a ball among their sacrilegious followers who finally hurled it to the floor." See "Actos sacrílegos en Santa Rosa," *La Prensa,* March 2, 1982, pp. 1, 14.

17. The July 23 edition of *La Prensa* carried an official communiqué from Archbishop Obando y Bravo stating that "those Catholics who participated in the events already denounced by us are criminals, subject to the penalties outlined in the appropriate sections of the current code of canon law.

"We are also stipulating that until further notice no priest can celebrate any sacred rite in the church building in which such profanations and sacrilegious acts took place." See "Curia sentencia excomunión y cierre de templo Santa Rosa," *La Prensa,* July 23, 1982, pp. 1, 14.

18. Cited in Teófilo Cabestrero, *Ministers of God, Ministers of the People* (Maryknoll, N.Y.: Orbis Books, 1983; London: Zed Books, 1983), 4.

19. "Documento de la Conferencia Episcopal de Nicaragua," in CEP, *Nicaragua: La hora,* 120.

20. Ibid., 132–33.

21. See "Entrevista a Fernando Cardenal," in CEP, *Nicaragua: La hora,* 52.

22. Cabestrero, *Ministers of God,* 49–50.

23. Fernando Cardenal placed this in context when commenting on the difference between the role for Christians in Cuba and that of Christians in Nicaragua: "I don't understand how the same ones who complain that Christians aren't allowed to join the Communist Party of Cuba then turn around and complain that the Sandinista Party in Nicaragua not only allows Christians to join but appoints them members of the Sandinista Assembly and entrusts the political directioning of its youth movement to be a priest! This ought to be seen as something positive. It ought to be recognized that if this were to be lost, the Church would suffer a loss." Ibid., 85.

24. See "Comunicado de la Conferencia Episcopal de Nicaragua," in CEP, *Nicaragua: La hora,* 165.

25. "Primera Respuesta," in CEP, *Nicaragua: La hora,* 169.

26. Teófilo Cabestrero, for example, cites the front-page story in the *New York Times* of December 3, 1982, which noted that "Pope John Paul II has demanded that Roman Catholic priests resign from positions they hold in the Nicaraguan Government as a condition for his visiting Nicaragua early next year, Roman Catholic Church officials here said.

"The Pope's ultimatum was personally delivered to the coordinator of the Nicaraguan junta, Daniel Ortega Saavedra, in late October by the Papal Nuncio here [Managua], Msgr. Andrés Cordero Lanza di Montezemolo, the officials said." Cited in Cabestrero, *Ministers of God,* 8.

27. See Andrew Bradstock, *Saints and Sandinistas,* 62.

28. For an insightful analysis of the effect of these changes on ACLEN and CONFER, see Williams, *Catholic Church and Politics,* 61–62.

29. "Jesucristo y la unidad de Su Iglesia en Nicaragua," in CEP, *Nicaragua: La hora,* 132.

30. See "Documento de las comunidades cristianas," in CEP, *Nicaragua: La hora,* 96.

31. See the "Comunicado oficial de la Dirección Nacional de FSLN sobre la religión," in CEP, *Nicaragua: La hora,* 108.

32. See the "Documento de la Conferencia Episcopal de Nicaragua," in CEP, *Nicaragua: La hora,* 115.

33. Phillip Berryman intimates that this document might well have been inspired by just one bishop: "Its rambling style gave the impression of having been written by one fast-typing individual not inhibited by the editing process inherent in genuinely collective statements; nevertheless, since it was approved by the bishops it provided a view of what was troubling them at that time." See Berryman, *Roots of Rebellion,* 253.

34. See David Close, *Nicaragua: Politics, Economy and Society* (London: Pinter Publishers, 1988), 86–99.

35. Ibid., 151.

36. Ibid.

37. See Michael Conroy, "Economic Legacy and Policies," in Walker, *Nicaragua,* 223.

38. William LeoGrande, "The United States and Nicaragua," in Walker, *Nicaragua,* 437.

39. Close, *Nicaragua: Politics,* 102.

40. Ibid., 152, 156.

41. See Williams, *Catholic Church and Politics,* 91–92.

42. Belli, *Breaking Faith,* 170.

43. O'Shaughnessy and Serra, *Church and Revolution,* viii.

44. "There's no incompatibility between Christianity and Marxism. They aren't the same thing—they're different—but they're not incompatible. Christianity and the system called democracy aren't the same thing, but they're not incompatible. . . . Marxism is a scientific method for studying society and changing it. What Christ did was to present us with the *goals* of social change, the goals of perfect humanity, which we are to co-create with him. These goals are a community of brothers and sisters, and love. But he did not tell us which scientific methods to use in order to arrive at the goal. Science has to tell us this—in our case, the social sciences. . . .

"I have said many times that I am a Marxist for Christ and his gospel, and that I was not drawn to Marxism by reading Marx, but by reading the Gospel. It was the gospel of Jesus Christ that made a Marxist of me. . . . I'm a Marxist who believes in God, follows Christ, and is a revolutionary for the sake of his kingdom." See the interview with Ernesto Cardenal in Cabestrero, *Ministers of God,* 31–32.

45. Canuto Barreto, *Nicaragua desde Nicaragua* (Mexico City: Centro de Estudios Económicos, 1984), 89.

Chapter 5

1. See William LeoGrande, "The United States and Nicaragua," in Walker, *Nicaragua,* 437.

2. See Catholic Institute for International Relations (hereafter CIIR), *Right to Survive: Human Rights in Nicaragua* (London: CIIR, 1987), 35.

3. Ibid., 37.

4. Quoted in "Vatican Offers Criticism" (UPI), *New York Times,* March 6, 1983, p. 14.

5. "Primeras palabras de Juan Pablo II en Nicaragua libre," *Barricada,* March 5, 1983, Supplement ("Edición Especial"), n.p.

6. "Saludo en la Catedral," *El Nuevo Diario,* March 5, 1983, p. 3.

7. "Laicado y educación (Palabras de Juan Pablo II en el acto de concelebración de la palabra en León)," *Barricada,* March 5, 1983, p. 7.

8. Vincent J. Giese, "John Paul II in Central America," *Our Sunday Visitor* 71, no. 47 (March 20, 1983): 4.

9. See "Testimonios y declaraciones," *Amanecer,* no. 16 (February 1983): 8.

10. Vincent J. Giese, "Perspective," *Visitor National Catholic Family Magazine,* March 20, 1983, p. 2.

11. See *Juan Pablo II: Viaje Apostólico a Centroamérica, 2–9 de marzo de 1983,* ed. Cipriano Calderón (Madrid: Biblioteca de Autores Cristianos, 1983), 103.

12. "Si quieres la paz, lucha por la justicia," *Boletín (Iglesia Guatemalteca en el Exilio),* no. 17 (April 1983): 11.

13. Philip Williams provides some useful insights into both the preparations for the papal visit to León and the Sandinistas' naïveté. In León, the medical campus was to be swamped with posters of Archbishop Oscar Romero and Father Gaspar García Laviana, the guerrilla-priest killed while fighting against Somoza. Eventually these plans were withdrawn, although the most common poster at the ceremony was one of the pope and Msgr. Romero (a snub to Nicaragua's own prelate, Archbishop Obando y Bravo). Official instructions were also given that it was acceptable to chant "Queremos la paz" during the passing of the peace in the service. "It was this chanting," notes Williams, "which ignited the disruption of the mass in Managua. In short, rather than turning out a success for the FSLN, the visit was clearly a disaster." See Williams, *Catholic Church and Politics,* 87.

14. "Juan Pablo II saludó a los millares y millares que no pudieron llegar," *La República* (San José, Costa Rica), March 5, 1983, p. 8.

15. See the interview with Cardenal, Tomás Borge, and Sergio Ramírez in the September 1983 issue of *Playboy,* p. 140.

16. See "Orad por verdaderos cristianos de Nicaragua," *La República,* March 5, 1983, p. 9.

17. *Playboy* interview with Cardenal, Borge, and Ramírez, p. 140.

18. Belli, *Breaking Faith,* 215.

19. Berryman, *Roots of Rebellion,* 274, 275.

20. Rosa María Pochet and Abelino Martínez, *Nicaragua. Iglesia: ¿manipulación o profecía?* (San José, Costa Rica: Departamento Ecuménico de Investigaciones, 1987), 66.

21. Dodson and O'Shaughnessy, "Religion and Politics," 136.

22. See "The Religious Attack on Nicaragua's Revolution," in Ana María Ezcurra, *Ideological Aggression against the Sandinista Revolution* (New York: CIRCUS Publications, 1984), 7.

23. Barreto, *Nicaragua desde Nicaragua,* 112.

24. See the Instituto Histórico Centroamericano's *Envío* 3, no. 30 (December 1983): 20b.

25. See "Consideraciones generales de la Conferencia Episcopal de Nicaragua sobre el servicio militar," *Amanecer,* no. 20 (September–October 1983): 7.

234 t Notes to Pages 157–68

26. Cited in "Hechos y situaciones," *Amanecer,* no. 20 (September–October 1983): 6.

27. See Michael E. Conroy, "Economic Legacy and Policies: Performance and Critique," in Walker, *Nicaragua,* 240.

28. See "Carta pastoral del Episcopado Nicaraguense sobre la Reconciliación," *Amanecer,* no. 26/27 (May–June 1984): 10.

29. "The materialist interpretation of mankind distorts both the human person and Christ's doctrine. It reduces man to merely material categories without any supernatural content, and so the human being remains subjected to material forces which they term the 'dialectic of history.' And so man, devoid of God and of his own spiritual values, remains disoriented, without any moral or religious reference points, any transcendent content—insecure and violent" (p. 10).

30. "A portion, although small, of our Church has abandoned ecclesial unity and has subordinated itself to the directives of a materialistic ideology. It sows confusion, both inside and outside our borders, and engages in a campaign to exalt its own ideas while defaming the legitimate pastors and the faithful who support them" (p. 11).

31. Cited in Belli, *Breaking Faith,* 222–23.

32. Richard Shaull, "Un llamado a la reconciliación que no es conciliador," *Amanecer,* no. 26/27 (May–June 1984): 14.

33. For a list of the basic principles outlined in the March 29 communiqué, see Ezcurra, *Ideological Aggression,* 176.

34. See "Two Models of Church," *Envío* 5, no. 50 (August 1985): 3b.

35. Penny Lernoux, "The Struggle for Nicaragua's Soul," *Sojourners,* May 1989, p. 20.

36. See "Vínculos de la trasnacional 'Grace' con Monseñor Obando," *Amanecer,* no. 28/29 (July–August 1984): 19.

37. Belli, *Breaking Faith,* 242. He continues: "In Nicaragua, a testing ground for liberation theology, it can be seen that radical liberation theologies have led Christians from opposition to right-wing dictatorship to support for left-wing totalitarianism. These theologies have identified themselves with a political force which seeks to repress and divide the Churches and which will improve neither the spiritual or material lot of the poor they claim to represent" (pp. 242–43).

38. See the "Testimonios y declaraciones" section of *Amanecer,* no. 16 (February 1983): 9.

39. See "La Iglesia de los Pobres en Nicaragua," *Envío* 5, no. 58 (April 1986): 4c.

40. See Mons. Pablo Antonio Vega, "No hemos avanzado desde la Conquista," *Amanecer,* no. 36/37 (September 1985): 25.

41. See Belli, *Breaking Faith,* 217–20.

42. See CIIR, *Right to Survive,* 93.

43. See "Sacerdote implicado en actividades terroristas," *Amanecer,* no. 28/29 (July–August 1984): 10.

44. Ezcurra, *Ideological Aggression,* 183.

45. For an analysis of the activities of these priests, see Belli, *Breaking Faith,* 228–29.

46. See Fernando Cardenal, "Carta a mis amigos," *Amanecer,* no. 32/33 (January–February 1985): 15.

47. CIIR, *Right to Survive,* 94.

48. Cited in Edward R. F. Sheehan, "The Battle for Nicaragua," *Commonweal* 113, no. 9 (May 9, 1986): 265, 267.

49. Ibid., 266.

50. See "Reacción de Mons. Vega ante el asesinato de seis niños," *Amanecer,* no. 30/31 (November–December 1984): 19.

51. See Sheehan, "Battle for Nicaragua," 267.

52. Cited in Connor Cruise O'Brien, "God and Man in Nicaragua," *Atlantic Monthly* 258, no. 2 (August 1986): 51.

Chapter 6

1. See "Atlantic Coast Autonomy Plan," *Latin American Regional Reports (Mexico and Central America),* January 10, 1986, p. 6.

2. See "Huge Devaluation of the *Cordova,*" *Latin American Regional Reports (Mexico and Central America),* July 14, 1988, p. 3.

3. See "Ortega Secures New Cuban Aid Package," *Latin American Regional Reports (Mexico and Central America),* August 18, 1988, p. 6.

4. "This [legislation] was a response to the complex situation inside Nicaragua, where the government judged it necessary to tighten political controls in order to insure continued success in the military arena. . . . The renewed state of emergency put some limits on the cardinal's feverish activity. If a visit included an open-air Mass or procession, the local parish priest had to ask for prior permission from the authorities. . . . With the renewal of the state of emergency, Radio Católica was prohibited from broadcasting the cardinal's homilies on his journey." See "Church-State Relations: A Chronology—Part 1," *Envío* 6, no. 77 (November 1987): 30–31.

5. Quoted in David Adams and Todd Gibb, "Peace Plan Dies, Civil War Flares On," *Globe and Mail,* August 9, 1988, p. A7.

6. See Peter McKenna, "Nicaragua and the Esquipulas II Accord: Setting the Record Straight," *Canadian Journal of Latin American and Caribbean Studies* 14, no. 27 (1989): 61–84.

7. John Medcalf, *Letters from Nicaragua* (London: CIIR, 1988), 8.

8. Miguel D'Escoto, "Mis razones para ayunar por la paz," *Amanecer,* no. 36/37 (June–September 1985): 36.

9. The letter, sent by Msgr. Bosco Vivas (secretary of the Nicaraguan Episcopal Conference) to the president of the Brazilian sister organization, commented: "The bishops of the Nicaraguan Episcopal Conference greet our fellow bishops in Brazil and request that they respect the authority of the local bishops, avoiding any interference in Nicaraguan matters that might bring even greater difficulties to the Church here, which has already suffered greatly. . . . The bishops of Nicaragua believe that ecclesial communion and charity are seriously damaged when some bishops in Brazil speak or act while ignoring the Nicaraguan bishops' authority." Published in *Amanecer,* no. 36/37 (September 1985): 22.

10. See *"La Prensa* Repudia el Ayuno," *Amanecer,* no. 36/37 (September 1985): 23.

11. See "Church-State Relations: Part 1," 34–35.

12. In his address to conclude the "Via Crucis," D'Escoto was even more direct in his criticism of Obando y Bravo: "And now the scandal is even greater, because the bishops are not saying anything. Not only are they not saying anything, however, for there are some among them who have taken up the obligation to appease the god of death and aggression, the god of foreign intervention in Nicaragua. They have gone to the United States and calmed the conscience of congressmen there, many of whom earlier had said that this policy of Reagan was not only illegal but also immoral. But along comes this poor Nicaraguan priest, Miguel Obando, who says to these legislators: 'Don't worry, for I am the Cardinal, and I don't condemn this aggression.' In the history of humanity has there ever been such an abomination? . . .

"Miguel Obando, brother in the priesthood that you have betrayed, brother of the people whom you have sold . . . The Lord and our entire people want your repentance, want you to occupy once again the place which is appropriate for you in our Church." See "Palabras del Padre D'Escoto al finalizar el Via Crucis," *Amanecer,* no. 40/42 (January–May 1986): 31

13. See "Obispo Vega justifica apoyo norteamericano a contras," *Amanecer,* no. 38/39 (December 1985): 4.

14. See "Church-State Relations: Part 1," 38.

15. See "Mons. Vega con líderes de la contra," *Amanecer,* no. 40/42 (January–May 1986): 13.

16. See "Church-State Relations: Part 1," 39.

17. Ibid.

18. Ibid., 41.

19. "This is the Sandinista Army's military aggression. That is what is making the people decide. . . . These people are defending their human rights. And it is an ideological system's aggression, snatching, as they say, their children from them, wanting to impose on them things that are not their own, that has led them to that decision. If a people is tormented, if a people is crushed, their

human rights eliminated . . . , if [they are left without] a homeland . . . , no other remedy remains to this person." Ibid., 40–41.

20. Ibid., 40.

21. Vega's condemnation was expressed in bizarre terminology: "While in Nicaragua the greater part of the hierarchy was definitely backing the dialogue as a way of resolving tensions, Bishop Vega, speaking February 19 on the contra radio station from El Salvador, compared the dialogue with 'those homosexual marriages they're talking about these days.' 'What is a marriage between homosexuals? It is simply a sterile masturbation, with no true hope of achieving a communion that will generate new life. In the same way a dialogue with people who are totalitarian Marxists is nothing more than a marriage—which can't even be called a marriage—between homosexuals. It's sterile, it doesn't lead to anything, it doesn't generate anything because it doesn't recognize that it is the meeting between matter and spirit that will truly make a new man.' " See "Church-State Relations: A Chronology—Part 2," *Envío* 6, no. 78 (December 1987): 40.

22. See "Cardenal Obando: 'Un mundo confuso; Dios lo sabrá . . . ,' " *Barricada*, July 6, 1987, p. 1.

23. Ibid.

24. See "Decepciona actitud de Cardenal Obando," *El Nuevo Diario*, July 7, 1987, p. 8.

25. O'Brien had gone to visit the cardinal and attend his weekly mass at his parish on the outskirts of Managua: "That morning, even when saying mass, the Cardinal seemed to be spoiling for a fight. As he put on his vestments, I thought he looked like a boxer getting ready for the ring. He is a small, powerfully built man, now running to fat, with decidedly Indian features. His most marked expressive characteristic—perhaps especially marked that day—is that the corners of his lips turn sharply down." See O'Brien, "God and Man in Nicaragua," 53.

26. See "El Cardenal Obando en Estados Unidos," *Amanecer*, no. 40/42 (January–May 1986): 12.

27. Taken from a shortened version of the letter published in *Amanecer*, no. 45 (November–December 1986): 35.

28. See the pastoral proper, "Carta pastoral del Episcopado sobre la Eucaristía, *Amanecer*, no. 40/42 (January–May 1986): 40.

29. Gaspar Calderón, "Iglesia de Nicaragua: ¿Reconciliación u opción por los pobres?," *Amanecer*, no. 45 (November–December 1986): 34.

30. See the "Documento 'Kairos,' " *Amanecer*, no. 45 (November–December 1986): 29. This document was drawn up by 111 South African Christians with the intention of showing that God does indeed take sides in cases of injustice. Its applicability to the Nicaraguan context seems appropriate.

31. See "Carta pastoral de la Conferencia Episcopal de Nicaragua con

motivo de la solemnidad litúrgica de los SS. Apóstoles Pedro y Pablo," *Amanecer,* no. 57 (July–September 1988): 14.

32. See "La carta del Papa," *Amanecer,* no. 40/42 (January–May 1986): 10.

33. In a December 1986 interview, Giglio noted: "It is necessary to have the rich and the poor, because the rich are destined to provide employment for the poor. If everyone were rich, no one would want to work. It's not possible for us all to be at the same level." See sections of the interview in "Church-State Relations: Part 2," 40.

34. See, for example, the official communiqué, signed on September 19, 1987, by Auxiliary Bishop Bosco Vivas, expressing distrust at the two hundred local peace commissions—and the reaction to it by Church and government leaders in "Church-State Relations: Part 2," 48–50. The official response to the murder of Tomás Zavaleta, noted earlier in this chapter, is a further example of this approach.

35. See "Nicaragua: Carta pastoral sobre catequesis familiar," *CELAM,* no. 231 (October–November 1989): 20.

36. "Orientaciones pastorales de la Conferencia Episcopal de Nicaragua con motivo del período electoral y de las elecciones de febrero de 1990," Managua, mimeo, September 29, 1989, p. 2.

37. Carlos Alemán Ocampo, "Daniel y Miguel: A votar por Paz," *Barricada,* February 25, 1990, p. 1.

38. "Cardenal vota exhortando a la paz y respetar resultados," *El Nuevo Diario,* February 26, 1990, p. 6.

39. "We congratulate the authorities of the present government both for the efforts undertaken by them to ensure that the elections could take place in a climate of stability and for their democratic attitude as they accepted the results of the elections. We also congratulate the new government, with the hope that mutual respect between Church and state can contribute to the well-being of Nicaraguans." Conferencia Episcopal de Nicaragua, "Orientaciones de la Conferencia Episcopal de Nicaragua en el Período Post-Electoral," Managua, mimeo, March 1, 1990, p. 1.

Prophetic Stance

1. See the April 25, 1991, issue of *Latin American Weekly Report,* p. 9.

2. See Julio César Armas, "Cardenal: 'Estoy de acuerdo con frenar inflación,' " *La Prensa,* March 3, 1991, p. 4. The cardinal concluded: "When the Word of God reaches the heart of a businessman, even when it is clear that he has to make a profit, he ensures that his profits are modest, that he is not exploiting the people."

✝

SELECTED

BIBLIOGRAPHY

In addition to the extensive citations found in the notes, there are several excellent sources of bibliographical information that are worth consulting. Of particular value is the well-organized and exhaustive bibliography in Philip J. Williams, *The Catholic Church and Politics in Nicaragua and Costa Rica* (London: Macmillan, 1989), 207–21, Also useful, particularly for a detailed bibliography of the prerevolutionary Church, is Manzar Foroohar, *The Catholic Church and Social Change in Nicaragua* (Albany: State University of New York Press, 1989), 239–53. An extensive bibliography of sources in Spanish can be found in Oscar González Gary, *Iglesia Católica y revolución en Nicaragua* (Mexico City: Claves Latinoamericanas, 1986), 385–99.

For an analysis of the prerevolutionary Church, the various pastoral letters published by the Nicaraguan Episcopal Conference are particularly important, as are the various commemorative albums and specialized reports. The limited issues of *Testimonio* and the *Servicio de Información y Documentación* (*SID*) are also extremely useful for a proper understanding of conditions in the latter stages of Somoza's Nicaragua. A different perspective can be gleaned from reading the monthly *Boletín de la Arquidiócesis de Managua,* especially the regular column of Archbishop Obando y Bravo.

The polarized nature of religious life (with a minority of clergy supporting Somoza, while most others were opposed or indifferent) can be best appreciated by comparing reports of *La Prensa* (edited by Pedro Joaquín Chamorro, an ardent foe of the dictator) with those of the Somoza-run *Novedades*. This radical division can also be seen today in religious coverage in *La Prensa* (conservative and prohierarchy) and in *Barricada* and *El Nuevo Diario* (pro-Sandinista and supportive of the "Church of the poor").

Three further sources deserve mention. The Puebla Institute, headed by Humberto Belli (a friend and adviser of Cardinal Obando y Bravo), has published several reports on the situation of the Church in Nicaragua. A totally different perspective is provided by the regular journals *Amanecer* (published by the Antonio Valdivieso Ecumenical Center in Managua) and *Envío* (published by the Jesuits).

What follows is an abbreviated listing of essential detailed studies on the Catholic Church in Nicaragua. Together with the material cited in the notes, these works will provide a useful starting point for interested readers.

Arellano, Jorge Eduardo. *Breve historia de la Iglesia en Nicaragua (1523–1979)*. Managua: n.p., 1980?

Barreto, Canuto. *Nicaragua desde Nicaragua*. Mexico City: Centro de Estudios Económicos, 1984.

Belli, Humberto. *Breaking Faith: The Sandinista Revolution and Its Impact on Freedom and Christian Faith in Nicaragua*. Garden City, Mich.: Puebla Institute, 1985.

————. *Christians under Fire*. Garden City, Mich.: Puebla Institute, n.d.

Berryman, Phillip. *The Religious Roots of Rebellion: Christians in Central American Revolutions*. Maryknoll, N.Y.: Orbis Books, 1984.

Bradstock, Andrew. *Saints and Sandinistas: The Catholic Church in Nicaragua and Its Response to the Revolution*. London: Epworth Press, 1987.

Cabestrero, Teófilo. *Ministers of God, Ministers of the People*. Maryknoll, N.Y.: Orbis Books; London: Zed Press, 1983.

————. *Revolucionarios por el Evangelio*. Bilbao: Desclee de Brouwer, 1983.

Cardenal, Ernesto. *The Gospel in Solentiname*. Translated by Donald Walsh. 4 vols. Maryknoll, N.Y.: Orbis Books, 1976–82.

Centro de Estudios y Publicaciones (CEP). *Nicaragua: La hora de los desafíos*. Lima: CEP, 1981.

Departamento Ecuménico de Investigaciones (DEI). *Apuntes para una Teología Nicaragüense*. San José, Costa Rica: DEI, 1981.

Dodson, Michael, and Tommie Sue Montgomery. "The Churches in the Nicaraguan Revolution." In *Nicaragua in Revolution,* edited by Thomas Walker. New York: Praeger, 1981.

Dodson, Michael, and Laura Nuzzi O'Shaughnessy. *Nicaragua's Other Revolution: Religious Faith and Political Struggle*. Chapel Hill: University of North Carolina Press, 1990.

Encuentro Pastoral. *De Cara al futuro de la Iglesia en Nicaragua (1o. Encuentro pastoral, Managua, 20–25 de enero, 25–1 febrero 1969)*. Managua: Fichero Pastoral Centroamericano, 1969.

Ezcurra, Ana María. *Ideological Aggression against the Sandinista Revolution*. New York: CIRCUS Publications, 1984.

———. *The Vatican and the Reagan Administration*. New York: CIRCUS Publications, 1986.

Foroohar, Manzar. *The Catholic Church and Social Change in Nicaragua*. Albany: State University of New York Press, 1989.

Girardi, Giulio. *Sandinismo, Marxismo, Cristianismo en la nueva Nicaragua*. Mexico City: Nuevomar, 1986.

González Gary, Oscar. *Iglesia Católica y revolución en Nicaragua*. Mexico City: Claves Latinoamericanas, 1986.

Instituto Histórico Centroamericano (ICHA). *Fe Cristiana y revolución Sandinista*. Managua: IHCA, 1979.

Jérez, César. *The Church and the Nicaraguan Revolution*. London: CIIR, 1984.

Lancaster, Roger. *Thanks to God and the Revolution: Popular Religion and Class Consciousness in the New Nicaragua*. New York: Columbia University Press, 1988.

Medcalf, John. *Letters from Nicaragua*. London: CIIR, 1988.

Nicarauac, no. 5 (April–June 1981): 1–196.

O'Shaughnessy, Laura Nuzzi, and Luis H. Serra. *The Church and Revolution in Nicaragua*. Athens, Ohio: Ohio University Center for International Studies, 1986.

Pochet, Rosa María, and Abelino Martínez. *Nicaragua—Iglesia: ¿Manipulación o profecía?*. San José, Costa Rica: Editorial DEI, 1987.

Randall, Margaret. *Christians in the Nicaraguan Revolution*. Vancouver: New Star Books, 1983.

Tayacán. *Historia de la Iglesia de los Pobres en Nicaragua*. Managua: CEHILA, 1983.

Williams, Philip J. *The Catholic Church and Politics in Nicaragua and Costa Rica*. London: Macmillan, 1989.

Wilson N., Franzella, Jilma Soza A., and Matilde Gutiérrez D. "Investigaciones para la historia de la Iglesia en Nicaragua." 2 vols. Master's thesis, Universidad Centroamericana, Managua, 1975.

Zúñiga, Edgar. *Historia eclesiástica de Nicaragua: La Cristiandad Colonial (1524–1821)*. Managua: Editorial Unión, 1981.

INDEX

ACLEN (Association of Nicaraguan Clergy), 119, 126
Agüero, Fernando, 84
Alvarez Osorio, Diego, 11, 219n8
Antonio Valdivieso Ecumenical Centre, 110, 124
Aragón Lucio, Rafael, 117
Argüello, Alvaro, 119
Arias, Oscar (Costa Rican president), 179, 182, 183, 202
Arias Caldera, Msgr., 118, 119, 123

Barni, Julián, 91, 148
Barquero, Antonio, 44
Barreda, Felipe and María, 168
Barreto, Canuto, 139–40; reaction to papal visit of 1983, 154
Batalla, Manuel, 117
Beadle, Elías, 28–29
Belli, Humberto, 110, 137, 165
Belzunegui, Pedro, 95, 117
Bobadilla, Francisco de, 8
Bosco Vivas, Msgr., 118, 167, 172, 230n16, 236n9

Cabestrero, Teófilo, 111–12
Calderón y Padilla, Octavio José, 37, 38, 46, 59, 224n23
Capuchin order, activities on the Atlantic Coast, 72, 91, 92
Carballo, Bismarck, 117, 145, 184, 188, 190–91, 195, 203, 205; involvement in the "naked priest" affair, 132–33
Cardenal, Ernesto, 67–69, 119, 123, 124, 126, 138, 232n44; admonished by Pope John Paul II, 147–48, 198; reaction to papal visit, 153

Cardenal, Fernando, 73, 81, 92, 100, 119, 124, 231n23; role during the literacy campaign, 108, 229n3; defense of his role in the FSLN government, 121, 122–23; expulsion from the Society of Jesus, 126, 170–71
Carranza, Clemente, 91
Casaldáliga, Pedro, 186
Casaroli, Agostino, 125, 203, 205
Castañeda, Francisco de, 8
Castellanos, Pilar, 117
Castrillo, Victor, 17
Cathedral in Managua, construction of, viii
Catholic Church in Nicaragua: role in the nineteenth century, 3; as a traditional defender of the status quo, 3–4, 13–14; earliest references to, 8–9; campaigns to convert Indians, 9, 10, 219n2; views of the *conquistadores,* 9–10; popular religiosity during colonial times, 10; role during the struggle for independence (1810), 11, 14; struggle to protect Indians from Spanish settlers, 11–12, 219n8, 220n12; polarization among Church members in colonial times, 13; division among Church members over independence issue, 14, 15–16; social position in Nicaragua at the time of independence, 15; reaction to William Walker's filibustering expedition, 20–21; effect of Concordat on, 21–22; reaction to U.S. intervention, 24–25, 27–29; development of, in 1910–40, 26; restructuring of, in 1913, 26; rejection of Protestantism, 27–28, 31, 40–41, 45, 47; views on Sandino, 29, 30; relationship with President Moncada, 30; views

Catholic Church in Nicaragua—*continued* on communism, 36, 40–43, 45; relationship with President Somoza García, 36–42, 43–51; views on social concerns, 38–40, 43–45, 47–51; development of Catholic Action, 47; situation in 1969, 52–57; development of lay role in post–Vatican II Church, 63; opposition to Somoza, 64–65; impact of Vatican II on, 66–67; grassroots developments, 67–75; campaign against progressive clergy, 116–21, 124–26, 171; support for status quo, 212–25. *See also* Episcopal Conference of Nicaragua; John Paul II; Liberal party; Obando y Bravo, Miguel; Vatican

CELAM (Latin American Episcopal Council), 4, 113; concern at FSLN government, 111–12; 1980 assistance plan for Nicaraguan Church, 112–23, 127. *See also* Liberation theology; Medellín

CEPA (Center for Education and Agrarian Development), 110, 124

Chamorro, José Antonio, 16

Chamorro, Pedro Joaquín, 48, 61, 94

Chamorro, Violeta, 108, 109, 110, 119, 134, 139, 179, 183, 210, 211, 217

Church hierarchy. *See* Episcopal Conference of Nicaragua

"Church of the Poor." *See* "People's Church"

Clark, Maura, 69

CONFER (National Conference for Religious Workers), 126

Conservative party, 18, 21; compared with Liberals in their treatment of the Church in the twentieth century, 25, 30, 33. *See also* Liberal party

Contreras, Rodrigo de, 12

Coordinadora Democrática Nicaragüense, 161, 162

Corral Prieto, Luis, 170

COSEP (Higher Council of Private Enterprise), 134, 139, 161, 212

Delgado, Santiago, 21

D'Escoto, Miguel, 92, 108, 119, 124, 126, 141; criticism of Obando y Bravo, 173, 236n12; "Evangelical insurrection," 185–87, 194

Díaz, Adolfo, 24, 221

Díaz, Agustín, 96

di Montezemelo, Cordero, 202

Duarte, José Napoleón, 182

Earthquake, December 1972, impact of, 61–62

Episcopal Conference of Nicaragua: pronouncements and pastoral letters by, 85–86, 155–61, 176, 196–201, 205–6; concerns of the bishops in the 1970s, 87–88, 90–91; growing opposition to Somoza, 92–95, 98–99, 101; early concerns about FSLN, 102–4, 108, 109–11; support of Sandinista social programs in November 1979, 104–7; criticism of Sandinista treatment of Miskitos, 114, 116; opposition to priests in FSLN government, 119–21, 124–26; opposition to FSLN government, 127–31, 138, 140, 159–60, 171–72; concerns about Sandinistas, 138, 159; attempts to reach an understanding with the FSLN, 174, 177, 178, 201–9

Espinoza, Francisco Luis, 96

Esquipulas II peace agreement, importance of, 182, 183, 184, 205

Fagoth, Steadman, 114–15

FSLN (Sandinista Front for National Liberation): plans for social reform, vii, viii, 180–81; support from Church sector, viii; development as an opposition group, 63; first contacts with Catholic Church, 74–75, 226n16; opposition of Obando y Bravo to, 102; educational reforms, 109; harassment of the Catholic Church, 114, 167–68, 169–70, 171, 184, 190–91; official statement on religion, 128–29; social charter under, 133–34; unrealistic expectations concerning Catholic hierarchy, 138; reactions to papal visit, 152, 153; economic programs of, 157; reactions to bishops' criticisms, 160; attempts to reach an understanding with the Church hierarchy, 174, 177, 178, 183, 201–9; electoral defeat to UNO, 183

Fuente, Rafael de la, 16

García, Donald, 95

García, Noël, 53–57

García Jérez, Bishop, 16, 17
García Laviana, Gaspar, 96, 172, 233n13
Giglio, Paolo, 193, 202–3, 238n33
González, José María, 95
González y Robleto, Vicente Alejandro, 37, 42, 48, 49–51, 52, 212
Gutiérrez, Gustavo, xi

Herdocia, José Hilario, 20

Instituto Histórico Centroamericano, 114, 124

Jara, José de la, 69, 81. *See also* San Pablo Apóstol community
Jérez, César, S.J., 1, 196
John XXIII, Pope, 4
John Paul II, Pope: conservative views of, 4–5, 165, 174, 214, 216; visit to Nicaragua in 1983, 28, 101, 140, 142, 146–55; meetings with Daniel Ortega, 108, 205; preparations for trip, 146, 152; addresses in Nicaragua, 148–50; goals of the papal visit, 151–52; impact in Nicaragua, 153–55; used as an opposition figure in Nicaragua, 172

Las Casas, Bartolomé de, 12, 18
Lezcano y Ortega, Antonio, 28, 36, 38–42, 223n7; support for Somoza García, 40, 41, 43, 222n31
Liberal party, 18; policies toward Church in nineteenth century, 19, 22–23; compared with Conservatives in their treatment of the Church in the twentieth century, 25, 30, 34; under Somoza García, 35–36. *See also* Conservative party
Liberation theology, xi, 4, 24. *See also* Medellín; Vatican
López Ardón, Bishop, 127, 150, 157, 168, 186, 187

McGrath, Marcos, 166
Medellín, importance of, 4, 52, 54, 65, 66, 75–77 passim, 79, 82, 95, 101, 105, 126, 165, 211, 216
Medrano, Luis, 117
Meehan, John J., 163–64
Mejía Godoy, Carlos, 101–2

Merino, Timoteo, 169–70
Miguelena, Benito, 17
Miranda, Otilio, 117
Miskitos, Nicaraguan bishops' support for, 114–16
Molina, Uriel, 72–74, 81, 95, 184, 226n12
Moncada, José María, 30
Morazan, Francisco, 19
Moreno, Juan Ramón, 157
Mother Teresa, 204–5

New Laws (1542), impact of, on colonial Central America, 13–14. *See also* Catholic Church in Nicaragua

Obando y Bravo, Miguel: viewed in world media, xi; opposition to Somoza Debayle, 2, 59, 83–84, 101, 161–62, 227n30; role of, 56, 57, 67, 82, 201, 209, 213; views on the Church's political role, 58; as mediator between FSLN and Somoza, 63; development of opposition to Somoza Debayle, 84, 87, 88–90, 95; assessment of first decade as Archbishop of Managua, 97–99; opposition to FSLN, 102, 123, 141, 157; criticism of progressive Church, 119–21, 124–26, 184; as leader of de facto opposition, 135, 137, 139, 145, 162–67, 169, 172, 174, 177, 193, 195–96; appointed cardinal, 142, 166–67, 175; views on the electoral process, 161; assessment of, 163, 165, 206–8, 237n25; criticisms of, 173, 187, 233n13, 236n12; "Crusade for Peace," 185, 194; contrasting opinions on murder of religious, 192–94, 205; following the UNO victory, 210, 211–12, 215, 218, 238n39
OPEN 3 (Permanent Operation of National Emergency), 76
Ortega, Daniel, 28, 63, 108, 135, 166, 194, 204, 205, 206–8, 209, 218

Pacheco, José María, 170
Pallais, Azarías, 46
Parrales, Edgar, 119, 124, 126
Pastora, Edén, 144, 165, 166, 174
Patronato Real, 13
Peña, Amado, 168–69, 171, 202

"People's Church," xi, 4, 67, 83, 95, 154, 157, 174, 177–78, 185, 196–99, 208–9, 215–16, 217, 218, 230n9; opposition of Obando y Bravo, 98, 176

Pereira y Castellón, Simeón, 23; reaction to U.S. occupation, 27–28, 222n27

Protestant Church: polarization among members of, 2; viewed historically by Catholic Church, 27–28, 31, 40–41, 45, 47; CEPAD, 81; Moravians on the Miskitos' situation, 115

Puebla, 4, 52, 65, 105. See also Medellín; Vatican

Radio Católica, 47, 184, 191, 192, 203

Ramírez, Sergio, 166, 203, 205

Reagan, Ronald: support for Obando y Bravo, 1, 214; opposition to Sandinista government, 107–8, 116, 125, 143; strategies used to defeat Sandinistas, 135–36, 143–45, 157–58, 168, 180–82; views on the contras, 157, 179–80

Reyes Católicos (Catholic King Fernando and Queen Isabel of Spain), 11

Reyes y Valladares, Canuto, 28, 32

Riguero community, 72–74, 81

Rivera y Damas, Arturo, 166

Robelo, Alfonso, 109, 134, 139

Rojas, José Ramón, 16

Romero, Oscar, xi, 172, 233n13

Ruiz, Tomás, 16, 17, 220n17

Sacasa, Juan Batista, 34

Salazar, Jorge, 134

Sandino, Augusto César: struggle against U.S. invasion, 3; criticism of Church, 29; influence in FSLN, 194

Sandoval, José Francisco, 96

Sanjines, José Antonio, 96

San Pablo Apóstol community, 69–71, 81, 82, 225n10

Santi, Carlos, 150, 157

Schick, René, 60

Schlaefer, Salvador, 91–92, 127, 157; flight to Honduras in December 1983, 171

Schmitz, Pablo, 127, 186, 192

SID (Information and Documentation Service), 76–77

Solentiname community, 67–69. See also Cardenal, Ernesto

Somoza Debayle, Anastasio: Church opposition to, vii, 34, 52, 60, 61; takes advantage of 1972 earthquake, 61–62; brutal rule of, 64, 88. See also Episcopal Conference of Nicaragua

Somoza Debayle, Luis, 51, 60

Somoza García, Anastasio, 30, 32, 34–52, 222n2; support for U.S. policies in Nicaragua, 34

Soto, Benito, 16, 17

Stewart, Bill, 64

"Sweating Virgin," 131–32

Testimonio: importance of journal, 76–81, 227n25

Tunnerman, Carlos, 109

UDEL (Democratic Union of Liberation), 63

Ulloa y Larios, Bishop, 22

United States: intervention in early twentieth century, 24–25, 27–28; support for the Somozas, 61; appeal to President Carter by Nicaraguan religious, 95. See also Obando y Bravo, Miguel; Reagan, Ronald; Walker, William

Valdivieso, Antonio de, 12–13, 18, 212, 216–17

Vatican: policy toward Sandinista government, 1, 124, 165, 170, 202, 203–4, 217; Concordat with Nicaraguan government in 1862, 21–22; importance of Vatican II reforms, 51, 52, 54, 65, 66, 67, 79, 82, 126, 165, 211, 216

Vega, Pablo Antonio, 56, 127, 145, 174, 184, 195, 203–4, 205, 209; criticisms of Sandinista government, 161, 162, 167, 168, 172–73, 188–90, 237n21

Vijíl, Agustín, 20–21

Vílchez, Pedro, 72, 167

Villavicencio, Rafael, 21

Walker, William, 3, 19–20; Church reaction to, 20–21

Zavaleta, Tomás, 192–94

Zelaya, José Santos, 22, 24, 26, 27

Library of Congress Cataloging-in-Publication Data

Kirk, John M., 1951–
   Politics and the Catholic church in Nicaragua / John M. Kirk.
     p.   cm.
   Includes bibliographical references and index.
   ISBN 0–8130–1138–8 (alk. paper)
   1. Catholic Church—Nicaragua—History. 2. Church and state—Nicaragua—
History. 3. Nicaragua—Politics and government. 4. Nicaragua—Church
history. I. Title.
BX1442.2.K57   1992   92–5131
282'.7285—dc20   CIP